The Good,
the Bad
and the Famous

The Good,
the Bad
and the Famous

Len Sherman

A Lyle Stuart Book
Published by Carol Publishing Group

A Lyle Stuart Book
Published by Carol Publishing Group

Editorial Offices
600 Madison Avenue
New York, NY 10022

Sales & Distribution Offices
120 Enterprise Avenue
Secaucus, NJ 07094

In Canada: Musson Book Company
A division of General Publishing Co. Limited
Don Mills, Ontario

Manufactured in the United States of America

Library of Congress Catloging-in-Publication Data

Sherman, Len, 1956-
    The good, the bad and the famous / Len Sherman
       p.   cm.
    "A Lyle Stuart book."
    ISBN 0-8184-0526-0 : $18.95
    Includes index.
      1. Celebrities--United States--Political activity. 2. United
States--Politics and government--1945-   I. Title.
E839.5S534   1990
973.92--dc20   90-1727
                                CIP

For giving me a lifetime's worth of blood, toil, tears and sweat,
this book is dedicated to my mom and dad.

Acknowledgments

I am very much obliged to the Park Hyatt in Washington, D.C., Bel Age in Los Angeles, the Ritz-Carlton in Palm Springs, and the Hilton in Sioux City, for making this book economically feasible through their generous hospitality. In a similar vein, I am indebted to the Pan Am Shuttle for flying me from New York to Washington and back, time and time again. Without their participation, I would have encountered considerable financial discomfort in doing research for this book.

On to individual co-conspirators: I am deeply grateful to everyone who consented to be interviewed. I have tried to present their individual opinions and actions as fairly and as honestly as my tape recorder and my judgment allowed. In addition, thank you to all the agents and assistants and associates of the interviewees who helped arrange these encounters.

Back at the publishing house, I would like to thank Steven Schragis for buying the book; Dan Levy for editing it; Jessica Black and Fern Edison for promoting it. A special word of thanks to Nancy Blum for getting the ball rolling.

And speaking of publishing, thanks to David Rosensweig, for ensuring that my contract was good for me, too.

Contents

Everyone loves power, even if they do not know what to do with it.

—Benjamin Disraeli

The Good,
the Bad
and the Famous

Introduction

Times have changed.

America has forsaken its traditional heroes—statespersons, explorers, soldiers and scientists—and anointed celebrities to take their places. One result has been that these new American heroes—actors, athletes, musicians, and so on—have stepped off the performing stage and into the political arena, to the platform to which American heroes have typically been elevated. To an astonishing extent, celebrities have become independent political operators. It is as if the public, finding politicians lacking in heroic qualities, has sought leaders who can still capture the imagination, regardless of these new leaders' abilities to perform the tasks of governance.

How will the ascension of stars to the pantheon of heroes affect the political process? Are celebrities who play at politics a significant force or merely performers in an amusing or distracting sideshow?

This is not a book of rigorous political analysis, but an attempt to explain subjectively a small part of the American psyche—its obsession with fame—and the political costs we have incurred as a result. The design for my work was to speak to a number of the leading players, in show biz and out, and let them speak for themselves. I tended to be provocative in my questioning, hoping to pierce the veneer of public relations hype with which I expected to be confronted.

Inspired by attending the major pro-choice rally in Washington in April 1989, where a number of Hollywood stars performed significant roles, I set out to speak to a few major players in the entertainment industry. Attempting to gain an historical perspective, I began my investigation with an actor who has been politically active for

1

most of this century—from the Spanish Civil War in the thirties through the Central American crises in the eighties, sharply punctuated by a fifteen-year blacklisting during the McCarthy era. After that, I spoke with two major stars whose professional and political lives have been part of the American scene for several decades, and whose differences have caused them to clash with serious consequences. Despite their dissimilar views and backgrounds, all three members of this older guard have proved themselves well-qualified to speak out on the relationship between entertainment and politics.

I interviewed several successful young actors, identified with Hollywood's "brat pack," who are just starting to stretch their political muscles. Their inexperience contrasts with both their enthusiasm and their influence, both of which are considerable enough that they must be regarded seriously. Of course, none of this would count for anything if the citizenry were not willing to listen to celebrities. Opinion polls suggested an answer; politicians routinely rank near the bottom of professions held in high esteem. Sessions with high school students demonstrated how deeply the cynicism has captured our youth, and perhaps our future. In order to better understand whether these low opinions are justified, I interviewed two former members of Congress who had been convicted of accepting bribes in the Abscam scandal and had been removed from office.

I spoke to a political consultant, an expert in shaping the images of politicians. His primary tool is television, for television has become the prime medium for fashioning images and opinions about everyone and everything. I discussed the impact of the camera's eye on our political process with a former Governor and one of the 1988 Democratic Presidential candidates, and with a top TV journalist, a man who garnered great acclaim covering Ronald Reagan's White House for eight years. I spoke with many others, including a young film executive, who organizes similarly youthful stars to talk to kids about drugs and sex; a public relations executive, who explained the Hollywood community's view of its central role in the world; a famed rock and roll impresario, who addressed the striking role of the music industry on the international political stage.

I traveled to the heartland to investigate the transformation of a prime-time television celebrity into a United States Congressman. There, in Sioux City, Iowa, it became undeniably clear that something has changed in our country, that something is profoundly different from the way it used to be.

It should be said that my opinions did not fundamentally change in the course of my investigation. By the time I finished my interviews, I still felt that America had let celebrities go too far in making their opinions part of the public discussion of politics. Of course, stars have just as much right as anyone to political involvement, and even to using available media as mouthpieces for their views. However, I remain unconvinced they will ever be equipped to take the lead, to stand in for our old heroes. I remain unconvinced they are the best our society can do. But perhaps it's gone a bit too far. By the time you finish this book, you might agree with me that America has paid a political price for its infatuation with celebrities. Perhaps we should encourage our traditional heroes to behave more heroically.

I believe that politics is essentially a simple business, an endeavor at least as emotional and as intellectual, as simple and as powerful as love or hate or passion or fear. On second thought, put in those terms, maybe politics isn't quite so simple after all. As I contemplate the phenomenon this book explores, I am confident that the truism expressed by so many writers and politicians and philosophers through the ages holds firm: whatever this nation's fate, whether the question concerns entertainment or politics or the pursuit of happiness, we shall inevitably get we want. More to the point, we shall get what we deserve.

October 31, 1989
New York City

Chapter 1

Washington, D.C.

Rally Round the Camera

They were all there. Well, maybe not all, but plenty, celebs, politicos and media mavens. Morgan Fairchild sat at one table between two female colleagues, all staring at the podium, all looking serious, elaborately coiffed, dressed in somber black (Hollywood somber: expensive, tight, with a splash of leather). On the other side of the room, Glenn Close, Marlo Thomas, Veronica Hamill, Bonnie Franklin and Daphne Zuniga were arrayed in two rows, unsmiling, unmoving, almost stern in their fierce concentration on the moment. Bella Abzug and Betty Friedan sat together, whispering, neither quite in step with the chic tone of the program, appearing more like veterans of an earlier war than comrades-in-arms marching alongside the glamorous Los Angeles shock troops.

Naturally, it was a special kind of glamour, earnest, sober, sincere—important—loaded with *meaning*, in the most contemporary, self-conscious sense of the word. This was Hollywood gone stone cold straight, straight to the heart of power and reality, straight to Washington, D.C.

Now this wasn't just some vague collection of Hollywood stars; it was the smooth-running, hard-charging monster of a political machine known as the Hollywood Women's Political Committee,

4

participating in "Choice Weekend," April 7–9, 1989, the weekend of the great march to support abortion rights. With Americans pouring into Washington from every state, it was projected that several hundred thousand women and men would be assembled on Sunday, making this one of the largest rallies in our history. HWPC had come to the Capital in force not simply to support the march, but to lead. In fact, talk among the pro-choice people frequently centered about the pushing for position among HWPC, the National Organization of Women (NOW), and the National Abortion Rights Action League (NARAL), all struggling for maximum visibility during the weekend.

Being from show biz, HWPC certainly knew how to play the game, and was playing it with gusto. The group operated a twenty-four-hour press office out of the Hyatt. Why it was deemed necessary to have some exhausted staffer always by the phone was unclear, especially to the several staff members imported from Los Angeles. After all, one could understand why the Pentagon never closed, but how many journalists would get the urge to schedule an interview with Michelle Lee at 4:00 A.M.?

Jockeying for media exposure is never complete without a self-congratulatory press release, and HWPC had one printed and ready. In case there were any doubts, HWPC explained that it was an organization with which to be reckoned:

In August 1984, a group of influential Los Angeles professional women—writers, attorneys, motion picture producers, studio executives, bank officers and others—concerned with the problems that might face the country if Ronald Reagan were re-elected, decided to form a political organization to affect change. They called themselves the Hollywood Women's Political Committee.

The Mondale/Ferraro dinner in Los Angeles gave them the opportunity to act in concert for the first time; they sold the dinner out, raising just under $1 million, and in so doing, created the activist base from which they have continued to function.

After Reagan was elected, the group began to crystallize. It became obvious that raising money for candidates was not enough—basic principles had to be forged. Meetings were held; plans were discussed; the need for a statement of principles became mandatory. A political advisor was hired. . . .

Within six months, membership increased so rapidly that it became necessary to hire an executive director and to open offices. In the Fall of 1985, a second fundraiser was held for Senatorial candidates. Its success, and the news of the group's fundraising ability and its increasingly high profile, began to interest political candidates from all over the country.

By the Spring of 1986, there were 72 members, all influential in their respective fields and most politically active in their own right. Well organized now and formidable, the HWPC, with the generous help of member Barbara (sic) Streisand, staged on September 6 a "Regain the Senate" event, which raised a total of $1.5 million in one night.

The press release continued on to list some of HWPC's other fundraisers and the amounts raised: $125,000 from the west coast premiere of Lily Tomlin's show; $150,000 from its First Annual Barbara Jordan Award for Political Courage and Commitment; $850,000 from "A Celebration of America," "a multi-regional menu and entertainment," proceeds targeted for six senate races and the Dukakis California campaign.

It was the Streisand event that put HWPC on the political map. While not exactly downplayed in the press release, HWPC hardly granted the evening, held at Streisand's home, hosted by Streisand and starring Streisand and her voice, its full due. Not only did more than five hundred show biz hotshots pay $5,000 per for dinner and a show, but Home Box Office bought the cable rights.

One would never have known that the concert was political from HBO's telecast. Senators Howard Metzenbaum of Ohio, Alan Cranston of California and George Mitchell of Maine, and Representatives Bob Edgar of Pennsylvania and Henry Waxman of California may have been displayed in the first row, shown every so often gazing up at the songstress with adoring eyes, but the political context had been left on the editing floor. Evidently, HBO decided that Barbra's political pronouncements were not quite as entertaining as her nonpartisan singing. HBO did eliminate one bit of vocalizing, when Streisand changed the lyrics of "Send in the Clowns" to include her feelings about Republicans: "Aren't they rich, Aren't they queer . . . Send home the clowns."

The ability of a single performer such as Streisand to raise so much money was not an unmixed blessing for HWPC, for while it demonstrated the group's fundraising ability, it also revealed its reliance on individual stars and their whims. No serious political organization can be held captive to the notions of a handful of individuals, disrupting all continuity of philosophy and procedure, and HWPC constantly asserted that all members were absolutely equal.

More practically, HWPC needed to prove it could transform money into power, a capability many in the political business doubted.

The Washington march was an opportunity to showcase HWPC's public reach and validate its political ambitions. A delegation was flown in from Los Angeles to represent the group. Actually, the number of HWPC members was never quite clear; *People* magazine reported that "more than thirty big names" attended, while HWPC handed out a sheet with ninety-two names attached, and then later claimed a much larger tally. Whichever was the truth, a bunch of them were present for HWPC's opening salvo, this press conference held Saturday afternoon, two hours after an orientation meeting for HWPC members.

Marge Tabankin, executive director of HWPC, stood at the podium. Before her was a roomful of celebrities and reporters and cameras—at least ten television news cameras and many more still photographers—and behind her was a file of impressive personages, seated on folding chairs, waiting their turns to speak: Kate Michaelman, executive director of NARAL; Molly Yard, president of NOW; Faye Wattleton, president of Planned Parenthood Federation of America; Ira Glasser, executive director of the American Civil Liberties Union (ACLU), and Gloria Steinem, chairperson of Voters For Choice.

"Hi, I'm Marge Tabankin. I'm the executive director of the Hollywood Women's Political Committee. I am privileged, proud and delighted to be in Washington this weekend and to be sharing this podium with the leaders of the pro-choice majority movement in this country. We have come from the entertainment community. The Hollywood Women's Political Committee is a group of a hundred and fifty equal women; we have no officers in our group, we have no elected members, board members, and things like that; we are a hundred and fifty co-equal women who share progressive concerns about the quality of life in this country."

There it was again, right at the top, this attempt to convince the audience that all HWPC members were created equal. Now down to business.

"This issue has become a litmus test issue for us. In the past, we have raised a lot of money for candidates, we raised a lot of money for causes, but now we are moving into an issue focus and an agenda that has a strategy, that has organizing, and that has movement as well as fundraising with it.

"Today, we are here in our capacity as enablers, as motivators, and as organizers, and as playing that role, we have helped to facilitate bringing two hundred fifty individuals from the entertainment industry from both New York and Los Angeles to Washington to share in the events of this weekend. We have singers, we have actors, we have directors, we have writers, we have producers, we have camera people, we have just about every possible type of lady who services the entertainment industry and that reaches out to entertain America.

"We are happy to be here; we understand that we are but a very small piece of a very, very, very large movement that is organized by the very brilliant people that are sitting behind me. We have chosen as our spokesperson to represent the Hollywood Women's Political Committee, Morgan Fairchild. Morgan has been an activist with the committee, as a member, on this issue for years. She is one of the celebrity chairs of NARAL and she chairs our reproductive freedom committee."

Fairchild walked to the stage to enthusiastic applause from her Hollywood friends and some hotel guests who had wandered into the room. The press was of two moods; the camera types were busy shooting away, while the print corps gazed around, trying to guess who these out-of-towners were. For the most part, the assembled newsies were political journalists covering a political event, the march, and more familiar with congressional administrative assistants than soap opera stars.

Fairchild recited crisply and emphatically in her high voice. "Thank you very much, and on behalf of the HWPC I wanted to really welcome everyone from the entertainment industry that bothered to come today. We really appreciate everyone being here, whether you're a member of HWPC or not. Thank you so much for showing up."

Fairchild smoothed out a paper and started to read HWPC's official statement:

"The Hollywood Women's Political Committee is proud to raise its Voice for Choice. We are writers, actresses, directors, producers and attorneys in the entertainment industry, who organized six years ago to apply our professional expertise and public visibility to effect political change . . . "

The statement went on to explain its advocacy of abortion rights in some detail. Near the end, the tale wound back to HWPC.

"For the Hollywood Women's Political Committee, the march tomorrow is only one step in our support of this cause. In these past six years together, we have learned how to be politically effective. We have raised millions of dollars for candidates who have supported issues which we felt must be given priority. In 1986, the year the Democrats regained control of the United States Senate, we raised $1.5 million for senatorial candidates. We have made countless public appearances to encourage voter registration. We have worked on committees and sponsored dozens of events with Presidential, Senate, House and state level candidates.

"We will continue to raise money for pro-choice candidates at every level, from state legislatures to the Congress of the United States.

"Towards this goal, we will use our time, our energies, our professional talents and skills. We will make our voices heard.

"Our commitment to choice is unyielding. Our future, our children's future and the future of the American family is at stake.

"Thank you very much," Fairchild said. The applause was long and loud and the television cameras, jammed together on a stand at the back of the room, whirred away.

Tabankin returned to the podium and got to the nitty-gritty, as far as the media was concerned. "I've been asked by the press to reassure you that there will be a time at the end for photo opportunities with the representatives of the entertainment industry delegation."

Around the room, the members of the fourth estate appeared relieved.

Tabankin introduced the leaders of the organizations who were seated on the dais. She lauded NARAL's Kate Michaelman for her

"vision," as well as her "media ability." The dynamic Michaelman lit up the room with her vigor and humor. She was followed by
Molly Yard, the venerable firebrand head of NOW, who vowed that
there would be no turning back in the fight. Yard was succeeded by
Fay Wattleton of Planned Parenthood, a striking woman, who gave
a long, reasoned speech, explaining the legal perspective. Despite
the appeal of these different women, the television cameras displayed a conspicuous lack of curiosity in what they had to say. The
camera operators had removed their minicams from the stands and
hurried to the front of the room, so they could turn around and film
the celebs watching the speakers.

This stark indifference was temporarily relieved when Gloria
Steinem was called up. Steinem, of course, is a celebrity in her own
right, and commanded media attention. Perhaps because she understood the rules of the game, she kept her remarks short and included
one guaranteed applause grabber: "I would especially want to thank
all of the entertainment industry people here today for showing
Washington that Ronald Reagan does not now and never did represent Hollywood."

Steinem done, Ira Glasser of the American Civil Liberties Union
had his chance just in time for the television crews to spin back for
more reaction shots from the glittering crowd. The celebs sat still,
playing their parts, pretending not to notice the lights and cameras.

Eventually, the floor was opened to questions from the press. The
room was silent, until a local television reporter asked Kate Michaelman if she believed the pro-choice side represented the majority view in America. Michaelman cited polls which indicated exactly that. Another local TV guy asked another easy question, and that
was that. The media seemed uninterested in performing their part,
to probe and joust, letting controversy fly. Instead, it was obvious
that the press regarded this as more a photo opportunity than a real
press briefing, and, with its customary grace, waited with noisy
impatience, adjusting its video equipment in anticipation of the next
shot, a better angle.

Tabankin announced that the podium would be struck and the
celebs summoned for the promised group picture. The press, sleep-
walking till now, rushed forward, the camera operators and still
photogs climbing over tables, each staking out a prime vantage
point. Things were returning to normal, as the press accelerated to

its regular frenzied pace and many of the celebs struck beatific, bland smiles as they ambled to the stage.

Someone declaimed each celebrity's name, though only the first name, as though this was a backyard barbecue: "Polly. Ellen. Leonard." (That was Bergen, Burstyn and Nimoy, though I do not know how Mr. Spock, along with a few other males, sneaked into HWPC.)

While the minicams and Nikons hummed and clicked and flashed, I asked a reporter from *The Baltimore Sun*, who was hanging back on the fringe, what politicians thought of celebrities.

"I think they're delighted to do anything that will get them press."

"Yes, but when they call celebs to appear before committees and that sort of thing, do the politicos actually listen?" I asked.

"Maybe they listen a little," she said. "Maybe."

Another room was available for the press to conduct one-on-one interviews with willing celebs. I asked Melanie Mayron, an actress on "thirtysomething," if she ever questioned whether celebrities should be involved in political issues.

"I think it doesn't matter if you're a celebrity or not if you believe in the issue," she replied. "I think if you are a celebrity and it means anything to people, that's great."

Did she think people listened to celebrities, as far as politics was concerned?

"I think they do," Mayron said. "I think it does affect people's consciousness if they like somebody a whole lot, or admire them, and they go, 'Oh, they think that way? Maybe I'd better take another look at that.' "

Not that Mayron believed that the public should take this to any extreme. "I don't think they should look to celebrities as experts unless they happen to *be* experts. Also, you know, I think someone can be a celebrity and also be a smart-thinking individual and be involved in other areas. But I don't think just because they're well-known . . ."

Mayron shrugged and her voice kind of drifted off and a television crew grabbed her for an interview.

I spotted Betty Friedan and told her about my book, which caused her to stand a little straighter and disown the idea of being a "celebrity."

"I don't consider you a celebrity *that way*," I said.

Somewhat reassured, Friedan talked with her customary rush of words about the propriety, or logic, of celebrities in politics. "The women that are here from the mass media, from television and movies, have such a profound effect on shaping our values and perceptions. The fact that the women who did come here are actresses and other people in the movie industry, there is something about this issue that they will come and put themselves on the line, and they kind of become symbols of people's values and so if you are trying to speak out on something, it's important. This is not an empty use of celebrity. This is legitimate. . . . Through the mass media, our perceptions are so much affected and symbolized by the characters of the movies and so on. And when we realize that the people who play those characters feel so strongly that they will come out of character to speak their own values that it adds an intensity to the debate and it is a way they can personally use their deepest values, and not just to sell detergent."

I pointed out that HWPC's opening statement suggested a political agenda strongly tuned to collecting and exercising power for no purposes nobler than the sake of the group.

"Well," Friedan said, "but I mean, you are for candidates if you raise money for candidates because you want to defend basic values. The women of the Hollywood Women's Political Committee, and I am sort of part of their family, I spend now four-and-a-half months as a visiting professor at USC—"

"But you're not a formal member of the group?" Her name was included on HWPC's press release.

"No, no," laughed Friedan. "It costs too much money." Membership dues were $2,500.

I asked Hendrik Hertzberg, senior editor (and now editor) of *The New Republic*, if he believed HWPC had any political influence.

"They've got their own money," he said, "and they've got a lot of money, and they're very, very big money in the Democratic Party."

"Is this a good thing?"

Hertzberg shrugged. "I guess it's marginally better than PACs and fat cats and big corporate types."

I wondered if he thought celebrities had become our society's heroes.

"There is a great useful distinction between celebrities and heroes," Hertzberg said. "A celebrity is somebody who, because of some more or less accidental trait, is elevated above the rest of us. A hero is somebody who, by dint of some force of character, has raised him or herself above the masses. So they are not really our heroes. And that's why an event like this is a two-edged sword, and an event like this always teeters on the edge of being ridiculous, because they are celebrities and they are not heroes."

The press conference was proof positive of Hertzberg's assertion. The cameras were glued to the celebs speaking or watching the speakers speaking or just sitting there looking pretty. No one else counted for anything but background.

"Yes, of course," Hertzberg said, "because this was a star event. You notice at the end there were no questions. It could have become a major embarrassment. The only reason there were any questions was because of self-aggrandizing local anchormen who wanted to be able to show themselves standing there. Because nobody wants to know, nobody takes seriously that these celebrities are here, doing this. It's great, but it doesn't necessarily convince anybody."

Hertzberg may have been right about the essential difference between celebrities and heroes. However, his distinction was more rational than real, for *effective* heroes, meaning those who have an impact on society, must have a broad popular acceptance—and that meant celebrities, and hero status.

I shared a taxi with four college kids from George Washington University on their way to a formal at my hotel. All four were pro-choice and the two girls planned to march.

They had heard something about celebrities also marching but no details, meaning no names, and I asked them if they thought the celebs would have any impact on the event.

"I think it does," one girl said, wearing a royal blue, frilly dress. "Because they are people's role models."

"Why are they role models?" I asked.

"Because they are in the spotlight," she said.

"I think that when people hear them talk," one of the tuxedoed boys said, "they can be persuaded to look at an issue again."

"Personally," the other boy said, "I don't care what they think about anything."

"Many people do," the other girl said, attired in a tight, black number.

"Yeah," the first girl said. "Poor, ditz-like people."

All four laughed in agreement.

Even if she didn't care, I wondered if anything could entice her to pay attention.

"Sure," she said. "If Tom Cruise got up there." This caused another round of mirth.

"What would happen?" her date inquired.

"I'd sit up and listen," she said enthusiastically, which, of course, brought the house down.

Back at the hotel, I contemplated the official HWPC rebuke I had received earlier in the day, when an HWPC press rep had accosted me, upset with my "belligerent" questions. "Hey," she said, "we don't need that." She stormed away, leaving no doubt that HWPC co-operation had just ended.

The outburst surprised me, since I viewed my inquiry as reasonable and my manner as acceptably polite, but then I remembered that celebrities do not appreciate even a hint of implied criticism. Mickey Kaus wrote of something similar in his description in *The New Republic* of a press briefing for Hands Across America, the attempt to create a four thousand-mile human chain from Los Angeles to New York for a few minutes on May 25, 1986, and raise $100 million for the homeless and hungry, where "a thick 'information packet' was handed out to virtually everyone who wanted it—*except* reporters. When I asked for a copy, a tight-lipped publicist assured me: 'You will be given all the information *you* need. . . .' " Later on, "reporters were made to feel like party-poopers if they declined to join hands during the emotional theme-playing."

Clearly, the show biz politicos had not learned the first brutal lesson of politics: when you enter the game, you become fair game. Celebrities are used to handling publicity, or, more precisely, having their press flacks handle other press flacks. Hollywood is a company town, and the company is entertainment, and everybody has a hand in promoting the product. Thus, unlike the natural antagonism between big business and the media, or government and the media, where the press works to ferret out unpleasant or unfavorable or uncomfortable facts about its subject, both sides play for the same team in L.A. The skepticism that is the media's badge of honor—the distance between its mission and the world that the press maintains as proof of integrity—has been abandoned in Hollywood. A symbolic relationship has replaced the search for truth; while many good reporters cover the show biz beat, their efforts are more often centered on the corporate aspect of the industry, leaving the celebs to the gossip columnists and other near-journalists, and that murky region where deals are struck so access is provided, interviews granted, exclusives arranged.

That might work just fine in Hollywood, but politics operates in an entirely different dimension. It was irrelevant that this group of celebrities was serious about the abortion issue, that they had demonstrated their knowledge and concern, and that they had traveled far from home. No one is forced to take a political position, no one is ordered to hold a press conference or issue a statement or speak out in any way; to do so or not is the right of every American. Though the true believer, celebrity or not, might be able to summon the press to pay heed to his ideas, he should not expect to control how the press responds or what the press asks. The press does not constitute an audience but is a participant, free and independent, a new and potentially dangerous variety of beast for many celebrities.

HWPC, NARAL and Voters for Choice were hosting a gala dinner that evening. The response had been so great that the Mayflower Hotel's Grand Ballroom could not hold all the paid guests, and a room across the lobby was pressed into duty. A giant TV screen was hung, so these exiled diners could observe the program.

The press hung around the lobby until the food was finished, attended only by knots of curious hotel guests. While we waited, I spoke to Wendy Reiger, correspondent for the local NBC station, who stood by with her crew to interview some celebs for the 11:00 P.M. news. Unlike many journalists, she was enthused about the celebrity involvement in politics and, more important, believed her viewers would find it "fascinating."

I asked her to explain what was fascinating, why the public cared what celebrities thought about anything.

"Because these are people we look at, and these are people who attract attention, and they are able to add some appeal to an issue," Reiger said. "I mean, what are the most popular magazines? *People*, *National Enquirer*, all these magazines that are personality magazines. People are interested in celebrities. I mean, that's why they become celebrities, because there is something about their lives that attracts our attention. They are the neon, the human neon signs, that we attach to issues."

Reiger contended that the "glitz" celebrities brought to an issue rendered that issue more interesting, though I wasn't sure if she meant it would be more interesting to the public or the media.

"Plus," she said, "some of them are articulate. . . . Glenn Close is a serious, respected actress, and Susan Sarandon is a respected actress and has a certain quality to her. And Morgan Fairchild is so tough and yet so Hollywood. I mean, she's beautiful, but she is *so* Hollywood."

Fairchild did have a tough streak, judging by a quote in *People* the week before the march. The actress left no doubt that the stars would play tit-for-tat with politicos who didn't support the pro-choice forces: "I'm sure the next time someone calls and wants me to fly across the country to slosh through snow for a fundraiser, I'll be too busy."

That decision would be her prerogative, though her tone sounded rather petulant. A fundamental frustration lay behind Fairchild's demand that HWPC's political allies fight beside the group: the problem political pros had in comprehending what issues were absolutely important to the group, what issues embodied the group's identity.

The dilemma was inherent in HWPC from the beginning, since it lacked the central, single reason for existing that ordinarily motivates the founding of a political group, particularly a group that raises and dispenses money. Unlike an organization that protects and promotes the corporate interests of its membership, like the Automobile and Truck Dealers Election Action Committee; or its vocational interests, like the AFL-CIO's Committee on Political Education (COPE); or its avocational interests, like the National Rifle Association (NRA)—HWPC can claim no such tangible and specific charter. Unlike a group that presses an intellectual interest—like the Heritage Foundation, or a scientific interest; like the Sierra Club, or an electoral, ideological interest; like the political parties—HWPC can claim no such philosophical basis for its formation. The unvarnished fact is that the Hollywood Women's Political Committee exists because it *can*; it has funding because its members have money; it raises more money because its members can raise more money.

Ironically, a group that bore more than a passing resemblance to the Hollywood Women's Political Committee was the Moral Majority. Though diametrically opposed to one another, ideologically and stylistically, both groups sprung from the impetus of their founders to aggrandize their positions and accumulate power, simultaneously appealing to and aggravating their powerful patrons and friends. The Moral Majority's method of fundraising might have been the opposite of HWPC's, Jerry Falwell soliciting five dollars from small donors instead of staging a high-ticket Streisand concert, but the result was the same—coffers filled with money but no firm political base or distinct rationale. Despite Falwell's success at amassing and distributing money to conservative candidates, the influence he and his group sought within the Reagan Administration was never attained, and their mission, clumsily articulated, never realized. From sharing in the 1980 Republican victory, raising $11 million in 1984 for lobbying efforts, and proclaiming itself ready for more triumphs in its battle against "secular humanism," "pornography" and anything else the Moral Majority judged detrimental to God, family and country, the organization began a slow decline which never stopped. Finally, in 1989, Falwell announced that the group would fold. Such is the fate of political organizations with appetites hungry for power and stomachs queasy with ideological indigestion.

Dinner was over, the doors were opened, and the press streamed inside, taking up whatever positions were available downstairs or in the balcony. The Grand Ballroom grew dark and a slide show began to the strains of "Pomp and Circumstance." Images of famous women flashed across the screen—Barbara Jordan, Golda Meir, Shirley Chisholm, Ethel Kennedy, Jackie Onassis, Jane Fonda, Gloria Steinem—and each received a burst of applause, punctuating the processional beat.

The music quickened and the slides revealed women in action, performing ballet, playing tennis, protesting, Jane Fonda protesting

the Vietnam War. Then "Pomp" returned again, along with pictures of more women, a somewhat more contemporary crop, like
Cher and Tracy Chapman.

Warm-up concluded and the crowd properly primed, Judy Collins
appeared on the small stage. Behind her a poster read, "Voices for
Choice." Collins sang "Amazing Grace," speaking the words first
so the audience could join along. Collins was followed by actors
Susan Sarandon and Tim Robbins, who welcomed everyone on
behalf of Voters for Choice, NARAL and HWPC.

Jane Fonda was introduced next, and the applause rolled over the
chamber. "I think that all of us feel that there is an energy and a
unity and a joy in this room that makes us very happy and gives up
great hope." Applause. "Also, such a breadth of experience, so
many generations. I don't know about you, but it's been a long time
since I've marched." More applause. And I've never marched with
my daughter." Her voice broke, and the applause was even longer.
"And there are a lot of daughters and mothers in this room. And
I've never marched with my sister-in-law . . ." The applause
flowed as she wiped a tear from her eye.

"It's been very special," declared Fonda. "And it's special to be
from a town, Hollywood, in which some very prophetic words were
said by Joan Crawford: 'No more wire hangers!' That would make a
great poster. Faye Dunaway should be here. Where is she? She
should have done this."

Laughter and applause mixed and overlapped to create a rousing
ovation. In about twenty years, Jane Fonda had made a remarkable
journey from home to Hanoi and back home again, from fiery
revolutionary to mainstream exercise video huckster. Fonda's reha-
bilitation attested to either the forgiving or forgetful nature of the
American people.

Fonda introduced Linda Ellerbee, sometimes newscaster, who
told a very long tale about her own abortion, and then presented "a
panel of witnesses" to address the subject. Judy Collins returned to
sing "Bread and Roses," which had been a rallying anthem for the
suffragettes in the 1920's. Actors Jill Eikenberry and Michael Tuck-
er from "L.A. Law" introduced writer Alice Walker to read her
poem entitled, "The Right To Life: What Can the White Man Say
to the Black Woman?" Walker left no doubt as to her opinion of the
"White Man":

When we have children you do everything in your power to make them feel unwanted from the moment they are born. You send them to fight and kill other dark mothers' children around the world. You shove them on public highways into the path of oncoming cars. You shove their heads through plate glass windows. You string them up and you string them out. What does the white man have to say to the black woman?

. . . Those of us who love life too much to willingly bring more children into a world that's saturated with death—abortion, for many women, is more than an experience of suffering beyond anything most men will ever know, it is an act of mercy and an act of self-defense. To make abortion illegal again is to sentence millions of women and children to miserable lives and even more miserable deaths. Given his history in relation to us, I think the white man should be ashamed to attempt to speak for the unborn children, for the black children. [Applause erupted from her captivated audience.] To force us to have children for him to ridicule, to drug, to turn into killers and homeless wanderers, is a testament to his hypocrisy. [Applause, applause.] What can the white man say to the black woman?

Only one thing that the black woman might hear: Yes, indeed, the white man could say, your children have the right to life. Therefore, I will call back from the dead those thirty million who were tossed overboard during the centuries of the slave trade, and the other millions who died in my cotton fields and hanging from my trees. . . . But I will go even further. For I know that until I treat your children with love, I can never be trusted by my own, nor can I respect myself. And I will free your children from insultingly high infant mortality rates, short life spans, horrible housing, lack of food, rampant ill health. I will liberate them from the ghetto. I will open wide the doors of all the schools and hospitals and businesses of society to your children. I will look at your children and see not a threat, but a joy. I will remove myself as an obstacle in the path that your children, against all the odds, are making towards the light. I will not assassinate them for dreaming dreams and offering new visions on how to live. I will cease trying to lead your children, for I can see I never understood where I was going. I will agree to sit quietly for a century or so, and meditate on this. *That* is what the white man can say to the black woman. We are listening.

The room exploded, the audience rose to their collective feet and clapped and cheered and shouted. I checked my watch; the ovation lasted thirty-one seconds—quite a long time.

"Was that racist?" I asked a newspaper reporter in the midst of the hurrahs.

She slowly shook her head up and down, still focused on the event. "I think so."

"And sexist?"

She answered with another affirmative nod.

I spotted several people crying. "And contrary to the spirit of the rally, which is supposed to be, We're all marching together, men and women, black and white, and all that?"

She nodded again.

"Right," I said. I had imagined that self-flagellation had been out of style since Leonard Bernstein's infamous radical-chic party for the Black Panthers back in the Sixties. I was wrong.

The program progressed with a few words from actresses Kelly McGillis, Marlo Thomas and Morgan Fairchild, as well as Gloria Steinem and Kate Michaelman. Michaelman pointed out the politicians in the audience including Senators Alan Cranston of California, Barbara Mikulski of Maryland and Tim Wirth of Colorado, and Governor Madeline Kunin of Vermont.

Finally, Melissa Manchester walked onto the stage to close the show. "I am the Encino representative for the Hollywood Women's Political Committee," she announced to the crowd's amusement. She sang her own composition, "Sometimes I Feel So Sorry for God" and then asked everyone to join her in singing "America the Beautiful."

Manchester said that they would sing the first verse and then the third. "It's just grand." She spoke the words on the third verse: "Oh beautiful, for heroes proved, in liberating strife. Who more than self, their country loved, and mercy more than life."

"Those are grand words," Manchester said, "because I'm so proud to be a part of the American potential, so proud to be a part of the female potential. I'm so proud of being in a system that is fragile and exquisite and worth fighting for and shouting for and singing about." Of all the words uttered that night, Melissa Manchester's resounded most clearly and eloquently.

A congregation of civilians waited in the lobby for their favorite celebs. The tourists, mainly middle-aged, pressed forward but remained respectfully quiet, and watched as the reporters cornered stars for interviews.

Actress Valerie Harper was talking to several print journalists, who were busy scribbling away. "Women's rights, women's equality, is the longest nonviolent revolution in the history of the world. It's been going on for centuries. And this is a milestone."

Having spent years working to alleviate world hunger, Harper spoke confidently about the relationship between poverty and family size, both here and in the Third World, and her take on the weekend. "We do a lot of work with hunger, and you get to be very connected to poverty and hunger and homelessness and health care. . . . I mean, it's all dovetailing. We must take humane and fair action."

"Look how skinny she is," an older bystander in a pants suit whispered to her friend, shaking her head in disapproval. "Too skinny, if you ask me."

"I don't know," her friend said. "I wouldn't complain."

The morning of the march dawned crisp and mostly sunny after a rainy night. An army of Americans poured out of buses and trains and planes and cars. The Hollywood Women's Political Committee and Planned Parenthood had sponsored a breakfast at the Russell Senate Caucus Room for, according to the HWPC Delegation Schedule, "HWPC supported candidates, Congressional leadership, Press," which included Senators Cranston and Mikulski again, and Senator Howard Metzenbaum of Ohio, Senator Bob Packwood of Oregon and Representative Don Edwards of California. Despite the political firepower, as well as remarks by actresses Donna Mills, Anne Archer, a Planned Parenthood board member, and Bonnie Franklin, a member of Planned Parenthood's board of advocates—not to mention free food—the real action was building outside and that was where everyone wanted to be. Shuttle buses waited to speed the HWPC members to the staging area near the Washington Monument; the rest of us made the relatively short trek on our own, by cab or on foot. HWPC ran the smoothest operation in the field, but then, its staffers were responsible only for the group's activities, not having to worry about the march itself.

The grassy areas between Constitution and Independence Avenues were gorged with people, mainly women, mainly dressed in white, in memory of the old suffragettes. Thousands, tens of thousands, hundreds of thousands, they walked around and waited, waited for the event to coalesce and commence. HWPC had set up a tent in the midst all this swirling humanity, near the front of the march, to shelter its members from the clutches of admirers. The press was allocated a small area enclosed by a fence, so journalists could scramble for space on the slippery ground and shout to celebs inside the tent to come out, come out, and be interviewed. As usual, many obliged; publicity for the cause was the primary point of their attendance.

Sometime after noon, the celebrities were called out to the starting line. Alone or in small groups, the stars emerged from the tent, shepherded by extremely protective HWPC staffers, bristling with walkie-talkies, shooing away reporters and interlopers. The crowd cheered their show biz favorites, who waved back.

A rough lineup took shape, as volunteers linked arms and held back the uninvited. Rapidly, however, the area was flooded with celebrities, pols, media, individuals wearing sashes inscribed "Honored Guest," people carrying Instamatics, families— everybody. A truck loaded with news photographers idled ahead of a row of police mounted on large, patient horses; helicopters hovered overhead; the crowd threatened to crush in on the center; time was passing, and the banners had to be held up for the cameras.

There were two banners. The one at the very front was of the generic pro-choice variety, while the second heralded HWPC. The first rank was naturally filled first, and with some of the highest profile types, including Fonda, Fairchild, Close, Hamill and Whoopi Goldberg. This left the HWPC staffers in distress, and they hurried to find appropriate hands, and faces, to hoist the flag.

Meanwhile, marchers-turned-fans roamed through the ranks, pointing out who was who.

"That's Morgan Fairchild," a mother insisted to her daughter.

"No," the teenager responded. "It's Dee Wallace."

"Dee Wallace?" her mother shot back. "It's Morgan Fairchild!"

One staffer was particularly upset by the dearth of celebs at the second position. She ran back and forth, sending one assistant scurrying for stars, and searching for press photographers to shoot the banner.

"Who cares about celebrities?" she yelled to the world at large, then spun to her assistant with a flash to impart to the missing celebs. "If they want the press, they have to make it easy!" She returned to her original cry. "Who cares about celebrities?"

"She's in 'Dynasty,'" a woman on my right said excitedly.

"Who?" her companion said.

"Her."

"Her? No."

"Yes."

"No. Are you sure?"

"Of course. Don't you think? Maybe not."

"Well, maybe."

"No. You're right. She's on that other show."

"No. Are you sure?"

The surge towards the front was so great that the lines were being split further and further apart. The march was going to start, ready or not.

Just then, the truck with photographers falling out the sides moved out, the police horses snorted and strode off, and finally the lead row took its first tentative steps. We were underway.

Constitution Avenue was jammed from side to side and the marchers proceeded slowly, as befitted their overwhelming numbers. The press jostled to stay a few feet ahead and beside the ends of the pro-choice banner, ensuring decent sight lines and pictures. Between the media and other people who wanted to get that close-up view of the illustrious company, the line was threatened with being overrun. Parade marshals threw two lines of volunteers into the breach, flanking the row. As the volunteers held hands, straining to maintain their chains, they folded inward, back against the pressure. More volunteers were rushed to strengthen the weak links and they held.

The press quickly found itself caught between volunteers, celebs and onlookers, complaining, cursing, stumbling sideways to maintain its bearings. This was the moment of glory, for star and reporter alike, embraced in their endless fox-trot, each knowing the other's steps and twists and turns, each depending on the other to make the dance complete, full of grace and ease.

Somewhere on Constitution, the banner line tenuously halted. Jesse Jackson appeared from the sidewalk, waving to the marchers as many applauded, and assumed a place near the middle of the front row, grabbing a piece of the banner. Jackson's tardy arrival guaranteed maximum media exposure.

I was at the front when the march revved up again, and tossed like a tumbleweed with the other writers and photographers as we moved down the street. An elbow from behind caused me to falter, and I stepped back and fell out of orbit. In seconds, I was left in the dust, standing in the midst of the masses. But despite being en-gulfed in a constantly moving river of humanity, I had no trouble holding my ground. There was no shoving, no pushing, just people without pause strolling down the avenue, laughing, singing, chant-ing, having a hell of a good time, the torso of the procession so different from the head. It resembled an ancient battle line, where the spear carriers in the vanguard fought to the death, while the soldiers in the next row, only a few yards back, lounged until it was their turn. Two treks were taking place, one for the media and national notice, the other for the marchers.

The march proceeded up Constitution, from Fourteenth Street to First Street, then aimed right and trod up the steps of the Capitol to a stage constructed just for the occasion. The crowd occupied the grass and the VIPs inhabited the stage.

Hours of speeches and songs followed, all provided by the usual suspects, from Hollywood to Washington. Some of the celebrity spots were duplicates of Saturday night. While the show went off up front, the media was scrambling for interviews in the back. The Reverend Jackson was first off the mark, opening with just one reporter and building to a pack, whose members dropped out after getting their fill, only to be replaced by colleagues. Thus, Jackson got to keep going, with nary a pause, winning a sizable chunk of air time.

I left for the airport.

I sat next to a lady from upper New York State on the shuttle home. She was a mother and housewife, who, perhaps inspired by the day's events, immediately told me about her own abortion some twenty-five years ago. She had been a Sixties activist, and had tried, along with Paul Newman, among others, to found a college for other activists. She described the actor as a "really nice guy," and said he was little and thin, with "electric blue eyes."

I asked her if she had seen any of the celebrities present at the march today.

"Celebrities?" she answered. "Like who?"

I mentioned a handful.

"Really," she replied, her voice more disinterested than questioning. "I guess not."

That night, the media reported estimates of the crowd size ranging from a couple of hundred thousand to over half million. National and local television news, which had demonstrated interest in the celebrity presence before the event, now concentrated on the march and its meaning. Perhaps because the print press had more space with which to contend, the stars received more space, in prose and pictures. Predictably, *People* magazine highlighted the celebrity presence to the hilt; eleven out of twelve photos in its article were of stars, nineteen of the twenty-five paragraphs of prose.

The weekend demonstrated that the relationships between celebrities, politicians, the media, the public and the political process had become confusing and intertwined. The public and the press loved their stars, and elevated them to the status of role models, of heroes. Nonetheless, did anyone actually pay attention to what they said? Who did they reach? How? Why? My essential concern was not the money trail, who raised how much for which candidates; while significant, especially to the Democratic politicians who were the main beneficiaries, that was more a matter of technique than philosophy. As a consequence of their fame, it is easy for celebrities to raise money for virtually any purpose, political or not. We shall explore this further.

Celebrity fundraising is the result rather than the cause, and I was after bigger game. Hollywood's central impact lay in a larger arena, the area of political opinion, communal values, societal expectations. The question remained: what was the nature of this impact? What was the result so far, and what awaited us tomorrow?

I needed to know more about the citizens of show biz. I had seen them on foreign territory; now I needed to observe them in their natural habitat. I needed to speak to people who could explain what made the wheels spin in Los Angeles, especially in people's heads.

It was time to go West.

Chapter 2

Los Angeles

Present at the Birth

John Randolph, actor and activist, has been standing at the center of Hollywood's political whirl for most of his professional life. Before delving into Hollywood today, I wanted to gain a view on its past. Randolph was the man who could provide an unparalleled—and entirely personal—perspective.

Whether the name immediately rings a bell, you know John Randolph. He won both the Tony and Drama Desk awards for his portrayal of the grandfather in Neil Simon's *Broadway Bound*. He was Jack Nicholson's father in the movie *Prizzi's Honor* and a police inspector in *Serpico*. He was Bob Newhart's father-in-law on the television series "The Bob Newhart Show," Mary Tyler Moore's dad in her last series, and John Mitchell in the mini-series *Blind Ambition*. Currently, he is starring in a new sitcom called "Grand." In the course of a career that has spanned five decades so far, his ruddy, expressive face and exuberant manner has become a familiar, welcome sight on stage, film and television.

But there is more to John Randolph. He was on the phone when I arrived at his Hollywood apartment. Waiting in his living room, surrounded by awards and mementos, I opened a booklet that was distributed at two luncheons honoring him, one in Los Angeles and the other in New York, both part of a tribute sponsored by the National Council of American-Soviet Friendship. The organization had recently named Randolph its national chairperson.

The inside page listed over two hundred friends and sponsors of the event, from Ed Asner to Senator Alan Simpson, Eli Wallach to Mayor Tom Bradley, Jack Lemmon to Representative Ronald Dellums, Stella Adler, Richard Dreyfuss, Jack Gilford, Raul Julia, Rita Moreno, Gene Saks and Rip Torn, on and on. The next few pages were copies of letters congratulating Randolph on the tribute and on his life and work, from Senators Bill Bradley of New Jersey and Alan Cranston, as well as official proclamations attesting to the same from New York and Los Angeles. A man of the political left, Randolph has intelligence, good humor and overriding, irrepressible decency that has attracted friends from all ideological ranks. And then there is his courage and his faith, for Randolph has championed his convictions and has suffered for it, suffered through some of the most frightening periods in our history, suffered and stood fast.

Randolph entered the room, a big smile gracing his face, and started to talk. It didn't take long to realize that listening to John Randolph was listening to a fair slice of the history of the entertainment industry, for better and worse.

He began with an enthusiastic rush, like an eager young man, full of hope and ideas, and told about being invited to speak at Iowa State University.

"I was asked to speak at the Northwest Drama Conference, which is a yearly thing, and be a judge of the best acting. And my agent said, 'John, don't be political. Now John, this is not a political thing.' I said," and Randolph's voice rose in astonishment still fresh, "How can I talk about myself as an actor without talking about being Jewish and having no theatrical background and coming from a middle-class family and so forth? I have to talk about the fact that during the Depression I got into the theater. The United States government, for the first time in history, had a WPA, Works Programs Administration, and they paid these people $23.86 a week, and they put you together to spend the money. And I, for the first time, coming out of college, began to see people more radical than I, people more conservative, but I was a part of that because I was in a theater group that charged twenty-five cents admission."

"What college was that?"

"City College [in New York]. I was a lower junior when I left in 1935. There's a perfect example of where my consciousness was beginning to be raised politically, helped by the United States government supporting the arts for the first time—not to support the arts, really, basically to put money into circulation. That was the whole idea of Roosevelt."

Randolph recalled the names of the innovative leaders of the WPA. "Under that kind of leadership, plus the leadership that came out of putting a hundred people together in a room and saying, 'Go ahead, rehearse four hours a day, you don't have to put anything on, just rehearse four hours a day'—out of that came an explosion in the arts that we have never seen in this country. There was a special excitement and vitality when you brought all of these people of different backgrounds together, without any hindrance of the Royal Shakespeare Theater," and Randolph's accent changed from pure New York to upper crust English, "where our tradition is to play Othello and so on and so on."

Randolph become American again. "You had nothing, you had kind of a raw vitality, and then you had the machinery that went into operation, you had a classic theater, you had an Orson Welles Mercury Theater, you had a one-act play theater, you had two black theaters opening up in Harlem, the Lafayette Theater, you had a Traveling Suitcase Theater, you had two Children's Theaters, you had writers, directors, you had a Living Newspaper, you had news-papermen and actors and producers and scenic designers, and they all got together and created the Living Newspaper. And it was all new forms. Well, this explosion, of course, was very exciting to me. Once I experienced that, I said, 'Jack, how can I talk? They want to know the truth! I can't tell them any bullshit! I'm going to tell them exactly about my experiences.' "

Randolph became quieter, more reflective. "Then, all right, now face it; now I get into show business and suddenly I'm blacklisted. How am I going to talk about fifteen years of my life?" Then he laughed and spoke strongly. "Why, I had no trouble at all. I spoke to those students, it was in my bio that I was blacklisted. They asked questions about that. I would say that amongst the theater people, there was a deep politicization, deeper than I had thought. So I found it easy to talk to them. And it was the first time I had done anything like that in a long, long time.

"I am interested in the youth, and I find that when I'm frank with them, I don't have any trouble being understood. I feel that when you level with young people, they understand better than we think. I think that I'm at a wonderful age where I don't have to lie as much as I lied when I was younger in order to get ahead. I may be an optimist; I *am* an optimist, in spite of all the shit that's going around. I don't get thrown too quickly, because I think things change much more rapidly than we think, and I think that sometimes we don't have complete control of those circumstances. But I think you are safe, as a human being, if you do what you believe in doing. I don't care if you're middle of the road or even conservative; I know where you stand, it's okay. I don't like people who are with me one minute, off away the other, when it is safe, when it is not safe. So I say, 'Okay, that's your problem, not my problem.' "

"Are you worried that the bad times might return again?"

"Am I afraid to get into trouble?" Randolph said. "Do I believe there's a blacklist coming out? I've been asked that over and over— 'You think, John, the same thing will happen that kept you out of Hollywood for fifteen years?' And I have said I don't think it can happen again like that. But then I had to qualify; somebody pulled me up short. An interviewer said, 'What about Ed Asner?' He's been having a rough time since he stood up for Medical Aid for El Salvador and the right wing began to smear him, saying he was using the name of the Screen Actors Guild, and he was using money from the union. None of which was true. And the the fact that he would talk to other unions, he would talk to the bakers, he would go to the steel workers. Ed has a working class background. He's proud of it. But man, when his show is pulled off the air—"

Randolph halted as he remembered and then his voice surged forward. "Kimberly Clark that does Kleenex were the leading blacklisters in the days when I was blacklisted, and they pulled their support, and suddenly syndication for Ed Asner's show was stopped. There was a ten million dollar negotiation. Everything's all figured out, you cannot do a show for five years or six years and not get it sold for syndication. I mean, that's what they meant. Suddenly, they can't sell it. Things stops. Not getting any movie jobs. I mean, not even offers. He did one movie about the Rosenbergs, with Sidney Lumet, practically no money at all. It was an extraordinary example of how there can be a blacklist. Hey, Ed's not starving, he's a millionaire. And he still sticks to his principles. But his is a name the right wing considers the curse. He's the enemy. And when they talk that way, listen to the poison that comes out. So it's there. It's lying under the surface. So I hope it is not naïve for me to say, 'Oh, I don't think it'll ever come back.' I say that because the union leadership today is all changed. The union leadership are all against blacklisting, both in AFTRA and SAG. And Equity has always been fairly liberal. But if the networks smashed down, I don't know what would happen. I'm talking too much, aren't I?''

"No. Absolutely not."

"If you say so," Randolph smiled. "More about that, I have doubts whether or not they can institute a blacklisting like they did before. Right now, the right wing is not organized like it was. They really were all geared up, they had the guys in the FBI, they had the president of Screen Actors Guild known as T-10 to the House Committee—I mean, T-10, the president of SAG, working with the FBI, fingering people who were against him! We have that information; under the Freedom of Information Act, it's all coming out." Randolph was referring to Ronald Reagan, who served as head of SAG in the 1950s, and whose role during that era has recently undergone critical scrutiny.

I asked him to return once more to his youth, to the 1930s, and discuss how he became immersed in the Spanish Civil War.

"I was deeply involved," Randolph said. "I volunteered to go to Spain. I was nineteen and a half. I remember speaking about the war at City College. My instructor in speech was a wonderful guy named Ralph Wardlaw—funny, I can remember names, I can't remember my lines—and I used to pick subjects that were always provocative for his class. Afterwards, he would call me in and he would not talk about whether I pronounced the words properly or my approach to the speech, but about the content. He left college and went and fought in Spain. He died in the battle of the Ebro."

"You volunteered but didn't go, I take it?"

"I went as far as Ellis Island and there they go through your bio. If you were the only one working in your family, they would not take you. I don't think anybody knew that at the time. The point was, they had real principles about that. That's why most everybody was either single, men and women. And I was working for the National Youth Act, it was like the WPA, it was a student thing, and I was getting fifty cents an hour. Going to City College and making fifty cents an hour, and contributing to my family. So they didn't take me and I was a terribly disappointed man, and I helped organize ambulances for Spain, that kind of thing. Spanish refugee movement. Medical Aid for Spain, like Medical Aid for El Salvador. Harvard sent an ambulance. NYU, too.''

"Was there any government or professional backlash because of your involvement?"

"It's very interesting," Randolph said. "Later on, people were called up for having helped in the Spanish Civil War. Veterans came back, they were on the Attorney General's list of subversive organizations. That came after the war. During the time of the war, nobody cared one way or the other. I mean, as a student, you went and raised money. It was a big cause. I think that we were right, historically, about what we were doing. I was involved in the student movement when the *Bremen* came into New York Harbor. You know about the *Bremen*, the Nazi cruise ship? The American Student Union, City College, Columbia and NYU, all worked together to go aboard that ship, with some longshoremen, guys who later on went to Spain. Now everybody could go on board ships in those days, so we went aboard the ship and at a signal, we all gathered around the flagpole. And bang, this guy, this longshoreman, climbed up. Bill Bailey was his name. I didn't know who he was. Later on, I found out he went to Spain. And he's still alive, a wonderful guy. He ripped down that Nazi flag and that night the *Bremen* left New York harbor. The chutzpah for them to come into New York City with two and a half million Jews, with the Nazi flag up there!" Randolph raised his hands in the air in unfailing outrage at the Nazis.

"As far as Spain is concerned," he said, "I think I have the plaque in the other room, it was given to me by the Abraham Lincoln Brigade for thirty-two years of anti-fascist activity and support of the Brigade. Because when they came back and were considered persona non grata, I entertained every year that they met on their anniversary, and we did readings, we did something always for Spain, as actors. But not many actors were doing that, because once you got on that Attorney General's list, you couldn't work anywhere else. Certain places wouldn't even let you rent a hall. I was a radio announcer in 1938 when the veterans marched in Boston, and they asked me, because I had a theater and would march with them, to help. Not because I was a veteran, but because my life had been to tied up with them. You want to go right up to date? Okay. June 5, this year, I'll be doing the fundraising for the Veterans Abraham Lincoln Brigade, to send more ambulances down to Nicaragua.''

I said, ''It's important for me to make the distinctions between then and now. I gather that people back then weren't against the U.S. government, they were against the Nazis and fascists.''

''We were against the Non-Intervention Act,'' Randolph said. ''I was against Mussolini and Hitler, who were experimenting with their weapons for World War II. Our government was saying, 'Let's stay out of it, both sides, all sides.' And that was wrong. It was the same old crap.''

''What would you have called yourself back then, politically?'' I asked.

''Me? I was a communist,'' Randolph said. ''A Marxist. I was not a member of the Communist Party, but I was very close, very impressed with the people that I met in the Communist Party. I mean, I was more careful only because I was middle class and I was told never to get involved with anybody. But they were the ones who had passion and, of course, like any student, I was involved in asking a million questions. I believe that they were right in Spain and I believe history proved them right. Many times they were not right. I'm talking about that particular war.''

I asked about the next decade, the 1940s. ''Tell me about your Army experience.''

''You're asking questions nobody else bothers to ask; even I don't bother to ask anymore,'' laughed Randolph. ''I volunteered after Pearl Harbor. I was in a show called *Native Son*, during which I married my wife. I volunteered right away, but they wouldn't accept me because I had a medical problem. Then, in April, when the show closed, I applied again and this time they accepted me.''

''Where did they send you?''

"I was educated at Scott Field, Illinois, where I became a tower operator. And then I was sent to Chanute Field, where the real training was. I was supposed to be in radio communications, but I didn't know anything about radios. They asked me what my background was and I said radio, but I meant radio announcer, and so they put me in radio. And let me tell you, my solution to anything mechanical is to kick it."

"Why didn't you join the acting arm of the service, and act in those training films and appear at bond drives?" I wondered.

"I didn't want to go into that," said Randolph. "I wanted to go into combat."

"Like Clark Gable." (Gable volunteered for the Army Air Corps and served as a gunner in a B-17 bomber, flying combat missions over Europe.)

"I was going to be a hero," Randolph said. "I applied for combat but it didn't make any difference. They looked at my background and sent me to radio school in Scott Field, Illinois. I asked to be transferred to the weather and control tower, and I was. I actually went to the tower for a short amount of time in Scott Field and then they sent me to Chanute, which was a really big field, with people coming back from the war and so forth. And I was a tower operator there for quite a while, then at Godman Field, Fort Knox, Kentucky.

"Suddenly, while I was sitting in Chanute, waiting to go to the Pacific Theater—the war had practically ended in Europe and they were sending people out to fight the Japanese and end the war there—and I wasn't moving. I was ready to go, but found myself not moving. Didn't know why. I applied to be shipped. Buddies in my outfit were all being shipped out to the islands. Finally, I complained about it. And they said they don't know why. In the meantime, I wasted a lot of time and then suddenly got shipped. I got shipped every three weeks to a new air base, to Lincoln Army Air Base, I went to North Dakota, I went to every fucking air field there ever was. And I'm asking everybody, especially from the Inspector General's office, 'Why am I being shipped out like this?' 'Oh, nothing.' 'Finally, one guy said to me, 'John, why do you think?' I said, 'Well, maybe they think I'm a goddamned socialist or a communist or a radical.' He said, 'That's right.' "

Randolph wore a rueful smile and his voice was hushed. It was clear that even after all these years, the mistrust of his government was a wound that had never completely healed.

"He said, 'I'll tell you, I'm a little socialistically inclined myself.' I'll never forget this officer. Guy about my age. He said, 'I went to NYU.' " Randolph paused to chuckle at that. "He said, 'You're not going to get anywhere. You're going to keep getting shuttled around everywhere. Your wife's not going to know where you are. Nobody knows where you are. I'll tell you what to do; change your job. We'll make you a firefighter. You want to go to combat? I said, 'Yeah.' He said, 'Well, you get combat as a firefighter, and as soon as they know you're a control tower operator, that's what you'll do. Cause on the line, they're not going to go with all of this shit with the generals.' So that's what I did. I became a firefighter.

"I became a firefighter and I went down to Wendover, Utah, in the Air Corps. I was in a base where, 'What you see here, what you hear here, will remain here.' It was a secret Army Air Corps base. They were experimenting with V-2 rocket projectiles, with B-29s. They built Japanese villages out in the desert and then bombed them with napalm, to see how fast they burned up. And I was in the fire brigade. In the three weeks I was there, I had already recommended different ways of loading B-29s to save time. I got a three-day pass and I decided to go to the West Coast. I decided to follow the path of *The Grapes of Wrath*. Highway 66." Randolph gave a soft smile, this memory happily supplanting the previous, less pleasant one.

"I loved Henry Fonda and all that stuff, and I took a three-day pass to Los Angeles, which was illegal. I should have only gone within a two hundred mile radius of Wendover, Utah. I went on a bus, rode twenty-four hours on the bus, saw the actors out here—never thought I'd get to California—and the Actor's Lab, lots of people I knew from New York. Watched shows for eleven hours, never slept, went back on the bus and came back. And the base was burned to the ground! I don't think I've ever told this story to anybody. This is all true. The base is burned to the ground except for the headquarters and the fire battalion headquarters. And everything else is gone."

Randolph had become very calm, almost still. "There were tents all over for the GIs. My barracks bag is packed, and I am shipped out within six hours. And the fire chief said, 'I don't know, we just got these orders. There's a team from Intelligence coming down here from Colorado Springs to check on the cause of the fire, and sabotage, and all this.' I have a feeling I would have been a dead pigeon, between you and me, if I were there. They saw my records, which indicated I was suspect. My background was radical and, at that time, whether people knew it or not, the government considered there might be a war against the Soviet Union and people like myself would be dangerous. I had an award as a control tower operator, for saving the lives of a couple of guys. I was the editor of the Army aircraft communications system newspaper worldwide. I mean, I was only a corporal, but I did all of those things, because I believed in this war against Hitler.

"But, I mean, if you want to see a dossier on me, man, I got it right in the next room. Under the Freedom of Information Act, you'll see what they have against me, including all the investigations they conducted while I was in the service. Didn't even know it. Scott Field, Chanute Field, how they opened up my barracks bag, took out my address book, all the names that were ever listed, and these were all considered contacts, whatever they did, examined all the letters my wife, my mother, my mother-in-law, my friends sent me. Copied them, resealed the envelopes. Same with anything I sent out. I had no idea; I mean, that's how naïve I was. I mean, they were shipping me around like I was a product of the railroad line. Shit, my dear wife didn't know where the hell I was. I come in there, soon as they find out who I am—I didn't know it, but what had happened was, they went through every record in headquarters and found out I'm not supposed to be there, I'm not supposed to be at a secret Army air base! Why, they had to take me out of the control tower, because it was considered security, in some sense. So, whatever my classification, I was considered dangerous in the control tower, where I had won awards for saving the lives of two pilots in P-51s. Suddenly, I shouldn't be at a secret Army air base! So they shipped me out before the Intelligence team came in, so there was no record there."

"That was a time all actors were helpful to the war effort," I commented. "We were all on the same side."

"We were all very good," concurred Randolph. "You see, there was a peace movement before Pearl Harbor. At that time, most people thought we were helping the English, who were eventually in that so-called stalemate with France, where nobody was fighting the Germans. We weren't fighting the Germans, but that line was really to tell Hitler, 'Go that way. Wipe out the Soviet Union.' Because we were no more for the Soviet Union than for the Germans. They were all the enemy. So there was a movement amongst the radicals called the American Peace Movement, against any involvement in the war on the side of England. Until Pearl Harbor happened, and when that happened, it changed the picture, so I was involved in all that. I was wrong. I was wrong in that.''

No doubt, involvement in the peace movement placed Randolph on the far end of the radical scale. I wondered if still considered himself a Marxist during the war.

''Well, if you say anybody who picked up Karl Marx is a Marxist. I would say I don't consider that I was a Marxist. I was impressed by what I was studying,'' Randolph said. ''I read a lot. I have a tremendous library. And I do think I applied Marxism better than a lot of other Marxists, because I hated phraseology and that kind of thing, and I was more flexible. I was impressed by what I had read. I do come from a conservative background, so I learned from both sides, and that was my great education at City College. We—the students and the teachers—we got involved, not just talked. It was the most stimulating, the most absorbing, the most realistic approach to politics.''

''So there is an evolution,'' I said. ''In the Thirties, when actors start getting involved in politics, often on the Marxist side, there is no penalty associated with it. Then the Forties arrive, when all that is forgotten, at least on your part, and everyone gets behind the war effort, whether they went off to fight or made movies.''

''Right,'' Randolph said. ''During that whole time, there were actors coming out here working. I mean, there was nobody being blacklisted then. People were more open. There were wonderful movies being done. There was Broadway, early television. There was nobody putting your name on a list, not for public distribution.''

''We wanted heroes, who symbolized certain values, and actors were more than ready to be those heroes. So it worked out very well for everybody's sake.''

''Right,'' Randolph said. ''My involvement in the Spanish Civil War didn't mean that I couldn't work.''

"Perhaps it gave actors a sense of empowerment, that they could be actors and be political, and everybody would applaud. Then the Fifties came along and it changed."

"Very rapidly," Randolph said.

"And today is so different again."

"I will tell you I never dreamed that I would see so many actors, producers, writers, directors, who are socially conscious and strong in that feeling. There is no shame. I can show you any list of supporters for groups defending El Salvador, South Africa, with congressmen, senators, artists, athletes, church leaders, etc. You want to see a list of names, these are the broadest fronts I've ever seen."

"Let's go back to the Fifties."

"Okay," Randolph said. "I spoke in Madison Square Garden for Henry Wallace, who was running for President on the Progressive ticket. I was a vet and represented the point of view of a veteran, for housing and progress and Henry Wallace. On that program was Gene Kelly. On that program, Frank Sinatra sang. This was in 1948, right before the blacklisting really hit. There were a lot of strong people, and then Gene Kelly was with a group, with Humphrey Bogart, Katharine Hepburn, Judy Garland—the Committee of Ten Thousand—they all went down to Washington in support of the writers, in support of those who had been subpoenaed. At the same time, Reagan, the president of SAG, went down to cooperate. So Humphrey Bogart, Edward G. Robinson, they were all in *Red Channels*, their names were in *Red Channels*, which was this so-called newspaper put out by a private group warning the media and corporate sponsors of actors and journalists judged by the group to be communists. So they were considered real Reds! Eddie Cantor—forget about it, Jack. But that was the kind of smearing that went on.

"But then they suddenly disappeared," Randolph said. I thought he was referring to the Red baiters, but then realized he was focused on his show biz colleagues. "Dore Schary suddenly became one of the boys who did a little blacklisting himself. He's supposed to be a liberal, he's a producer, head of a studio. So they changed quietly. In New York, we didn't do that kind of about-face. Suddenly it was one hundred eighty degrees and where are you, Jack? That means the studios got at everybody here quickly. But not only the broadcasting studios, but also the studios here, MGM, Warner Brothers, so on. They put the pressure on and it was open and frank. *You don't work!*

"I'm not bitter about the guy who mentioned my name because he was a nebbish; the FBI said, 'We'll drive you back to Canada unless you give us some names,' and he named some people, and his testimony was so vague and so weak and had nothing to do with anything. He said he tried to join the Communist Party and they refused to take him. Finally, he insisted. They said, on the stand, 'Why did you do that?' He said, 'Because they were standing up for white and black sharecroppers to unite and fight and I thought that was a wonderful thing.' 'And what did you do in the Communist Party?' He said, 'I went to a couple of fundraisers and that was all.' That was the *big deal*, enough to drive people into insanity, to suicide, drive people overseas, and cause people to lose everything, including the ability to work. Now that I talk about it, I hear how nonsensical all of this was."

Nonsensical and dangerous. I believed Randolph when he said he harbored no bitterness towards the man who gave him up to the House Committee like some sacrificial lamb. In contrast, his anger at his colleagues who betrayed their friends remained livid.

"It must have been a stunning thing for you to be confronted with all this."

Randolph slowed for a moment, his brow furrowed. "We were pioneers, we didn't have any background. We knew communists had to flee, we knew about the witch hunt, but we never thought the grounds of guilt by association would become power weapons."

Randolph shook his head vigorously. He was back up to speed. "I mean, you get up there and you say, 'I'm against so and so, I think he stands for just the opposite what any decent actor stands for,' and there's a guy writing your name down. You try to run against the opposition of the union and if you ran on the blue ticket you were finished. You were put on the list. Sometimes the list worked, sometimes it didn't. But it was that kind of fear. Everybody got up and said, 'I'm not a communist, I'm an anti-communist.' Anything! It didn't matter. If you wanted to have shorter rehearsal hours, whatever you want to do, it was always qualified by that phrase, it kept crawling in. And those self-appointed watchguards kept talking about the poisoning of the

bloodstream. Anybody with a radical idea was poisoning the bloodstream of America. And the phrases they used: 'infected,' 'you
were infectious.' It was like AIDS.''

"Did you or most other actors think actors had that kind of
power?''

"Nowhere near,'' Randolph answered quickly. "We never even
thought about that. Now that is an interesting difference. Now Ed
Asner becomes a target because he really is known universally.
Lucy, of 'I Love Lucy,' was progressive. Then she became, I don't
know what she became, but she suddenly just disappeared from
speaking out about things. Even her, with her sickness now, the
mail that comes in—she is powerful. She really reaches into areas
that no left-wing group ever could.''

Lucille Ball had been sick for some time, and her condition was
monitored around the world. I did not tell Randolph that I had heard
on the car radio that she had died that day.

"So in your own mind you were just speaking out or marching or
whatever as a citizen, not as an actor or star?''

"That's right,'' Randolph said. "Just as an American.''

"But you are pretty famous.''

"Well, I'm not famous, but I'm well-known. My face is well-
known. Nobody knows *me*. 'John Rudolph—Fred—what's his
name?' They don't know. But they know my face and I can go
anywhere and if I speak, it is pretty clear I am known. It's a shock.
It's a wonderful thing. Most people go through their lives, nobody
knows whether they're living or dead. London: there is a bobby
telling you he saw you on 'Dynasty.' Or you go to Spain or even
behind the Iron Curtain. In Germany, a film club: they saw *Serpico*
playing when I was in East Berlin. The world is shrinking, symbol-
ically.''

"In the 1950s, you didn't have a lot of power and you were
punished severely. Today, actors do exert more power and literally
get away with anything.''

"I would say an exception is Jane Fonda,'' said Randolph.
"What she did in Vietnam hit a nerve of people who might even
have been progressive.''

"Nowadays, actors raise money for causes and politicians, and
even testify before Senate subcommittees,'' I noted. "It seems
actors have more power than ever before.''

"We have!" Randolph agreed. "For example, Dukakis came to speak at Norman Lear's house. There was a tremendous amount of people who came, who were invited. I didn't expect to see some of the people I saw. Debra Winger. Martin Sheen. Georg Stanford Brown. Mike Farrell. Okay, we were all activists. But I saw Michael J. Fox. Justine Bateman. Burt Reynolds."

"Is this a good thing?" I asked. "Not that the opposite of that is bad; after all, they're citizens and have a right to be politically active. However, is it good that they are our heroes, our main heroes, and they have real power?"

"Do you know of any other industry," Randolph said, "do you know of any other weapon of communication that can reach more people?"

"But are they supposed to be the instrument of that weapon, or are they supposed to be the weapon itself? They don't only speak the words, they've become the live characters themselves."

"When they are in the mouth of Ronald Reagan, they become a weapon on the other side," Randolph said. "Lies can be told by somebody who's low-key and quiet, who says stupid things about the Abraham Lincoln Brigade, doesn't know what he's talking about, makes stupid remarks that are almost obscene and yet gets away with it. He's called the Gipper and he's a figurehead, he's in there all the time, gets a wonderful press. Knows how to read, and communicate on television; he was, really, a tremendous communicator. I mean, I recognize it. It pissed me off."

Randolph related that Reagan had stated that the Americans who soldiered in the Abraham Lincoln Brigade had fought on the wrong side. Considering that Hitler backed Franco and his fascist forces on the other side, it was, to say the least, an inexplicable remark. Of course, if the left could abuse the media, so could the right; what was good for the goose was good for the Gipper.

"Did you ever get invited to the White House?"

"I was invited to the White House, yes, when I was on Broadway with *Broadway Bound*."

"Did you go?"

"Yes, and I see in your eyes a certain surprise," Randolph said, a smile forming on his lips. "They announced that the President of the United States would love to meet the cast of *Broadway Bound*. Because we were a hit, right? He would have seen anybody. We put up a sheet next to the invitation, so the actors could sign up, and Linda Lavin comes to me and says, 'John how can you sign your name to come to that den of iniquity?' '' Randolph was laughing heartily, laughing through his words. ''Now I'm much more radical than Linda Lavin, I've really been involved, I've been put in jail and all the rest of it. I said, 'Linda, he doesn't own that place. I mean, that White House belongs to me! If I don't want to go in there, I'm kind of giving up my right to be there.'

''Well, she wouldn't go anyway. We went. He was upstairs. Suddenly, the President of the United States sends his love but he can't meet with us—there's a crisis, matter of national security. We did the tour anyway.''

''What do you think changed from the Fifties to the Sixties that made actors think anybody would want to hear what they had to say?''

Randolph nodded, smiling and serious. ''Deadly, deadly, Len,'' he said. ''When I toured with *Inherit the Wind* right after being a hostile witness, an extremely hostile witness against the House Un-American Activities Committee, the country was already devastated by McCarthyism. I didn't know the devastation of the country; I knew the devastation of actors. But we accepted that. We had never been rich, we had always been unemployed. But I was able to work on the stage. But I remember traveling with *Inherit the Wind*, and trying to make contact with progressive people to tell them the actors had turned back the Committee. The Committee walked out of New York saying, 'Well, somebody put the pressure on them, they wouldn't cooperate with us.' Actors and writers and directors were the first to turn back the Committee. I wanted to bring that message across to other progressive people. I thought it was important to get the names of whoever was liberal or radical in any area, and I would call them up when we hit Cincinnati or Chicago or Detroit.

''Man, I was talking to deadly fear. 'Who is this?' That kind of thing. I said, 'I'm in *Inherit the Wind* with Melvyn Douglas. I would love to meet people out here, tell you what went on in New York.' 'What's your name?' I'm talking to people who were afraid, who had been hurt, whose names had been smeared in the newspapers because they had supported Henry Wallace at one time. I saw devastation I never believed I would.''

"How did that turn around?"

"It turned around in 1962, 1963, around that time. I began to notice when I got a call from [the TV show] *The Defenders*, because by that time they had done a show on an actor or writer who was blacklisted in Hollywood. Jack Klugman played the guy and he won an Emmy. It won all these awards. And the day they won their awards, I got a call. I was in a show called *A Case of Libel*, playing a sports writer who sued another writer for calling him a communist. It was a real case of libel; the guy was smeared for advocating a second front against the Nazis, in order to help out the Russians. It was an interesting play, which I believed in, because that kind of shit was going on.

"So I got this call," Randolph went on, "and my agent said, 'Johnny, are you available for a CBS show *The Defenders*?' That was the phrase that was used—'Are you available?' Then they crossed you off the list and said, 'Oh, they changed the part to a midget or they cut it out.' But I said yes. I hadn't put blacklisting behind me. I mean, I sneaked through on a couple of shows by accident, but basically, that word 'available' was like a red flag to a bull. You get to get all sorts of Pavlovian reactions inside."

Randolph chuckled. "And I don't hear anything. They said they'd call back in an hour. My agent called back in an hour and a half. 'Johnny, let me ask you something. You did an *East Side, West Side* with George C. Scott. Who was that for?' I said, 'For CBS.' 'Good, darling, for CBS. I'll call you back.' Nothing. Nothing. I walk on that fucking stage and I am playing this reporter and the scene is where I come in, with my wife, and ask Van Heflin, who played the attorney, to take this case." Randolph's voice was rising and it was clear nothing would stop it.

"Van's sister and brother-in-law had already been blacklisted and he was scared stiff. So now we're in this play, and this is all legitimate, this is a real case. And he says, 'Well, I don't know whether I want to make a fuss about something like that, the second front is a dead issue.' You know, he's an ambitious man, he's not stupid. And I say, 'Have you lost your courage?' " Randolph was shouting, as though he were back on that stage, or maybe back in that time. " 'You don't want to take a stand on any issues that are important? You call yourself a liberal?! And then on an issue like this, you're going to back out!' "

Suddenly, Randolph smiled and he was here again. "And I am giving it to Van. And after the first act, he goes, 'Hey, what's the matter, Moose?' " Randolph laughed. "He used to call me Moose. 'Anything wrong?' I said, 'No,' and I told him about *The Defenders* and he got kind of nervous himself.

"That was when I first began to break in on TV. I have no idea why at the particular moment. It took time for McCarthyism to begin to fade; the Committee was not getting as much reaction, it had already exhausted the biggies, they weren't getting as much publicity. There was beginning to be a counter-movement against it all, because it was destroying the movie industry, destroying live television, destroying everything. This was '62. But the thing that was different about the Sixties, the contrast was I offered to speak with Melvyn Douglas, who himself had secretly and quietly been blacklisted because his wife, Helen Gahaghan Douglas, had run against Nixon for the Senate. He was told to denounce his wife by Louis B. Mayer and he refused to do that. Melvyn Douglas, who *kissed* Greta Garbo. And the first real job he had in a long time was to replace Paul Muni in *Inherit the Wind*. A wonderful man, a wonderful guy, and I loved him. And we offered to speak anywhere. Not one fucking offer from a tour of nine months throughout the United States, from any college, from anybody, from any group. The colleges were the worst. I will tell you there was a fear. This was 1956, '57. Not one single offer to speak. They were afraid I was going to be picketed, but there was no trouble. Melvyn Douglas was picketed by some veteran's group because he advocated fluoridation in the water, which was supposed to be a communist plot to poison the water."

"Tell me more about some of your troubles in the fifties."

"I was called before HUAC in 1955," Randolph said. "I was picketed in New York in a show called *Wooden Dish*. I was the first actor to get a job who had defied the House Committee. They didn't know I was going before the Committee when I got the job." Randolph chuckled. "Louie Calhern was a wonderful man, he was the star of the show and the director. I was picketed opening night and for a short while by a Brooklyn committee against communism, run by Roy Cohn, who later turned out to be a fantastic jewel on the horizon." Of all the emotions Randolph could effortlessly convey, sarcasm seemed least compatible with his personality.

"But nobody thought, I never thought, I would ever work again. It was bad enough I couldn't work anywhere on television or movies or radio. But not to be able to work on the stage, where we had an anti-blacklisting clause that came out of this particular period, was the end, as far as I was concerned. I mean, there was no solution. My wife would be blacklisted. So you teach, you look for a job, any job, to keep you alive when you have a kid. But I must say, when I got a job in *Inherit the Wind*, I wasn't getting paid a great salary, man, I had to pay the rent in New York and on the road, and had a wife and a kid and another one coming. But it was a job. For eleven months. From that point on, I never stopped working. When I got that job, I had thirty-eight dollars in the bank. Christmas coming, all that kind of stuff. So I had gone through the lowest point in my life, in one way; I didn't consider defying the Committee a low point. I mean, I was pretty proud of myself. But I didn't think in those terms; the low point was having thirty-eight bucks in the bank and a three-and-a-half-year-old daughter and Sarah pregnant with the next one. So that I've been through that period and that period was a low point in the United States. It began earlier, in 1948, '47, with the Hollywood Ten, began to go into Broadway in 1951, hitting the whole Broadway theater and television, and it didn't end for me until 1963 or so with *The Defenders*, and I ended up doing five more *Defenders*.

"If someone had said to you in 1957 that ten years later an actress would be going to an enemy capital and speaking in favor of that enemy, what would you have thought?"

"I think the depth of the feeling against the war in Vietnam speeded up the opening up process," Randolph said. "Not in the beginning, but slowly. The government apparatus couldn't do anything against you just because you were against the war in Vietnam. I was put in jail, in Kennedy Compound, for demonstrating. What's his name, our friend, Attorney General John Mitchell, issued an order. Luckily, somebody recognized me as an actor and I was in and out in fifteen minutes. Later on, I played Mitchell in *Blind Ambition* on television. I got a fucking kick out of that. I loved to do that.

"On the other hand, Jane Fonda was photographed posing next to a North Vietnam anti-aircraft gun. Even though everybody today says we didn't belong in that war, it was a terrible war, we still have great compassion for the veterans because they really suffered. So she was, and still is for a lot of people, a real, visual enemy, because of what she did.''

Randolph had led me on a tour through the decades, and through the political evolution of Hollywood. His life and career encompassed a good part of the century, in the course of which he had experienced triumph and tragedy, eventually, finally emerging vindicated and victorious. Though I did not agree with him politically, though I saw American history and policies in a different light, I cold not help but like and respect him, and admire his humanity and courage.

As I got up to leave, I noticed his sleek, modern telephone, so out of step with the decor of the apartment, and commented on the discrepancy.

''I have an automatic dialer,'' smiled Randolph. ''One number's for the President of the United States. I got a secret number for him from a supporter. Then I got one for Cranston and one for Jim Wright and Henry Waxman, and I just press the button.''

''Do you ever get any of them?''

''Sometimes,'' he laughed. ''You've got to keep trying.''

Chapter 3

New York City

Lightning on the Left, Thunder on the Right

John Randolph had provided a vibrant picture of the history of political Hollywood. I wanted to know more about what had led up to the current state of show biz politics, more about the past few decades, and I turned to two men who could tell me.

Charlton Heston and Ed Asner: when one talks about the big guns of the Hollywood political scene, the heavyweights, the champs, one is talking about these guys. Stars of the first magnitude, these two gentlemen long ago reached the top of their profession—Heston, star of *Ben Hur*, *The Ten Commandments*, *The Agony and the Ecstasy*, not to mention *Planet of the Apes* and a plethora of other movies, and Asner, star of "The Mary Tyler Moore Show," "The Lou Grant Show," and his own flock of films.

In addition to professional success, both men share an acute interest in politics and are well-known to the public for working to further their strongly held beliefs. Both men have served as president of the Screen Actors Guild, Heston before Asner.

Heston is the foremost Republican in Hollywood. Just in the month of August 1989, he could be seen on television touting

46

William Buckley's conservative journal *National Review*, along with Tom Selleck and another renowned Republican, President Ronald Reagan. He had also appeared in magazine ads for *Insight*, a conservative publication, and print ads and TV spots for the National Rifle Association.

Asner is as liberal as Heston can be considered conservative. Among his many political acts was helping found the controversial Medical Aid for El Salvador, a group which actively opposes U.S. involvement in the Salvadoran war and also assists victims of the conflict. Asner's political life began early.

"I had sisters who were social workers and they may have done a great deal to influence my conscience," Asner told me over the phone from London. "Three other factors I think affected me very strongly. I went to the University of Chicago; my liberal aspect was probably piqued there. I think the two main factors were that I was a young Jewish boy in the time of Hitler, being in America, and therefore very lucky, and that I was a young, unknown actor at the time of McCarthy and the blacklist."

"The civil rights movement was the first time I took an active part in politics," Heston told me a few days later, also over the phone, from Los Angeles. "I was active in support of Adlai Stevenson during his two campaigns for President, and then in 1968 I worked for Jack Kennedy. But that was more of a routine thing; it was understood even back in Roosevelt's day that actors could support Presidential candidates. But the first social issue in which I took a public stand was the civil rights movement in the Sixties. And I picketed in Oklahoma and in the South, and I led the arts contingent in the March on Washington [the 1963 rally where Martin Luther King made his 'I have a dream' speech]—which was a very interesting thing, because you would be surprised at the people who didn't do it. For good reasons. Friends of mine said, 'For heaven's sake, this has nothing to do with making movies, what do I want to get into this for? Naturally, I agree, but why do I want to go to Washington?' The list would surprise you."

Heston told me that Bill Cosby did not attend the march. I asked whether he thought it was because Cosby did not want to jeopardize his budding career.

"I have no idea," Heston said, "and I make no suppositions. I'm just telling you he didn't go. Sidney Poitier didn't go, though Harry

Belafonte did. To the best of my memory, the arts contingent comprised twenty to thirty people; call it a couple dozen. Burt Lancaster and Jimmy Garner and Marlon Brando. James Baldwin was there, the wonderful black writer, who died last year. As a matter of fact, I was enormously impressed with him. Jimmy Baldwin was pretty radical, even for that time—really radical. And I was elected leader of the arts contingent, probably because I was president of the Screen Actors Guild; although, at the time, I made very clear every time I spoke—*every* time I spoke—that I was speaking for myself and not for the Screen Actors Guild.

"We were trying to divide up public chores, once we got to Washington. And Burt Lancaster made a statement, Marlon made a statement. Very short, because we were a small group, but a highly visible group. I was going to make a statement on behalf of our entire group. They said, 'Could Jimmy Baldwin write your statement?' I said, 'I don't know if he could write something I would be entirely comfortable reading, but let's take a look at it.' And I have to say, to his immense credit, he wrote the kind of thing I would have said, better than I could have written it. It was dead on. I always respected his understanding of what his task was in that particular hundred-word statement. I think the march is conceded to be the high-water mark of the civil rights movement and certainly one of the most exciting, fulfilling days of my life."

Other than Heston, who has grown increasingly to the right over the years, high-profile conservatives are not easy to find in Hollywood. The list of prominent Republican or conservative activists in show biz is short indeed, and not particularly youthful. I tried Arnold Schwarzenegger, who emphasized his support of Bush at a campaign rally by declaring, "I only played the terminator. George Bush is the *real* terminator." Unfortunately, Schwarzenegger was spending the summer in the jungles of Mexico shooting a film.

I sought out Tom Selleck, but his publicist was neither enthused nor amused about my interest in exploring the actor's political side. I pointed out that Selleck was famous for his Republican views. The publicist disputed my contention, even after I pointed out that Selleck had addressed the Republican National Committee, introducing Nancy Reagan to the delegates and to the television audience.

"That was personal, no political."

"How can you do anything on national television at the Republican National Convention and not have it be political?"

"It was personal, not political," she repeated, and that was the end of the discussion.

In an appearance on "The Donahue Show," Selleck provided a much clearer accounting of his political acts in response to a question from a member of the audience:

"No," Selleck said. "I don't have any political aspirations. In fact, I don't think I quite fit in the box that I seem to be getting put in. And I've tried very hard not to abuse my access to the media. I think you should stand up and be counted, but at the—I said before I don't think my opinion should matter more because I happen to be in the public eye. At the same time, I don't want it to matter less.

"I was at the Republican Convention. I did support President Reagan. And President Bush. I would have stayed away from the convention, quite honestly, because I didn't think I belonged there, except for one reason. If I want to go to a convention, and I happen to be an actor, then I should spend the time and become a delegate. But in this instance, the First Lady, who I'm very fond of, and did a lot of drug abuse work with her—"

"You speak of Nancy now?" interjected Phil Donahue.

"Nancy, yeah," Selleck said. "She asked me if I would introduce her. And I think when you're asked something like that by the First Lady, or the President, you go. And no matter how you think or feel. In this case, I also feel knowing her as I do, and knowing her to be a warm, lovely woman, that she's gotten a very bad rap in the press, and this perception about her is so far from the truth, that I felt I would be weaseling out of something by not going. So I went, I tried to talk about Mrs. Reagan and leave it at that. And I'm proud that I did it."

The next query from the studio audience wondered what Carol Burnett was really like, which ended the political discussion.

I asked Charlton Heston about the past, suggesting that actors used to represent basic American values and had generally refrained from speaking out in vigorous opposition to U.S. policy.

"There's a very significant reason for that," he responded. "Performers were often overpaid, but they were under the control of the studio owners. When I came into the business, I was the second actor, after Marlon Brando, to have anything other than an exclusive contract with a studio. Marlon came out in '48 or '49, and I was right after him. And after that, things began to change. Actors could make pictures at different studios, we could play what we wanted, even though there were still some obligations to the studio. The significance is, prior to that time, the studio could and did, more or less, control what you said and did. Now, obviously, we have a First Amendment, but if your livelihood depends on not making waves, you don't make waves, even if you're Clark Gable.

"And, you know," Heston continued, "I don't think it came up much. I've worked with a lot of those guys, Gary Cooper, Jimmy Stewart, I knew Gable slightly; it just was not what you did. Because whatever position you take on an issue, roughly half the population will disagree with you, right? So it just was presumed to be a bad idea to go out on a line on any issue, on either side of the issue. As you say, actors were against Hitler, but that was about it. During the war, actors went on war bond tours, USO tours, that was a given, you had to do that. If you didn't do that, you were not a good guy, and just about everybody did. But that was it."

"Well, that was the extraordinary thing, everything changed in the sixties."

"Yes," Heston said, "you were either strongly for the Vietnam War or strongly against it. And I think that more significant issues when you are talking about celebrities—and we are talking more about actors than athletes, because I think athletes, by and large, avoid any public involvement. The more I think of it, I can't think of any, can you?"

I mentioned Roosevelt Grier, who was with Robert Kennedy when he was shot, later turning into a conservative Republican and supporter of Pat Robertson in the 1988 Presidential race. Of course, the foremost examples of athletes in politics are former Buffalo Bill quarterback Jack Kemp, ex-congressman and current Secretary of Housing and Urban Development, and former New York Knick forward Bill Bradley, now United States Senator from New Jersey. Still, Heston was right; many more actors than athletes are publicly involved in politics. Not that athletes don't generate the same mindless enthusiasm enjoyed by actors: recently flipping through the channels, I came across a professional volleyball game, played on some beach before a couple of bleachers of fans, and paused just long enough to hear a CBS commentator exclaim, 'These athletes get to play in front of large crowds wherever they go, and they are worshipped as gods!' Gods, he said, no less—and that from a CBS man, the network of Edward R. Murrow.

"Athletes don't tend to be as effective communicators," Heston said. "Communication is the actor's skill."

I posed the same hypothesis to Ed Asner, how we used to have many heroes and now we do not, and how actors have become more outspoken and political.

"I think it is more difficult to maintain heroes anywhere today," Asner said, "once they enter the public limelight of expression, be they actors, be they politicians."

I asked him if actors functioned as heroes today.

"I don't think they're our heroes anymore than they used to be," he replied. "People worship them."

Asner asserted that few actors take political stands, and that fewer still would dare if the national political climate changed for the cooler.

"During the blacklist days," Asner said, "there was the Committee of the First Amendment, and those people really got their heads bashed in. But they did exist for a while. If the HWPC took a really unpopular stand, if the terror descended upon us and the HWPC took an unpopular stand, those people belonging to the HWPC would be squashed."

I asked Asner why Hollywood is so chock full of Democrats and liberals.

"Well," Asner began, "actors, for the most part, wherever you are, are identified with the liberal thought of the nation—the arts. There is an innate understanding that actors survive best with liberalism. They operate best, they flourish best, under the most liberal of regimes, no matter where it may occur, behind the Iron Curtain or in front of it."

"That's self-interest, or self-interested domestic policy, but that doesn't explain why they'd be more liberal on Central America or any issue that has no direct effect on their lives," I said.

"I'm not saying I'm one of the founders of Medical Aid for El Salvador because I'm an actor," Asner said. "It's not because of that. Once again, that goes back to those early years, whatever made me a liberal, whatever made me a concerned citizen.''

Charlton Heston made the transformation from Democrat to Republican a long time ago, just like his good friend, Ronald Reagan.

"Well, I think a great many people did," Heston said. "In my view, it isn't that there are suddenly more Republicans in the country, but that the Democratic Party moved radically leftward. That accounted for my switch. I can pinpoint it to you exactly.''

He related how he had labored hard on behalf on Democratic Presidential candidates Adlai Stevenson and John Kennedy, and had voted for Lyndon Johnson. However, it was during Johnson's 1964 campaign that Heston discovered his true political home.

"It was like an epiphany," Heston said. "I was filming a picture in upstate California, in a remote area. I was living in a motel, and every morning I would drive to the location along the same road and there was only one stoplight. And at the stoplight there was a big billboard put up by Barry Goldwater's people. And it was a picture of Senator Goldwater with a lot of white space and only one line: 'In your heart, you know he's right.' And I looked at the billboard every day, I'd look at it going out and I'd look at it coming back. And I cast my vote for Johnson as an absentee ballot, from that location. And after I cast the vote, the billboard was still there, and I looked at the billboard and said, 'That son of a bitch is right.' ''

As Heston was lodged in the very small and perhaps permanent conservative minority, I figured that maybe he had really pondered why most actors are liberals.

"*Why* are they?" Heston said. "You're not questioning that they *are*? Producers and studio heads are less so," Heston said. "As far as actors are concerned—and this is my own theory but I'm pretty confident in it—it has to do with the fact that actors make their livings with their emotions. Thus, they learn to depend on those emotions, as well they might. And they tend to say then, 'Well, what I feel is reliable. It makes me a living and therefore it must be true.' Many actors rely on their emotions for reaching decisions about the world, and they leap to simplistic conclusions. Similarly, you have to resolve a sitcom in the last five minutes, and that's done in emotional terms. I remember, gosh, twenty years ago, when the nuclear freeze was a hot issue, I debated an actor. It was not Paul

Newman; I always have to make that disclaimer, because I debated him too, on 'Nightline.' I said, 'Now, have you read this survey and these statistics?' He said, 'No, no, I don't have to read anything, this is a gut issue.' And I said, 'Okay, then we have nothing else to debate. You feel this and that's your conclusion.' And he realized he had made a dumb blunder. But it's the way many actors think. And I can understand that.''

"But that implies that being emotional is liberal."

"All I'm saying is actors . . ." said Heston, then paused and started again. "It might not be. We all had an emotional reaction to Pearl Harbor."

"But if you use that as an example, then you're saying that the emotional reaction is the inherently correct reaction, that there is something logical in what your emotions tell you."

"It depends on the issues, doesn't it?" replied Heston.

"Yes, but why would your emotions make you liberal? After all, people said that Ronald Reagan didn't so much study the facts as rely on his emotional response to events and symbols. That his world view was shaped by his career as an actor."

"That's another issue I want to touch on," Heston said.

"He reacted emotionally to things and it made him conservative."

"I think this point must be made on this question of why actors are liberal," intoned Heston, his voice flowing more smoothly again, evidently having gathered his ideas. "First of all, they rely on their emotions to make decisions. Second, an acting career is a very precarious, insecure kind of living. Every job, even to a successful actor, conceivably could be his last job. You know, it's possible. In any event, I promise you, every actor thinks that. I remember I did a series for ABC a couple of years ago, and it was a very expensive, highly touted series, and it ran for two seasons. ABC pulled the plug on it, I suspect, because it was so expensive. And there was great consternation, great speculation; why did they do it, how terrible for everybody. And I got phone calls from journalists who said, 'My gosh, what are you going to do, how do you feel, how are you going to react to this?' And I said, 'Hey, this is the longest job I've had since the Eleventh Air Force in World War II.' ''

It was a funny line that Heston had used on other occasions to illustrate the actor's dilemma. "Actors lose jobs all the time, so I never had a job a longer time. Actors constantly face up to what to many people would be a crisis. If you'd been working for the phone company for twenty years and you lose your job, that would be a major crisis. Actors lose jobs four or five times a year. Now you're out of work. They tend to turn to the victim status. They think of themselves as victims of circumstances beyond their control which to a certain extent is true. See, if I were a writer, a novelist or a painter, I could do my work whether anybody buys it or not. If I do a great piece of work, it's going to sell. If I'm an actor, if somebody doesn't send me a script and say, 'Chuck, we want you to star in this film,' then I don't get to do the film, right? Now, I've dealt with that all my life. Happily and fortunately, I continue to be able to make a good living at it. But seventy-six percent of the Screen Actors Guild made less than $2,500. That's well below the poverty line. So most actors, even working actors, tend to be very anxious about the fact that it all may end at any moment."

"So they identify with the victims, which tends to make them more liberal?"

"I think so," Heston said.

"Isn't that a good thing then? Isn't it better to identify with the victims rather than with the bosses?"

"I don't think you should identify with either victims or bosses," countered Heston.

"Don't our great leaders inevitably identify with the victims of suffering or injustice? Think of Abraham Lincoln."

"Well, remember what Lincoln said. He was indeed the Great Emancipator. But he said, 'My concern is to save the Union. If I can do that by freeing all the slaves, I will. If I can do that by freeing some of the slaves, I will do that. If I must do it freeing none of the slaves, I will do that.' Now I call that a very reasoned statement. He had his priorities in order."

(Heston came pretty close to Lincoln's actual words: "My paramount object in this struggle is to save the Union, and is not either to save or destroy slavery. If I could save the Union without freeing any slaves, I would do it; and if I could save it by freeing all the slaves, I would do it; and if I could do it by freeing some and leaving others alone, I would also do that.")

It did not seem reasonable to use the mortal danger of the Civil

War to say that Lincoln was not fundamentally opposed to slavery and did not identify with its victims. Putting that aside, Heston's point still did not advance his concept that identifying with the victims makes one more liberal.

"I'm afraid a lot of it has to do with fashion," Heston said. "In the Sixties, it was civil rights. There were those of us who marched and picketed, and those of us who didn't."

"Civil rights has always been a liberal agenda."

"Well, I don't know if it was liberal or not," he said, "but call it what you like, it seemed to be the right thing to do and I did it. It seemed to a lot of people the right thing to do, but they didn't, though they carry on about it now."

The next day, Heston called back to say he had thought of another ingredient in the making of a liberal actor.

"I think there's another factor, and that is guilt. Unlike most fields of achievement, where you can measure your capacities, demonstrate your skills on an objective scale, this is not true of acting. What somebody else thinks of a performance you give is . . . I mean, there's nothing there, it's all smoke. Even when you make a movie, the complete film is just a roll of blind film. Acting can only be experienced in time, unlike a book or a painting, or even an athletic performance, which can be measured and demonstrated to be whatever it is. Acting is what people think it is, when they see it. And all actors know this and we all tend to be faintly bemused at how it all turned out. Now at the very highest levels, there is no doubt. Laurence Olivier knew perfectly well he was the greatest actor alive. But most actors are faintly surprised by success, or even employment."

"But often the people who speak out the loudest are the ones who don't have to worry about money or employment."

"That's exactly what I'm getting to," Heston said. "How do they speak out? They speak out as liberals. They feel subconsciously guilty that somehow it worked for them and it didn't work as well for those people. And how come? How come the guy who won the sonnet reading contest at Northwestern is selling aluminum siding and I didn't win it, and I'm acting? You know. And they think, 'God, let me slip through the cracks somehow, or it could end any day.' The fact of success is a faint burden of guilt: 'Hey look, I'm sorry, I know you studied just as hard as I did . . .' Well, maybe they didn't, but there's always that anxiety. An attitude of confidence is important, is crucial in anything you do; but the absence of confidence, or the presence of guilt, I submit is more likely in actors, especially working actors, triple especially in very successful actors, and I think the fact of it, the guilt factor, can be overlooked.''

Ed Asner told me that younger actors pretended to have no fear that their political activities could adversely affect their careers.

"They're full of crap," he said. "If a young actor, or any actor, went around saying a year ago, certainly two years ago, 'There should be a state on the West Bank and we should conduct talks with the PLO,' he would hear about it. So I would say, in terms of bottom line, their thoughts and activism have been proscribed.''

I brought up Jane Fonda, who has certainly prospered despite some extremely dubious political acts. "Do you think another person, a person who is not a star, might have suffered a lot more for what she has done?''

"Of course," Asner said. "I don't think anyone else could have survived.''

"How did she?''

"Well, wealthy, first of all," he said in clipped, precise tones. "Also, Henry Fonda as dad—his respect within the community. The fact that she wasn't in TV, she was in features.''

Asner's last comment meant that there were many film producers who had the ability to hire her, as opposed to being hostage to the whims of the few and almighty television companies.

In fact, Heston expressed a somewhat similar opinion as to the secret of Fonda's success, and added a few more ideas.

"Professionally, her career peaked just at the time it didn't matter," Heston said. "Jack Warner would have hired Adolph Hitler if he had made a successful film. But what I was thinking of, I think Jane Fonda, riding the anti-aircraft gun in Hanoi and all that, permanently eliminated her husband from consideration for statewide, let alone national office, though I suppose it might be different now that they're separated.''

I told him about my conversation with John Randolph, who had said that all of his political acts were performed as a private citizen, and not as an actor.

"I think that's a fair comment," Heston said. "John's an old-fashioned Thirties Marxist, but a lovely actor. By God, he is. I've worked with John and he is a lovely man."

"So why was he blacklisted and a few years later Jane Fonda was in Hanoi?"

"Jane is an actress of enormous ability," replied Heston, "who just happened to be coming on to the very peak of her career. Also, by the time this happened to her, the media was inclined to be very easy on her. Which is not true when John got into trouble."

"You mean that the media sympathized with her anti-war stand?"

"Well, the media, during that period, was becoming increasingly liberal in its orientation, as it certainly is to this day."

I reminded Heston that for years, conservatives have often claim-ed that the media had a liberal bias, while liberals have insisted on the opposite.

"I've heard a couple of liberals say that," concurred Heston. "I don't see how you can make a case for it." He claimed that the media had been strongly pro-Dukakis during the Presidential campaign; before that, the political cartoonists "had had a field day with Reagan."

I reminded him of Reagan's "Teflon Presidency," but Heston asserted the tag simply referred to Reagan's invulnerability to the media's unkind attacks.

Ed Asner had a concise answer to the question of media competence.

"They suck," he said.

Asner was recently seen on the daytime talk show "Attitudes." Appearing on behalf of a revival of *Born Yesterday* in which he was starring, Asner broached a very serious subject on a TV program apparently designed for tackling subjects of a different nature.

"I know there's a big death penalty process going on in this state," Asner said, "and I spoke against it recently for Amnesty International. There's a great button that ACLU is putting out, which says, 'Execute justice, not people.' "

The two hostesses watched Asner with rapt attention. "Ohhh," one commented. "Hmmm," the other said. "Yeah."

That didn't last long. "Good luck on the play," the first woman said. "Nice to have you back in New York." She turned to the camera. "Coming up next: everything that's new 'afoot'—the hot-test trends . . ." And before one could spell out ACLU, Asner was gone and pretty girls were displaying the latest fashion in shoes.

Asner laughed at my account of his appearance. "My duty is to be as learned on the subjects that I speak out on as I can be," he said. "To talk as knowledgeably as I can and to admit that I don't know anything about it when we get into an area that I have not studied."

"Do you feel you are accomplishing what you want? Do you feel you are reaching people? Do you feel you have an impact?"

"I think so," said Asner. "I hope so. The point is, I don't want to sound pyrrhic, or heroic, but even if I don't achieve anything, if I believe in it, I still have to speak to it."

"What if you're on a talk show and they just want to hear about your latest movie?"

"Well," Asner said, "they're the ones who always ask me. I never volunteer the information."

"Do you think the press is not liberal?"

"I certainly don't," Asner quickly responded. "I don't think it's liberal at all. Centrist at best, generally right of center. I gave a press conference in New York and I mentioned a lot of things. From the press conference, AP came out with a story saying I blamed the Reagans for the cancellation of 'Lou Grant.' I did not do that. So a stringer from AP wrote it up that way, and it was circulated in a number of papers. In the L.A. *Times*, it was in the upper corner of the third page, fairly prominent headlines, etc. And then I kept debating, 'What should I do, what should I do?' And then, to its credit, AP must have listened to the stringer's tapes or whatever, and put out a retraction. The retraction took place in the lower right-hand corner of the third page, about the same size story. The headline this time read, 'Asner Denies White House Influence.' And I realized, once again, they didn't say 'AP is full of shit, Asner never said it'—words to that effect. By their very headline, they've got me denying something I never said in the first place! In other words, the headline itself became damaging and harmful to me, just by its very nature. So finally I realized what the fuck's going on; if you control the thought processes of five hundred, one thousand rewrite men, copy editors and headline writers in this country, you control the news in essence."

Asner recalled a 1982 press conference in Washington in which he and other entertainment figures condemned the Administration's support of the government in El Salvador.

"Howard Hesseman, Ralph Waite, Lee Grant, Bill Zimmerman, another one or two people, we went to Washington and gave our talk, which was to a hostile press, merely on the grounds that we were challenging the Administration's position. The doomsday point came for me in the press conference because I evidently became the spokesman for the group. I read the unified message of the group, saying what we were dedicating ourselves to. Then, in the question-and-answer afterwards, a cable reporter said, 'You say you're for free elections in Salvador; what happens if these elections achieve a communist government?' "

Asner sighed. "And I thought long and I thought hard, and I thought to myself, 'Oh God, this is the question I've been avoiding all my life and I have to now deal with it . . .' So I tried to weasel out of it with my first answer and went on to the next question. Then I realized, how can I be there talking about this if I weasel on answers? So I went back to him and said, 'I felt I didn't give you an adequate answer. I want to say that if it is the government those people elect, then I say let them have it.' And then we went on and finished the press conference. Afterwards, a gal came up to me, a middle-aged gal, and said to me, 'What did you think of the questions? How'd you feel about them?' I said, 'Well, I don't know. What'd you think about it?' She said, 'I thought they were rough on you.' And I said, 'Oh, thank God, I do agree with you but I didn't want to be a crybaby.' 'Yeah,' she said, 'I thought they were very rough on you.' And she walked away. And I asked somebody who she was, and she turned out to be Mary McGrory, a columnist whose work I respect very much. So I was pleased to hear her assessment."

I asked Charlton Heston if there was something dangerous about actors speaking out on political matters. What was the point? "Why would 'Nightline' have you and Paul Newman on to debate the nuclear freeze issue?" Their desultory exchange did little to enhance the populace's understanding of the highly technical issue. ("Nightline" was unable to provide a transcript of the show because, inexplicably, ABC News had no record of the event, as though the computer had seen fit to permanently erase any evidence of the actors' appearance.)

"How come I get to go on a talk show that a senator might have trouble getting on?" Heston answered. "The reasons is obvious: because the audience is more likely to watch an actor. And that's the reality."

"Isn't there a danger in that?"

"Of course," Heston said.

"So, is it a good thing when actors speak out?"

"I think it's a good thing when *I* speak out," Heston said. "It depends on the actor."

When he finished chuckling, Heston elaborated. "I value the right to speak very much and I feel a responsibility to inform myself on whatever issue I might be speaking."

"Fine, but you, like any actor, are not responsible for the ultimate decision. A politician has to suffer the consequences of his decisions in a very tangible sense, i.e., whether he's going to get re-elected or not."

"Well," Heston replied, "it was thought in the 1960s that I might suffer for my demonstrating for civil rights, and that's why other people didn't do it."

"Is that true any longer? Does anyone feel they are going to suffer for their beliefs? John Randolph said Ed Asner's show was canceled because of his politics."

"I know Ed says that," Heston responded. "And Ed and I have had our ups and downs. At the time, Wayne Rogers had his show, 'House Calls,' canceled, and his ratings were higher than Ed's show. But I know that Ed feels that, and it cannot be proved or disproved."

Asner had a very different perspective on the issue of whether his political work has had specific repercussions on his career.

"I know it has," he said.

"Do you think that's why your show was canceled?"

"Yes. And why it took a year and a half before anybody picked up the show for syndication. It explains the reduction in the number of jobs I got afterwards."

Asner's voice was becoming even shorter, more precise, revealing his excitement. "Well, you know, my little theory is that whenever a blacklist exists, it exists with the help of liberals; and I've talked to liberals who admit to this, who become aware of having done it." Asner slowed, became calmer again. "In my own way, as a liberal, I've betrayed my principles in other areas. But on a talk show in Washington four years ago, I was saying that liberals participate in a blacklist by different methods. Take me; I'm proposed for a job and they are in the hiring mode. They look at me and they think, 'No, he's too fat, he's too old, he's too gray, he's too bald,' or as one big casting director said, 'He's too overexposed.' And they find reasons whenever they feel that I would not be right or good for their very special baby, their property—and thereby don't hire me. There's really no way you're going to find that unless each and every one of those people goes through intensive examination of themselves and their motives.''

''You mean their real agenda was political? They didn't want trouble?''

''That's an unconscious psychological agenda,'' Asner said. ''This agenda was proved to me after I made this statement on that talk show in Washington, oh, six months to a year later. I got a request to narrate a documentary in Boston. I was busy working on the documentary and the producer gave me a lift at one point back to the studio, and he was telling me that a few years before, he was on another documentary and he put my name at the head of the list of those he wanted as narrator, and his bosses returned the list to him with my name scratched off. And he didn't do anything, he didn't fight it, he didn't say anything. And when he heard me on the talk show, he realized that he qualified under that list of people. And then he came forward with this other documentary to try to atone for the past. And in my opinion, I think that goes on all the time. And I'm not saying anything can be done about it, but I think it happens.''

''So you'd say that though a lot of Hollywood people are liberal, the people who control the purse strings are conservative?''

''Yes,'' Asner said. ''They control the purse strings, they control the publicity, they can merely look upon the choice as not a wise choice, not a palatable choice.''

Heston had also said that the money people, the producers and studio executives, were more conservative than the more public members of the Hollywood community. Unbeknownst to either, Heston and Asner agreed on a lot of things, coming from opposite sides to reach the same conclusions.

However, on certain subjects there could be no agreement. Their sparring began when Asner became president of SAG at the end of 1981. They differed over union business: giving an award to Ronald Reagan, helping the air traffic controllers fired by Reagan, joining SAG with the Screen Extras Union. And then there was Central America.

"The shit hit the fan when I read the prepared statement for this group in Washington," Asner said, referring to the D.C. press conference on El Salvador, "because I hadn't properly stated before I made the declaration that I was not speaking as the president of SAG, which was the technique Charlton Heston always used for everything he used to stand up for. I made my declaration in the middle of the speech, or maybe towards the end; couldn't have been more than five or ten minutes of our being there and I made it quite clear that I was not speaking as the head of the Screen Actors Guild. Heston made a huge hullabaloo about it, that I should have said it before the speech. Nobody walked out, nobody printed their story without hearing it all, so there's nothing lost there. He saw his chance and I, ever the honest man, responded honestly, saying I didn't say it at the beginning of my speech, I said it at the end of my speech. So what? Same results are there, same ears were there. But the storm of controversy that was generated in the papers made people think I had committed some great boo-boo, that I had truly sinned against God.

"Actors wrote me letters saying, 'Who the hell do you think you are? You're not spending our money without my saying it's okay, blah, blah, blah.' There was a lot of that. That controversy was fed through all the papers and generated a lot of misinformation in people's minds. It lasted for several months and in May the show was canceled."

Through it all, according to Asner, one incident loomed over the others. "Charlton Heston," he said, "with whom I had rubbed shoulders at our strike only a year before, and seemed very sympathetic of the strike and everything we stood for, began lying about me in the press on Latin American subjects, that I was discussing Latin American subjects in the board meetings, as union business. A total out-and-out lie. I never had once mentioned Central America at the board meeting. So they were distinct lies."

"I take it you and Heston don't have much to do with one another."

"Oh, no," Asner said. "A man who once was regarded as a moderate now seems to find all right-wing causes worthwhile."

Charlton Heston listened later as I repeated Asner's allegations with distinct calm, seemed fairly uninterested, and then denied ever misrepresenting any of Asner's words or deeds.

After so much time and so much argument, it might not have been possible to determine who was wrong, who was even lying, but that wasn't important. SAG political feuds—internal union matters—held little appeal. Yet the dispute between Asner and Heston was indicative of the depth of the political commitment of these major Hollywood figures.

I asked Heston if he had considered running for office.

"Yeah, that's come up a couple of times," he said. "My joke answer is I've already been President three times. My real answer is it happens I've been approached by both parties to run for the United States Senate, though obviously not in the same year. The last time was, I think, four years ago, by the Republicans."

"So you don't want to."

"No," Heston said. "Primarily because I would have to give up acting and I don't want to do that. And the second reason is you can't be a successful politician and not be absolutely crazy about being a public figure. I remember, I had gotten on Air Force One after President Reagan's last election swing in his final campaign. He always ended his campaigns in San Diego. It was a tradition. And everyone on the plane was exhausted. Nancy was exhausted, Baker was exhausted, Deaver—everyone except the President. And the President's eyes were dancing, his cheeks were rosy; I mean, he was having a marvelous time. He loved it. And I thought, 'That's what it takes.' Churchill felt that way. Churchill lived most of his public life on the losing side, fighting. Because he loved it. And I don't feel that way. I know what I like. I get to act, but I get to go on TV talk shows, my letters-to-the-editor get published, and people call me up and ask for my opinions about books they're planning, and that's fine. I get to stay a private citizen."

So did this mean that Heston believed that the whole idea of actors getting involved in politics was essentially benign?

"My theory is," he replied, "that in a democracy, everybody gets to speak out. Overall, I perceive this as a good. A lot of people don't know what they're talking about. I point out to you a lot of people elected to the Congress don't know anything about it either. You know, democracy is a tricky draw.''

Ed Asner told me that he had once considered running for office.

''I quickly decided absolutely not,'' Asner said. ''First of all, it would be a terrible burden on me to have to represent a constituency on a number of issues I wouldn't give a good hoot for. That's number one. I would fear having to represent a constituency in which there would be constituents I would despise, but still have to represent. To be a good politician, one has to compromise with one's so-called peers. Maybe I'm a snob, but I'm very ineffective at it and would probably fail at being able to be a good politician and comfortably rub noses with sons of bitches whose politics I disagreed with.''

''Actors often speak of politics and politicians in awful terms.''

''Yes, I know,'' Asner said. ''There are politicians who I think are the greatest thing who ever came down the pike. Politicians who I regard as liberal, politicians who I feel dedicate themselves not to waving banners like I do and attracting public attention—because that's my job, to attract public attention—politicians who go home, study the problem, have their staff study the problem, come up with a plan, come up with a bill, compromise with their opposition if they have to, but in the end, try to cure the disease. And for those politicians, I am in undying awe. But they are in a very small minority.''

''What do you think of the idea of actors running for office?''

''I think they can be prepared as anyone else,'' Asner said.

Heston also believed that actors could be adequately prepared for political office; in fact, they might even have an edge. ''Politicians must rely on performance,'' Heston said, ''and most great leaders are great performers. Politicians will not say that and they are very uncomfortable when you compare them to performers. Obviously, political leadership significantly includes performance skills. You can't do it if you can't perform. And this is because one of the primary duties of a political leader is to inspire. Who are the most successful heads of state in the twentieth century? Winston Churchill. Charles de Gaulle. Hitler. Castro. Castro hasn't been in the Sierra Maestras for over twenty-five years, but he still wears the combat fatigues, and he's right. So he should. De Gaulle always, or almost always, appeared in uniform, as did Hitler. Roosevelt had his old hat and cigarette holder. Churchill had his jumper suit and bowler.

"Churchill was maybe the great man of the century. And it may well be that his most valuable contribution to his country and the West was not his strategic abilities, but rather his speech at the nadir of Western hope, after the fall of France. And he said ''—and Heston's voice became richer and more dramatic—'' 'We shall fight on the beaches. We shall fight in the streets. We shall never surrender.' '' (Heston hit fairly close to the mark again, picking up Churchill's address in the middle: ''. . . we shall fight on the beaches, we shall fight on the landing grounds, we shall fight in the fields and in the streets, we shall fight in the hills; we shall never surrender.'')

"Now he didn't make that up on the spot," Heston said. "He wrote it, he rehearsed. Unlike most politicians, he memorized it. And he gave that same speech twice. Now if that wasn't performance, I don't know what is."

"But there is a difference," I challenged Heston. "For one thing, he wrote his own speeches, unlike most politicians today. More importantly, Churchill knew he had to inspire his people, he had to embody the best of the nation and sweep up and raise up the nation with him—again unlike today, where most politicos look at polls and then decide what most people want to hear. Today, maybe they are just playing a part. Churchill might have performed, but it was secondary to his character, to his beliefs; his performance came out of something much greater than simply the need to perform."

"I see what you are saying," Heston responded. "I would sign that anytime, but what I am saying is that Churchill was a great leader and a great performer. I see what you are saying, but I hope you see my point."

"Yes, but first he decided what was right, he accomplished something, and then he performed."

"Sure," agreed Heston.

Winding up the second of these two interviews, I felt I hadn't reached the heart of the issue, the fundamental relationship of celebrities to the public and polity. In one last attempt, I tossed in my usual comparison of how the Founding Fathers were heroes who lived and worked within society's rules and acted as examples to be emulated, whereas modern celebrities, who stood in as heroes, often lived outside the rules and did not necessarily promote societal values.

I finished and Heston did not immediately reply, and then said something that was seriously funny, or serious and funny, not to mention kind of deep.

"Well," Heston said, "it's asking a lot to expect Don Johnson to live up to the example of Thomas Jefferson."

Now, Charlton Heston knew as well as I did that using Don Johnson, most recently of "Miami Vice" fame, wasn't fair because he wasn't a political type, but the point was well-taken. How many people, in show biz or out, live up to the standards of Jefferson and the other Founding Fathers? More to the point—how many people, in show biz or out, try?

By this juncture, I had talked to three people whose intellects and experiences entitled them to be heard on matters of politics. They were surely among the most prepared in Hollywood to enter into such discourse. But what about the rest of the entertainment community? In particular, what about its younger members? Many possess power, money and media savvy; did this translate into a desire and ability to influence the public and the political process?

I realized that to understand the citizens of Hollywood, it would be necessary to understand something about their city, the hothouse in which they live, the place in which they talk and debate and form their attitudes and beliefs.

Chapter 4

Los Angeles

Hollywood Hubris

"Hollywood is high school with money."

With those few words, a famous actor—who requested anonymity—summed up his community and its citizens, east coast and west.

Now that was a hell of an opening line.

Michelle Bolton is the public relations director of a chain of luxury hotels around L.A., a favorite of visiting CEOs, foreign potentates and show biz folk, either in from New York, hiding out from the press, or holing up while the beach house is being re-painted. Her job is to get the hotels into the media as often and as favorably as possible, so she ends up throwing a lot of parties, starring a lot of celebs, luring a lot of press. Hollywood is a place of eternal insecurities, of never knowing who's going to hire you next, or fund your pet project, or why or when. Hollywood is a place where everybody says yes and few mean it, because nobody wants to be remembered as the guy who turned down *Jaws*. Hollywood is a place where there is no objective measure of ability, no diploma on the wall which certifies the recipient knows what he is doing. In Hollywood, you are what you say you are, as long as somebody buys it. In such a place, parties are not simply for fun; who is invited where, who speaks to whom, and who gets prime press coverage, matter to the Hollywood tea leaf readers in the same way Kremlinologists examine the Red Square reviewing stand on May Day parade to see who's up and who's down.

In such a place, public relations directors count.

Bolton told a story that explained something about her celebrity acquaintances. She commenced with a cautionary prologue.

"So many people make their decisions for them throughout their lives," Bolton said. "They are pampered and have certain expectations, and when those expectations are not reached, you hear about it. Some of them are so demanding, it's just incredible."

Bolton recalled a national sports magazine that wanted to shoot a cover at one of the hotels, using a television actress as the model. The magazine asked Bolton to contact the actress on its behalf. The actress, whose career had hit its height twenty-five years before, a point which corresponded precisely to the cancellation of her TV series, should have been thrilled. She wasn't, not exactly.

"And she said," Bolton related, the amazement still fresh in her voice, " 'Well, what's in it for me besides the publicity value?' Now, there was a tie-in with a television manufacturer, and she said, 'Can you get me two color TVs?' "

Bolton kind of laughed. "Two color TVs. We're giving you a cover and you want television sets . . ." Her voice trailed off and she shook her head.

Nonetheless, Bolton went ahead and made the request to the manufacturer, because that's the way things are done.

"They've just been given, given, given," Bolton said. "They don't think anything of it. 'I want two color TVs!' "

Bolton offered more clues into the art of dealing with celebs.

"First, you have to get to them," she said. "As you know, unless you have a personal contact, you have to go through a whole slew of people, from the publicist to the manager to the agent, just to get a letter sent over inviting him to the event. They always confirm; you just don't know if they're going to show up. There are some people, not too many, who are always supportive and will actually come without having their whole entourage telling them yes, sir, or no, sir."

Bolton agreed that that was a strange way for celebrities to live.

"People make their decisions for them. And I think they feel it's almost an honor if they attend a function and we should be happy if they, in fact, come. And if they don't come and they had confirmed yes, we shouldn't really worry about it."

While Bolton said she would not accept such behavior from anyone else, a celebrity is different. "That's the way this industry works," she said.

She added that if she did call to complain about a no-show, the star might be insulted and decline to attend an event another time. On the other hand, if a celebrity arrived at a party uninvited, Bolton admitted she would probably let him or her in anyway—complimentary, of course.

"I'm not going to say if it's right or wrong," she said. "It's unfair, certainly, but it's standard."

"Well, unfair is ordinarily considered wrong," I replied.

Bolton shrugged, serene in her comprehension of her world. "It's the rule," she said.

I had one last question. "That actress—did you get her the color TVs?"

Michelle Bolton laughed. "Let's just say, just like she asked, we asked."

Now that's show biz.

Though William Atherton starred in Steven Spielberg's first feature, *Sugarland Express*, as well as *The Day of the Locust* and *Real Genius*, he is best known for playing the mean guy from the EPA in *Ghostbusters* and the unscrupulous TV reporter in *Die Hard*.

In reality, however, Bill is not mean; rather, he is a friend to me as well as to my political left, and one of the smartest people I have met in the entertainment industry.

"The main thing now," Atherton began, his tone distinct and unequivocal, "and I think it is more now than even twenty years ago, is that an actor is seen as a person who is useful for somebody with any kind of a platform, for that platform will be heard if he has a famous person talking about it, and the most famous people in the country are usually actors. And, at the same time, a person will give credence and remember that, but he also won't give much substance to it because, after all, who's saying it, but an actor?"

That was classic Atherton, one thought running after and into another, all rather reasonable. His manner suited his presence, which was tall and solid and fiery, with red hair on top and sometimes all over his face.

"Why don't people regard actors as serious, thinking individuals?"

Atherton first laid some of the blame on his fellow actors. "The money is so enormous and a person's fame can be so complete, that an actor's vanity can go through the roof, and he takes on more accoutrements than really he is entitled to. And it can happen to the best of people. It's a very intense situation, and it's a different situation in the last fifteen years than I think it ever was before."

Essentially, however, and not surprisingly, Atherton defended his fellow thespians. "In terms of this century, if an actor has been political, it has usually had an unfortunate consequence. When the political actors all came before the House Un-American Activities Committee, it was a terrible time. Also, there's a difference in each person's personal history as an actor. If you're from the stage, you're given a certain intellectual weight that actors in the movies— I'm not saying this is warranted at all—are not. It's unfair to people who are very smart, who have very rich intellectual backgrounds. Not that there aren't dumb actors, just like there are dumb anything."

Atherton went on about a problem unique to being an actor. "You are in a very odd position, because you can be so accessible and so remote at the same time. And the more accessible you are to a person in his living room in a theatrical way, the easier it is for people to have contempt for you, to make less of you, to feel, in a sense, often unconsciously, that they own you."

That was intriguing about being accessible and remote at the same time, because I regarded that as one definition of a hero, somebody who is familiar and yet different, somehow smarter, stronger, better, somehow untouchable. I gave the example of Franklin Roosevelt on the radio, so warm, so reassuring, so much one of us, and yet so commanding and, fundamentally, Presidential.

Atherton nodded in agreement. "In his time, people were very circumspect about FDR. Very respectful. Nobody took a picture of him on his crutches. It wasn't exactly forbidden, but it was a gentleman's agreement that nobody would do it. To do so was perceived as contempt, it was showing him as weak in a way that was unfair. That doesn't happen now. Anything is fair game. It's probably one of the terrifying things of our age, because, politically speaking, you're not going to have anybody other than a homogeneous, very bland person for the most important office. We don't elect a President any more, we elect a figurehead, a king, someone who's going to get the Academy Award for playing the best President. That's what is happening now, and that is what's so terrifying. It's the kind of thing where anybody of any substance, for Christ's sake. . . ."

Atherton paused to shake his head. "I found Gary Hart objectionable in many ways, but the fact of it was, there was a huge gang-up on somebody's sex life; it had nothing to do with the larger questions, you know—is he going to push the button in a way that's stupid? Does he see Central America in a much better way than his opponent? Because he had a sex life that may not be up to people's liking—frankly, there were some things one could have criticized him for legitimately, that were important. But that's not what happened; the way the press latched onto his sex life made it the same thing as whether he could run the country. These two subjects were joined together somehow, but they were very, very different subjects."

He caught a breath and kept talking at the same time; I figured it for some actor's training. "The press encourages that type of thing. There's that instant notoriety, for things that have nothing to do with acting. And in the midst of all this, there are a lot of actors who are very serious about what they do, who have some intellectual substance and basis for it. I think what frequently happens is that many actors speak out about an important issue because the material they have to do with as actors is usually not very good, and nobody likes to think of themselves as lightweight, people want to care for something of substance and be seen as having substance themselves. They want to be sensible, and they want, if they're working in something, they want to have a good effect on people. They want to feel that it matters somehow, that it isn't just vanity. Sometimes, unfortunately, it can be just vanity, but it's not easy to be honest about it. Nobody wants to see themselves that way."

Astonishingly, Atherton was picking up speed.

"The other thing that can happen," he continued, "is that an actor wants to say something of substance, feels he can be articulate

and powerful on an issue, and at the same time feels he is used and
insulted. A person can very much have a feeling for something, get
to the event, and have some press agent say, 'Well, we don't think
of you as important today as we did yesterday, we have somebody
else who we think is more important than you today speaking.' And
that has happened to a lot of people.''

"But that's the name of the game.''

"But, you see,'' Atherton said, "it may be the name of the game,
but I tell you, from an actor's point of view, it isn't seen that way.
It's the name of the game in the actor's *business*; the actor is often
disappointed when in politics, somebody says they're running for
justice, then doesn't show much respect for the actor who's helping
him. There's a difference here.''

"No, that's politics.''

"Often here, people think of politics as a forum for the ethics
they would like to have. It's often very naïve how people see
politics here. Unfortunately, some actors aren't erudite enough,
they're not well-read enough. It's not that they're not smart enough,
they just don't have the street smarts of politics. In show business, a
person has to have street smarts. He gets involved in politics to get
away from that, and finds it requires some of the same kinds of
skills.''

I started to compare the political sophistication and intentions of
entertainment political groups with other political groups, such as
the Machinists Non-Partisan Political League, but Atherton interrupted, suggesting I was comparing basically dissimilar groups.
Instead, he offered the clergy and the military. "People who are
accustomed to a sense of presenting themselves or an idea in a
public way—in an obvious way they're very different,'' he
plunged on, anticipating objections, "but at the same time, they
both have a similar relation of public to private. One of the reasons
I'm making this relation is that I've discovered that the predomi-
nate backgrounds of actors, the family backgrounds, cultural backgrounds, are often the clergy and the military. They all have to do
with pageantry, I think, it has to do with largeness of expressed
feeling, it has to do with a kind of emotional order and logic, it
has to do with many things. Acting is an art that's different from
other arts.''

"Based on what I saw in Washington, people often seem to ask celebs their opinions without being interested in the answers, quite content to simply stare at them. Why?"

"They don't think the actor is real," he said. "They don't think a person really thinks about issues. They think the biggest thing in a person's life is being a movie star and advancing himself."

"Isn't that true?"

Atherton laughed. "Isn't it true about every professional?"

I conveyed my impression that our elected officials weren't too fond of actors who blow into Washington, make a speech, tell politicos what they're doing wrong and then instruct them on how to correct their mistakes. Finished, they head back to Hollywood to shoot another movie and rake in another ton of money.

Atherton saw it differently. "That's the other thing that makes a lot of actors angry. They feel, 'All right. He needs me. He'll use me. And then he'll throw me out again.' The anger of politicians towards actors is very suspect, very self-serving. They want it both ways. They can't have it both ways. And an actor has a right to go back to Hollywood and make a living.

"The problem with politics is," he continued, "usually a politician, by his very nature these days, is so 'two ways,' is so adroit and adept, he doesn't know what he believes himself, and neither do we. There's very little sheer ethics in politics. A person wants to assemble himself in a way that's cosmetically acceptable to people and will sometimes use an actor to do it. And often try to seduce an actor into feeling there's some intellectual or ethical integrity they have, when they really do not. And that happens over and over again.

"Actors are smart that way, in terms of seeing how people will use them. If an actor feels there is something in this politician— given contemporary, late twentieth century American politics—that can have a good effect on people, the actor may jump into it, knowing this person isn't perfect. This happens a lot.

"So it isn't just one thing, there are whole combinations of events, of feelings, of emotions, that go into an actor going in and representing somebody. Because, I mean, face it, part of the problem in the last fifteen years has been a degeneration of politics, and the ethics in government as a whole. It didn't exist the same way when I was a kid. And here I am, talking like I'm ninety-five years old, you know."

"Don't actors use pols, too, to get their points across and reach a great many people they could never reach otherwise?" I asked.

"That's a little too cynical," Atherton replied, "because an actor isn't going to just jump in; of course, there are vain, silly people everywhere. However, the minute you say you're an actor, you're given certain colors that may not have anything to do with you at all. It's like saying to someone: 'Well, he's only an electrician, so he's never been to an art gallery.' I mean, it's insulting and it isn't true. And that's what happens."

"That doesn't mean actors don't use politicians," I suggested.

"In my experience," he said, "it has been that when a person really does believe in something, he is automatically graceful. I don't think it's necessary for a person to know everything. I don't think it's necessary that a person has to be Albert Schweitzer to have a sincere passion about something. That's one of the things I feel is so disproportionate; a person can have a feeling about one thing and mean it and feel it and be useful on it.

"What happens often when you're a celebrity," Atherton continued, "is you're subjected to tabloid mentality. A person can say one good thing and thirty seconds later, one not-so-good thing, and the not-so-good thing will be exploited by the press and presented to people, or taken out of context or changed. You're not really hearing an issue sheer. You're not hearing it. There's so much noise, so many voices, it's like a cloud. It's like trying to hear a violin in the *1812 Overture*, single, good, sincere violin in a badly conducted *1812*. What is going on? What is really true? An actor, myself included, prey to all the wrong things, is often made very unsure of himself professionally—I mean businesswise, not artistically. And at the same time, you can't present yourself as unsure. Then they'll use that to have contempt for you. It's a very ruthless platform to begin with, and the ruthlessness can be underestimated. It's so intense that way. So an actor going out to campaign for the life of a worker who is dying of pesticide poisoning, for example, he's exhausted by the time he gets there and he doesn't even know how tired he is! That's what happens so often and that's why I have such feeling for people, for actors, who do go out and do some good. And many of them do extraordinary good, like John Randolph."

Atherton was winding down. "A lot of yuppie politicians want to use actors, actors will use them back. They'll architect a certain kind of false intellectual pretense for themselves. I feel it's unfortunate; I'm not going to say everybody does it, but I am saying it is seductive.''

I asked Atherton to try to explain in a phrase the whole experience of Hollywood turning political. How did he understand this trend, which flowed from serious business to raging melodrama and back again?

Atherton chose to reply indirectly, succinctly capturing the relationship between actors and politicians, and actually capturing a lot more than that. "It's the court of the Sun King," he said. "And everybody wants to be Louis.''

Atherton had explained a lot about show biz, show biz people and their political motivation. Now I wanted to speak to some of the younger members of the community, to see how they were stepping forward to test their political power and assert their political roles.

Lesley Bracker works for International Creative Management, one of the big three agencies, along with Creative Artists Agency and William Morris; ICM handles actors and directors and producers and writers and the other components of the entertainment industry machinery. She is in her mid-twenties and soon after our interview was promoted to story editor at the agency.

Bracker is also on the board of directors of a group called Young Artists United and has served a term as president. What I had already heard about YAU was impressive. Comprised of about 400 members, YAU had defined its objectives and focused its energies from inception; the results were dramatic and inspiring, particularly because almost all members were in their twenties. All worked in show biz, at different jobs and different levels. Even given the startling upward mobility frequently found in Hollywood, a surprising number occupied positions of real preeminence. From every indication, YAU appeared to be among the most successful sort of celebrity-driven groups, both in conception and implementation. Its focus was on young people helping young people, and its members forayed into schools to talk bluntly about drugs, sex, parents, peers, education, work and other issues confronting American youth. By all accounts, YAU visits were keenly anticipated, enthusiastically greeted and gratefully acknowledged.

YAU was started in 1986 by Alexandra Paul, actress and co-star of *American Flyers* and *Dragnet*, and Daniel Sladek, former Hollywood publicist and currently an executive with Spectacor Films, a production company.

"YAU started because Daniel and Alexandra were sitting around one day and talking about what they would do when they were rich and famous and had millions of dollars, and what they would do for kids and charities," Bracker said. "They were becoming very frustrated with what was going on in high schools with drugs and suicides, so they decided, heck, we don't need to be rich and famous, we can just gather all of our friends together and go out and speak to these kids in their high schools."

So about thirty-five friends were gathered for a meeting.

"These were the people who shaped the group," Bracker told me. "There were several different committee meetings, basically to start the groundwork and write the by-laws. People like Meg Ryan and Anthony Edwards and Judd Nelson were meeting one or two times a week, very, very active in setting the groundwork for Young Artists United."

A tax-free foundation was established, along with a thirteen-person board of directors who not only set and implement policy for the group, but also vote themselves on and off the board.

While most YAU members were undoubtedly serious about their efforts, I wondered if many people joined the group hoping to network and advance their careers.

"People do," Bracker said, "but we discourage that. We try not to give them any opportunities to do that. For instance, people keep saying they want a directory of all the members' phone numbers and occupations. We don't do that. Everything has been strictly business."

Business as defined by the board, of course.

"Board meetings are open to members," she said. "We can go into closed session if we feel that we need to. Otherwise, members are always welcome to speak or hear what anyone has to say. If they have complaints—there was recently an instance where twelve people got together and wrote a letter saying they weren't happy with something, and we invited them to our board meeting and gave them an hour to discuss with us what they thought was wrong. You're always going to have people who are upset with the way things are running. Always, always, always. I mean, it's always the same faces, the exact same faces. And we always change, we take their advice and we change accordingly, as much as we can. You know, one step was to open our board meetings. Whatever. And they're still not happy, so at this point, it's just . . ."

Bracker shrugged.

"Ultimately," I suggested, "they probably want the membership to vote on things."

"Of course they do," Bracker concurred. "But then you end up having people running the group, running the board, who are not truly qualified to do the work. We know who's doing the work. We know that thirty—it's funny, no matter what, there're thirty core people. And when people run for the board, it's discussed who actually pulls through, you know, who commits themselves. When you open it up, it's too easy to win people over with your charm, but not actually be a true worker."

Dues were twenty-five dollars per annum, which covered the cost of printing and mailing of the monthly newsletter and notices of committee meetings and special events. The substantive work of YAU was supported by the budget, which had climbed from $12,000 the first year to $30,000 in 1989. The group was capable of raising that much money through a single annual event, featuring a movie premiere and a party.

Board members were assigned to chair the twelve committees which did YAU's work, and board members and their committees worked pretty hard. I asked Bracker to explain the tasks assigned to the major committees.

"Media Relations," Bracker said, "which is run by somebody who is an expert at media, where we sit around and decide what we should publicize and what we shouldn't, how we should approach different reporters. That's something I formed when I was president. Special Events. Inter-Education. Inter-Education is when we have our forums and people come to speak to us. Speakers Network, that's when people go out and speak to kids across the country. Public Service Announcement Committee, they do print, radio and television ads. We had a voter registration ad that Sarah Jessica Parker and Alexandra Paul were in and it ran like crazy until the Presidential election.

"Foundation Committee looks toward the future. We go into

these runaway centers around L.A. and hold acting classes, teach them painting, things like that, creative things that make them feel good about themselves. We're looking to open up our teen drop-in center in Los Angeles. Also, we need a place where YAU can be centered; right now, everyone works out of their own homes. The Foundation Committee is really looking towards that, plus they're forming something called Youth United, something we would leave behind when we go the high schools for the kids to form their own sort of SADD, you know, Students Against Drunk Driving. A place for kids to talk to each other and to have peer counseling.''

As was so typical of these groups, the functioning of the committees pointed up that while celebrities were not the prime movers of the unglamorous, fundamentally essential work, the work which made the group viable, they inevitably took center stage when the group reached out to the public.

''Well, obviously,'' Bracker said, ''if we have a press conference, it's stars only. The news people don't want to see anybody who's not a celebrity. So if we have a press conference, like when there were so many copycat suicides—that was when I was president—in two days, we put together a press conference. And the Comedy Club gave us their space and we had a lot of celebrities come together and hold up an eight hundred number for kids to call if they felt suicidal or depressed. And that was celebrities only. I was there, but they didn't want me up there on that podium. They wanted Eve Plumb and Heather Locklear and whoever.''

I had one more question. How would a group of ''young artists'' determine an age cutoff for members? Would people be booted from the group when they hit thirty or thirty-five or forty?

''We haven't dealt with that yet,'' Bracker said. ''We have to figure out a structure.''

Now that was going to be an interesting board meeting—closed, I imagined.

Daniel Sladek, one of YAU's founders, rustled through his files and emerged with a small stack of newspaper articles and letters heralding YAU's accomplishments. *USA Today* ran a picture of Heather Locklear and Eve Plumb at the press conference to combat teen suicide which Bracker had mentioned. Plumb, who played the middle sister on the television series ''The Brady Bunch,'' was quoted as saying, ''I considered suicide. Young Artists helped me get the attention off myself.'' *The Denver Post* reported on an appeal by Sarah Jessica Parker and *Torch Song Trilogy* star Bruce Toms, as well as others, to raise money for a runaway center. Local New Jersey papers recorded a tour by several members of YAU to schools in southern New Jersey. At Morristown High School, the celebrities exchanged feelings about a wide range of experiences and problems with students. In order to foster ''a feeling of comfort and confidentiality,'' teachers and press were excluded from the sessions. Later, the visitors revealed some of what they had said:

Doug McKeon, twenty-one, co-star of *On Golden Pond*: ''I told my group about how it felt to grow up with an alcoholic father. For me, acting was a way to express my emotions. It was my escape valve in a very, very tough situation.''

Alexandra Paul: ''I was anorexic at fourteen and bulimic at fifteen. I want kids to know that I'm not perfect. I want them to know that I'm vulnerable too.''

Brian Varaday, twenty-six, who appeared in the film *Breathless* and the television show ''Eight is Enough,'' recalled teenage battles with cocaine, alcohol and dyslexia: ''I heal myself and my wounds when I talk to kids.''

''I thought it was really good,'' a high school junior said in praise of a YAU presentation. ''The message was just to be mature enough to make intelligent decisions, try to make your life worthwhile.''

A press clipping from *Variety* related that YAU was presented the National Commission Against Drunk Driving's 1987 distinguished service award. The commission cited YAU for ''its distinctive role in the increasing public awareness and action in the efforts to reduce the tragedies caused by drunk and impaired driving.''

Then there were the letters thanking YAU for its work, from school principals and school board members and local government officials. Sladek showed me a handwritten note from a teenage girl who had attended a YAU meeting in her Arizona town: ''I am writing to you to thank you for your advice on my suicidal friend. She called me one night, and she said she was going to kill herself. Thanks to you, I was able to talk to her without sounding scared, and convince her to seek help. She is slowly but surely recovering from her pain. I am very grateful to you, for helping me understand that I had to help her. Please write back, or send a picture! Thank you!''

Sladek made clear who controlled the speaking engagements. "The speaking tours really are very well-defined and the people who I select to go out are very handpicked."

He also had some definite ideas about the nature of politics in the days prior to this era of celebrity involvement.

"Politics was basically a pretty untouchable organization," he said. "I think that politics was an inaccessible area to reach from most outside avenues. It was its own world, its own corporation, if I can use that word freely, and existed within it and of itself, whereas I think today it has been infiltrated as well as the hands within have reached out. Because there's too much going on in this world just for the politicians to take care of without disturbing the public and making them want to be involved."

Sladek stated that his strong opinions on life and politics were a direct result of his background.

"I'm twenty-three years old, I'm part of the yuppie, Me Generation," he said. "Okay. I grew up that life, I grew up with absolutely not a trouble in the world, from my perspective, one-on-one trouble, to hamper me in any way. I had no threat of being drafted, I had no threat of war, I never thought I would ever starve. I grew up as part of this claustrophobic, taken-care-of generation, that in some ways I really pity, because I can say that most of my peers have no sense of belonging and no sense of willingness to contribute back to society, because they have basically been conditioned to take things for granted."

"I take it you think celebrity political participation is a good thing?" I asked.

"I think it's a *damn* good thing," asserted Sladek.

"Do you think it's a good thing that celebrities are heroes?"

"I think it's an important thing," he said. "It's important because it really creates a sense of fantasy, a sense of mystery and mysticism, that I think people need. I think people need heroes. The Egyptians needed gods or whatever. It was mysticism, it was spirituality. Those were their heroes. I think that forever, people have always depended on some element to use to escape reality, and I think that the arts is that element. If you push that a little further, I think there's a sense of excitement and a sense of intrigue and a sense of desire that is built around celebrities. It's something exciting, it's something that's just a little untouchable, it's something that maybe gives you a little hope that there is some good in this world.''

"But isn't that the problem, that our heroes come from fantasy?'' I asked him. "It's okay to have a few like that, but they're not the real thing.''

"Okay,'' Sladek said. "I was going to get to that. I think there is a need for celebrity and the need for hero status for everyone. Everyone has their heroes, everyone has people not necessarily they look up to, but look to. Right? The Depression—what industry survived the Depression? Arts and sports industries survived.''

"Other industries survived, too. And we still looked to FDR, the President, to save us.''

"Okay,'' Sladek said, "you still looked to FDR to save you, but it's a different world now. You have celebrity talent, like Brooke Shields and like Jonathan Silverman and like Doug McKeon and all these kids, who go to college and they're getting their degrees in political science and history.''

I reminded him that Jimmy Stewart graduated from Princeton (Class of 1932, Bachelor of Science), and that he is hardly the only actor of his generation with a degree.

I offered Sladek a rather more skeptical view of young celebrities in politics. "It's a different society today and most people don't know what's behind the faces they see. And most people aren't willing to look far enough to find out what's behind the faces. When they see Rob Lowe on the campaign caravan for Dukakis, they think that here's a young hotshot who's trying to ride on the wings of a Presidential campaign, who doesn't know jack about what he's talking about.''

Sladek nodded in regret. "He's a friend of mine—I'll defend him.'' In Sladek's defense, his championing of fellow show biz citizen Lowe occurred several weeks before the infamous videotape starring Lowe surfaced. Shot in the course of the Democratic National Convention, which the actor presumably attended because of his conspicuous interest in national affairs, the short film showed Lowe and a pal having sex with a minor. Regardless of the impact this incident would have on Lowe and his career, it was certain to put a crimp in his political bona fides.

"The guy's [Lowe] talented,'' Sladek continued. "The guy's *really* talented. Actually, I can honestly say the guy's one of the best-read people I've ever met in my life. I've never seen him in a casual situation, sitting at his house, hanging out with him, traveling with him, where's he's not reading a book, an *important* book about something that happened in this world some time ago.''

Whatever one construed of Sladek's conception of politics and celebrity, let alone Rob Lowe, YAU performed a valuable service, and that was what really counted. Not only was this service of frequently life-changing and sometimes life-saving benefit to many young people, it cost the taxpayers absolutely nothing. YAU had chosen its audience and task with exactitude and intelligence, and the results were dramatic and conclusive. That was the point, not whether Sladek favorably compared the denizens of a weekly soap opera with the pagan gods of the ancient Egyptians; not unless YAU ceased to be a nonpartisan organization, dedicated to issues which did not require intellectual reasoning or exist in a distinctly political context.

Success fires ambition in individuals, corporations and bureaucracies, and perhaps YAU would be no different, seeking to expand its scope and influence and prestige. Was it inevitable that the group's leaders and members would become just like their Hollywood elders, forcing YAU to change and eventually become yet another collection of moneyed show biz citizens, intent on thrusting their opinions into the political arena? YAU was smart; would it stay that smart or become too smart for its own good?

Chapter 5

Los Angeles

Youth Will Be Served, Hollywood Style

Talking to kids in a school auditorium about drugs is one thing; talking to millions on national television about nuclear war or the federal budget or the Presidential campaign is quite another. It is time to shift the focus from the relatively low profile Young Artists United to three high profile individuals, all successful actors in their twenties who are obviously aware of their position in the entertainment industry and their potential value in the political process.

I was seated in the home of Robert Downey, Jr., and Sarah Jessica Parker, situated in the Hollywood hills. Downey had recently starred with Cybil Shepherd in *Chances Are*. Parker was a regular on the television series, "A Year in the Life." Also in attendance was Judd Nelson, who achieved fame in *The Breakfast Club*.

"Some people really investigate the issues and others do not, but speak anyway," I began.

"Are you being kind?" Judd Nelson said with a smile.

"Yes," I replied. "The convention was an example. A lot of bad press came out of that." Nelson had been at the Democratic National Convention in Atlanta.

"Of course, you don't have to be a total idiot to get a bad rap from the media," I said. "You in particular should know something about that." I was directing my remark to Nelson, who was midway to a beard and wearing, rather inexplicably, especially on this hot spring day, both a tie and work boots.

"What magazine are you talking about?" His manner was playful, for we were all well aware which magazine had ravaged him.

"*Spy*," I said.

"Oh," he said, still smiling. "*That* magazine."

Spy magazine, an irreverent New York monthly, had trumpeted its opinion on the cover of its February 1989 issue: "The Importance Of Looking Earnest: We're Serious, You're Serious, Everybody's Serious—Especially Judd Nelson." Inside, the title of the article left no conceivable doubt: "If I Only Had a Brain."

The piece detailed an interminable catalogue of celebrities who were attempting to prove that they were sober, somber, thinking citizens. More often than not, at least according to the cruel and hilarious article, the celebs ended up falling on their faces, tripped by their own extravagant gestures and statements. Sylvester Stallone, responsible for several of the more pointlessly violent movies of recent years, was quoted on the reason he keeps a "well-publicized journal": "I like to really embellish the human spirit." Morgan Fairchild explained why she was qualified to appear before a Senate committee and discuss Alan Cranston's California desert protection act of 1987: "I am an actress. I am very interested in the environment. . . . I have also had extensive visits to the Arizona desert, spent some time in Israel last year where I was making a movie. . . . As a child I dreamed about becoming a paleontologist. That did not happen, but I have maintained a strong interest in science, the environment and human interactions. . . . As an actress, I have spent most of my professional life in dramatic situations which imitate real life. I have become very sensitive to human interaction in a world that is increasingly crowded." A taste of the poetry of Charlie Sheen, actor-son of Martin Sheen, was provided: "Crying and yellin' from daylight till night/One giant shit sandwich, 'Fuck you,' take a bite." *Spy* said a volume of Sheen's literary output was being circulated by the literary department of the William Morris Agency to publishers. A phone call to the agency to discover what progress had been made revealed that the work had been removed from an unappreciative marketplace.

Nelson was an easy mark and his pronouncements were strewn generously through *Spy*'s article, though one will suffice here. "Suddenly I realize I cannot formally interview the PLAYERS," he wrote regarding the Atlanta Hawks for *In Fashion* magazine. "I don't want to be talking with THEM about LAME OLD-HOME NEWS. Why insist on talking to a professional only about his profession? We are what we do? We are what we eat? I am what I am? Green eggs and ham? I have no interest here in criticism or commentary. I just want to hang."

Robert Downey, Jr. was not neglected by *Spy*, quoted as saying, "You've got to change the mass consciousness. That's what I want to do."

"It must be difficult dealing with that sort of attention," I said to Parker, Nelson and Downey.

"Well, there's a certain amount of ego involved, if you put yourself on the line with your beliefs," Downey said, also in need of a shave. "But then, I think it really comes down to whether you wholeheartedly know what you said and felt was true. And then it's kind of like a film, you know, you try to say what you can in the film and then it's up to the critics and they can say what they want. I think to me it's more about the experience of what feels good. See, I'm a high school dropout. I need to say that because on any of these issues, I'm just learning as I go along. And so, say for abortion, inherently I know that it's unconstitutional to take that choice away. So for me, I feel that I can stand on that issue, but at the same time, I know that I listen to the other side. I don't want to be someone who's just like uninformed but passionate. To me, it's really about becoming informed."

"Let's put abortion aside for the moment," I interjected, "because it is essentially a moral choice as opposed to a technical or political issue, such as arms control or Central America. Would you speak out on other issues?"

"I don't even really know about those," Downey said. He kept glancing at his hands, clearly uncomfortable. "To me, what seems to make the most sense, if I'm asked to lend my name or energies or time to things that I feel I can't really go wrong with, are issues like voter registration. To me, it's environmental issues that are the most key or personal issues, and they take precedence. I just want to be informed and protect what I believe to be my rights. As far as the environmental issues, I saw this thing on the [*National Geographic*] 'Explorer' series about a Mayan city. And as the city expanded more, it kept eating up the environment around it. And this great civilization really was lost because of its disregard for the environment. And to me, it just seems to be exactly what's going on now, you know. But then again, when it comes down to facts and figures, I just want to do what feels right and be as well-informed as I can."

"Let me get this right," I said. "Actors don't have to investigate; they feel, therefore they know."

"That immediately makes me defensive," Sarah Jessica Parker jumped in quickly. She was thin and delicate and rather intense, and her words had a habit of tumbling out, sometimes bumping into one and other. "You know, I can't and I don't want to stop people from speaking, who, I think—inevitably, it's going to be interpreted that's how I feel, because it's a young actor speaking about any number of things. Central America, you know, I campaigned for Dukakis, nuclear disarmament; I mean, there are a whole range of topics that I don't say, 'I feel therefore I'm right.' I don't think for me that's the thing." Parker sighed with frustration. "These blanket statements—I try not to make them in my own life."

"Why do you think most actors are liberal rather than conservative?"

"I don't think that's necessarily the case," Nelson said. "We had an actor who was President, who was as about as far right as you can get without flipping back over in an Einsteinian way. I think that then it depends on the actor, to be the kind of actor that depends on his feelings more. I know for myself, I might be an actor by profession but I use facts much more than feelings."

I had heard politics compared to everything from love to war, but never Einstein.

"I want to answer what you asked before," Nelson said. "You know, the price you pay to speak your mind. You can say, if you can't stand the heat get out of the kitchen. Granted, we're given a forum because we are public professionals and that forum is sort of a hot seat, to a certain degree, where you are provided an opportunity to speak your mind, but then you leave yourself open to more abuse if people disagree with you."

I thought about the bitter irony of how John Randolph had suffered publicly for his private political acts, committed not necessarily as an actor but simply as a citizen.

"The thing is," I mentioned, "actors were never given a forum before. They were expected to represent American values, to be symbols, but it was never before inevitable that they would speak out. Now it's different."

Echoing an observation I had heard Charlton Heston make, Nelson said, "It's different for a lot of reasons. There was a studio system that didn't allow Cary Grant to pick the films that he made. Columbia or United Artists or Warner Brothers told him what films he was going to be in. When he did publicity for the films, he was told what to say. When the studio system broke down, when actors became producers as well as actors, they are, we are, given more freedom to do the projects that we want to do and then, to a certain degree, we have to defend those choices. Young actors are more susceptible to being led. We are also forming out of the embryo stage, or the tadpole stage, so we can be convinced or swayed to follow anything. I don't think that actors of my generation are necessarily more liberal or more conservative than our counterparts forty years ago or the general population today."

I had to challenge Nelson's observation. "Young actors are certainly more liberal than most young people today. More young people who voted, voted for Bush, yet more actors worked for Dukakis."

"More actors who are vocal," Nelson said.

"Well, that is our only measure."

"I meet people all the time who are Republicans," Parker insisted. "I mean, something I just worked in, two out of the three young people on the project were Republicans—were conservative."

"You don't see young Republican actors getting together to support the contras," I said.

"Because they're the winners," claimed Nelson. "It's sort of like, America likes the underdog, sure, everyone jumps on: 'We're gonna win, we're gonna win,' and as soon as it's decided, then, 'Yeah, we'll support him anyway.' We all like the underdog until the final result comes in, then people sort of jump ship and switch. I mean, I don't know whether it's really important that we agree whether there's a larger percentage of young actors that are more liberal. I'm willing to agree that it seems that there are a lot of those actors that are more conservative that seem to be a little bit older, like Charlton Heston, and they're not really pro-anything, they're more anti. And I think that the older generation has fallen prey to the, 'Let's make a long list of the negatives and win,' as opposed to what it is the candidate can do positively and win.''

"A lot of people that I know, that I work with, are political,'' Parker said. "I'm not a recent convert. Long before I came to Los Angeles, I politically had the same links that I have now. It was part of my upbringing and I was exposed to both sides and it's a choice that I made, I mean, in 1972, literally, in looking at my country. I mean, it's nice that there's a network and a resource out there of people that in a lot of ways, feel the same we do, or agree or want to work for the same things or to, you know, work against something. So a lot of us are progressive.''

"Let's take a negative view of why most actors are liberal,'' I offered. "We can probably agree that in our society today, actors get away with actions no one else can.'' I rummaged through a grab bag of standard examples, including actors wearing sneakers in a fancy restaurant and actors Don Johnson and Melanie Griffith making the cover of *People* for conceiving a child out of wedlock, where a politician in the same circumstance would be disgraced and ruined.

Everyone signaled agreement with the proposition.

"So if this is true,'' I said, "then this is more than ordinary liberty, this is license, and license can be seen, though it doesn't have to be, as liberal. Taking advantage of this license and seeking to continue to enjoy its pleasures is what renders most actors liberal.''

"Probably more liberal by definition,'' Nelson said, "meaning more things are allowed, but this is not necessarily more politically liberal.''

"Yeah, it's not that recent really,'' Downey added. He pointed out that, for whatever reason, the acting community has long lived by different rules.

"But it's different today,'' I said. "In the old days, it was quiet. People at least pretended to lead normal lives, with families and homes and pets. They didn't advertise on the covers of magazines.''

"Because they didn't have those magazines,'' Nelson said. "If they had *People* magazine—we were talking about this a while ago—if they had *People* magazine fifty years ago, Zelda and F. Scott Fitzgerald would have been on it *every week.*"

The assemblage laughed at that and Nelson continued. "If they weren't on the cover, it was because maybe Fatty Arbuckle was killing somebody that week. And they have those little, you know, what do they call them, at the top of the cover?"

"Corner insert," Parker said.

"Yeah," Nelson said. "Corner insert, inset. Zelda, with a bottle over Scott's head." The image was probable enough to cause another round of laughter.

"But you are right," he added. "Actors can get away with almost anything."

"Do you think that because they can get away with almost anything, they feel confident they can get away with talking about things they don't know anything about?" I asked.

"Yes," Nelson said. "Yes."

"Sure," Parked agreed.

"Because some people will listen," Nelson said. "Because some people will go, 'Yeah, I like him, he's against wearing furs, so I won't wear them.' Sure, it's the cool factor. I'm not sure if there was a cool factor before. Jennifer Beales cuts her shirt, everyone goes out and cuts their shirt. Stallone, Schwarzenegger get big muscles and they're cool, so we'll get big muscles so we'll be cool. It's that fame by association."

"Stars have always helped set fashion," I said. "Remember Veronica Lake and her hair style in the Forties? Let's take it politically—do people listen to actors? Or do they just like to look and listen?"

"I think it's just to see them," Nelson felt.

"Yeah," Downey said. In contrast to his friends who were participating with some enthusiasm, Downey had remained detached and uneasy. "When we did the Vote '88 thing, most people who came out weren't even of age to vote and it didn't really seem like so much of a, a—"

"Educational process," Parker interjected. They had both been involved, along with other celebrities, in a voter registration drive during the 1988 campaign season.

"Educational consciousness," Downey said, "or anything. Of

course, some people were there just holding up posters of films you'd been in or whatever, but I think the real issue is that—and I'm in no position to consider myself an activist—I think it's even funny that I'm sitting here, but I just want to be an active citizen, you know, and to get these kids out there. I don't care what gets them there, I really don't care if they're there to see me or whatever, but they're going to hear words and they're going to make up their own choices anyway. And a lot of them are going to go back to a conservative household or whatever, but at least those questions are being raised, at least there's options to make the choices, and that information is, in a way, experience.''

Downey had shown some passion in the course of speaking; now, he sat back and became quiet again.

''Why they come, and how they leave,'' Nelson said, ''are not necessarily the same thing. I think that that's our possible impact— that they may come because they've seen twelve movies that they like; they may leave with, let's say one percent of them leave with a new idea.''

''They will register to vote,'' Parker noted.

''Now those kind of odds,'' Nelson said, ''if we were medical researchers, would be unbelievably high odds. You know, so it's really . . .''

Uncharacteristically, Nelson had failed to finish his thought. I moved to fill the gap. ''That's an incredible responsibility. People are coming to you, not because you have anything to say they want to hear, but because they like you, or their picture of you. Then all of a sudden, you speak out on an issue and somebody might actually listen and act on it.''

''That's why I choose to educate myself,'' Parker insisted. ''I won't speak unless I feel that I have really educated myself so that if somebody asks me and I'm putting myself in the face of adversity, I don't feel in the end like a complete asshole, like I've minimized or negated fifty, forty hours or years of a lot of hard work that a lot of people have been doing, people who are known and people who are not known. Because it's so easy to take it away.''

''That's why we are an easy target,'' Nelson said to Parker. ''You are rare, in that sense, that you feel the need to educate yourself before you speak. Most people do not feel that way.''

''Some issues are easier to learn about on your own than others,''

I said. "Voter registration, for instance; bottom line, you need to know it's important to vote because if you don't vote, you can't have an impact on government. Other issues, like Central America, are more complicated. To understand Central America is another matter."

"It could take years," Parker felt. "Maybe."

"How old are you?"

"Twenty-four," Parker said.

"Twenty-four," Downey said.

"I'm twenty-nine," Nelson said.

"There aren't too many people in their twenties who get a chance to speak out on anything, let alone issues of national and international import."

"That's why it's important to draw that distinction between what you feel and what you think," Nelson said. "I think that Central America, for someone to be in a position to speak out on Central America, 'I feel' makes me cringe. 'I feel, you know, we have to put them down because they are close to the Rio Grande.' I'm confident the Texas Rangers will handle any Sandinistas coming across the Rio Grande. I mean, there are certain subjects, moral-slash-political issues, that are much easier to 'feel' about, but I think when you know more of the facts, like the mother's life is in danger and you're trying to protect something that's basically two teaspoons full of blood and tissue, you know, I don't see it as a 'feel' issue."

I brought up the Democratic National Convention, attended by Nelson and Parker, and the special treatment celebrities received. Among other perks, the Hollywood contingent was accorded a briefing by leading politicos each morning. I reminded them of the infamous Justine Bateman story.

As widely reported, Senator John Kerry of Massachusetts had concluded his lecture explaining the indirect Presidential balloting of the electoral college and solicited questions when Justine Bateman, of the television series "Family Ties," raised her hand. I quote from *Spy* as to the gist of her query: ". . . Bateman said, 'Like, a lot of us are making a lot of money now, and so we're paying a lot of taxes, you know. Is there, like, a way I can just write on the memo line of my check what I want my taxes to go for, like for school?' " I pick up the tale from an account in *Spin* magazine.

" 'No, I'm afraid not,' the senator says. It doesn't really matter. The actress isn't listening. She's passing a note to her friend and giggling.''

This was hardly the only tale that made one wonder what celebs were doing in the heat of the action—but more that later.

"That's the danger in people making fun of us,'' sighed Parker. "You know, that makes me upset, that makes me upset that she just . . . But what am I going to do?''

"You have to expect it,'' I said, "because of the composition of the group.'' Tom Hayden had organized the Hollywood caravan, transporting to Atlanta his personal collection of stars, many of whom are identified as *ex officio* members of the "Brat Pack,'' a group of young actors regarded as brash, opinionated and self-satisfied. "Did you all go under Tom Hayden's auspices?''

Parker nodded. "Yes, but more importantly for me, I did a lot of things outside of an umbrella situation. You know, outside of Tom Hayden or Jane Fonda or lots and lots of other things. And I was given an opportunity to go to the convention. Now, had I been given an opportunity, you know, ten years ago, I would have gone to the convention.''

I suggested that their special treatment in Atlanta might have provoked some resentment among journalists who had been granted more limited access than the Brat Packers. "If you were trying to cover the story and you couldn't bribe your way past the guards and get behind the podium, but Justine Bateman strolled by wherever and whenever she pleased, you'd be really annoyed too.''

"Sure,'' Parker said.

"And as members of your industry,'' I continued, "I don't know if at the time, with all the excitement, it occurred to you that this might not be a good thing.''

"Sometimes it's embarrassing,'' Parker interjected.

"Yeah, it's interesting that it's the three of us that you're talking to,'' remarked Nelson. "Like Sarah said, she was involved in this stuff before she was acting. I was involved in this stuff long before I was acting. It took a lot of careful thought on my part to get involved whatsoever in politics since becoming an actor. Because, myself, when I see an actor stand up for a cause I turn the channel, because I don't really give a shit about what actors have to say. And I care a little bit more about what politicians have to say, but not a whole lot. I'm more issue-oriented than candidate-oriented, and so it's hard to get behind issues without having a politician be there as well.''

"Ed Begley, Jr. was there as a delegate and had nothing to do with the Hollywood contingent, because he said he didn't want to get labeled that way.''

"He's been doing this for a while,'' Nelson said. "He understands from his firsthand experience more than we did then. We are learning now about the kind of trade-off in credibility that's granted in a democracy, as opposed to a capitalistic republic.''

Nelson explained what he meant. "Athens was a city of sixty thousand at the height of the Greek Empire. And a group of thinkers got together and figured out a way of running the society that would protect everyone. Plato said the polis does things for the individual and the individual must, in return, do things for the polis. That's why they could draft people from Sparta.''

This interpretation of history and philosophy was bewildering, considering, among other facts, that Athens was a city some five to six times larger than Nelson's estimate, of which half the populace were slaves and aliens, and two-thirds were disenfranchised women and children.

"Exactly,'' Nelson answered. "So it was not a democracy. It was a democracy by the chosen people. That's why Thomas Jefferson and Benjamin Franklin were very comfortable in adopting the principles from a slave society two thousand years ago to today, because today we're in the same position. Thomas Jefferson had a lot of people, including his slaves, who had no vote, in this system that Thomas Jefferson was trying to construct in America.''

Now I understood why some celebrities, even intelligent and sincerely interested ones, received such bad press. Judd Nelson was a smart fellow and three out of four statements he uttered proved that; however, while three out of four wasn't bad, that fourth was the killer, that fourth was so dopey or arrogant or plain incorrect that the press could have a field day if it so desired. Some stars seemed untouchable, I suppose as a result of their extreme popularity, while others were not. Not that it mattered, really; untouchable or not, nobody ended up sacrificing or suffering for his opinions. Still, who wants to sound like an idiot?

"You're talking about very complicated ideas and historical events very glibly, and not always correctly. If I printed only this part of the transcript, it would not look so good."

"Well, I trust this isn't *Spy*," Nelson said with a smile.

"I'm not talking about that. I'm saying that you're speaking with extraordinary confidence, especially for someone who isn't an academic. Where did you get this confidence?"

"From years of academia," Nelson replied. "I mean, as opposed to what I'm paid to do, I'm a reader. If I could do any job, it would be Robert Redford's in *Three Days of the Condor*. Sit around all day, read books." (In the film Redford played a CIA analyst whose duty entailed reading and digesting all types of books.)

"You could have that job," I said. "Perhaps not with the CIA, but you could go into academia or academic work. Why don't you?"

"Well, you mean, why don't I today? Or why don't I three years from now?"

"Now."

"Well, I have commitments."

"And three years from now?"

"Three years from now," Nelson said, "I'm sure I won't be acting. If I had my druthers, I would not be acting now. This is another subject, but it's very Faustian in that sense of like, right in that one second Faust realizes, 'My God, I had a little bit of this and I've given my soul for eternity over to the Devil.' He realizes that in the one second before he dies. That one second, for me, has been extended to four years. It's like pushing that rock up the hill and it rolls back down again."

"So what do you think you'll be doing?"

"I don't know, but I don't think I'll be a dancing bear anymore," Nelson said. "I have a big interest in making documentary films. I don't see film as necessarily entertainment. I see it as a learning tool, an instructional tool. I don't think I want to make industrial films for IBM. My concerns are much more, like Robert's, more environmentally oriented. That's sort of a finite thing we're working with."

"It's really hard to raise money for documentaries."

"Well, you see," Nelson said, "I'm in a situation where I can use my profits from my bubble gum to make aspirin or penicillin. So—oh, you were saying I'm glib. My glibness is more a defense mechanism.''

I suggested to Nelson that silence might be a more appropriate defense mechanism.

"Robert Kennedy taught us that silence is, in fact, a communication of guilt," Nelson quickly replied.

"From what I understand," I responded, "Robert Kennedy only spoke when he had something to say. And he was not glib."

"No, he was not glib," Nelson said. "But anyone that pleaded the Fifth was guilty under his Justice Department."

"People who pleaded the Fifth when Kennedy was Attorney General were on trial. Your situation is different. If you say nothing, nobody will care, nobody will ask why didn't speak."

"Yes and no," replied Nelson. "When you are in these shoes, silence is waiting for the axe to fall."

"Hold on. You are all in a very unusual position. Ordinarily, for people in their twenties, there are older, wiser people checking you, checking what you say and do. You are all remarkably independent and there is no one above checking you."

"I do feel like I have somebody checking on me," Parker said, "and that's me. Believe me, that's punishment enough."

"But it's often good, often useful, to have someone older and wiser looking out for you, someone with whom you can consult."

"Sure," Parker said. "And that's why I appreciate a lot of the people I have met through being involved in California politics, in national politics. People who are older, people like Mike Farrell and Kris Kristofferson and a handful of others. I will go to a half a dozen or a dozen different lectures or group forums where people speak, and I'll listen before I choose to speak or get involved."

"Older also doesn't mean wiser," added Nelson. "And also, we are, by profession, more bold. In order to stand up and make believe you're the King of England and speak iambic pentameter before four thousand people a week—this does not a coward make. You know, I will be more guilty of strangling myself with my own tongue than most people."

"But your political statements and involvement do not affect your career," I reminded them. "You can say or do *anything*, smart or stupid, and it doesn't matter. There are no penalties. Look at Jane Fonda; she gave aid and comfort to the enemy in time of war and so what? She makes a fortune in movies and exercise videos and achieves national respectability. I mean, she said things about our soldiers that were not only mean and anti-American, but so stupid that it is mind-boggling.''

"Not stupid," Nelson said. "Misinformed."

"Uneducated?"

"Yes," he agreed. "Uneducated. But then, you have to be careful with a high-brow attitude." He adopted a simpering, mocking tone: " 'Well, of course if you had an education and you had read and prepared, then you wouldn't have made those silly mistakes.' ''

Parker was agitated. "Are we going to take away the vote of people because—"

"We still have a vote," Nelson interrupted. "Even though we are public professionals, we still have a vote, you know. I would love to see brickmasons get a chance to stand up and say what they think."

"Me, too," agreed Parker. "And I would love to see plumbers."

"No one would write about it," Nelson said. "Because people believe that brickmasons are less."

"I participate on a much more basic, civilian level than only being involved in something as an actor," Parker said. "To me, the question is, am I going to stop people at the polls and say, 'Do you know about Proposition 65, 66, 67, 68? Well then, what right do you have to go in there and vote no or yes?' ''

Parker said all that very fast and took a breath before proceeding. "Well, the right is that I may not understand the language of the proposition, though in layman's terms it has been explained to me by my neighbor, my cousin, my father, my sister, my brother. And I feel that it is not in my best interests, so I'm going to vote against it. Now, standing up and speaking on behalf of something, or because you feel a certain way, leaves you really vulnerable and open to criticism. But, you know, on the Central American issue, a large portion of Americans were opposed to aid to the contras. Now, unfortunately, you know, there aren't news cameras in Newark, New Jersey, or Clifton, Ohio, lots of different places, but those people also feel a certain way. And to remind people, to just make them aware for just a few minutes out of the day, you know, to write their Congressman, or to galvanize at a grass roots level, it's to me a show of support or mobilization that's important.''

I stated my contention that celebrities constitute the only group who have joined together without a personal or professional interest in an agenda, who feel that they not only have the right to speak but deserve to be heard on virtually any political issue.

"You're right," Parker said.

"And that's also part of the job," Nelson said. "You can play a killer, you can play a hero, you can play—"

"And that's part of America," interjected Parker. "That is part of the choice of Americans, in a way, because number one, they'll listen, and number two, they're the people that buy the movie tickets and the people who watch the television shows. They're supportive in a way. Now, I'm not saying that they want me to speak on their behalf, but that's societal, too."

"Do you think celebrities are our heroes today?"

Parker answered quickly. "I think the difference between celebrities and heroes is that celebrities play heroes."

"Who are our heroes? Who are America's heroes?"

"Do you mean," Nelson said, "who are considered heroes?"

"I'm interested in which groups, which categories of people are considered heroes. It used to be soldiers were heroes, and explorers and scientists and political leaders."

"And now it's sports figures, athletes, actors," Parker said.

"And major entrepreneurs," added Downey.

"Money," stated Nelson. "I mean, the dollar is the god we worship, as opposed to the human spirit. If the human spirit is what is worshiped, then the heroes are what are close to being the personification of the human spirit, period. If you love the human spirit, then Hillary, the first guy to the top of Mount Everest, becomes a natural hero. If the dollar is worshiped, then Donald Trump becomes a hero."

"One hundred years ago, robber barons were heroes, but there were other heroes, too."

"Yes," Nelson said. "Today the anti-hero is a hero, that is in fact not a bad guy to the general populace."

"Who else are heroes? Are politicians heroes?" I asked them.

"The guys who pulled Jessica McClure from that well in Texas are heroes," Parker said.

"Let's stick to classes of heroes. When I was growing up, JFK and other politicians were heroes. John Glenn and other astronauts were heroes."

"Well, it depends," Downey said. "That's your perception, if you really want to get down to stuff where you're filtering through what you believe. That's why feeling to me—see I feel that feelings are—I mean, if you go and you learn all the facts and this and that, ultimately what are your decisions left up to? Well, I guess that's very provincial, but to sit there and judge if what we say is right or wrong, whose perception is that? Okay, or is it an objective perception and who can take responsibility for whose perspective is objective or whatever?"

It was evident both from Downey's countenance and his words that he was not enjoying the conversation.

"A politician's job," I said, "is to formulate and implement national policy and no one else has that job. A pol is the one who has to stand up and say this is the way it's going to be and take the heat."

"If they didn't waffle so much," Nelson felt, "they might reestablish their heroic nature."

"Yeah," said Parker, "you know, generals and all those things might have been heroes long ago, but I grew up in a time that that didn't exist. Vietnam—"

"Westmoreland killed every single general as a hero that there was," Nelson broke in. He mimicked a deep-throated general's voice: " 'Let's take this mountain and then let's give it away and then let's take it again at tremendous human sacrifice but, uh, we're here to fight communism. We're not here to win the war.' "

"César Chavez," Parker said. "The migrant farm workers' activist. And also the guy who won the Nobel Peace Prize."

"Oscar Arias of Costa Rica."

"Right, I think those are heroes. But they're few and far between."

"Look at the 1940s. We had many heroes. Why don't we believe in them now?"

"Because the people saw decisions being made and they saw leaders standing up for those decisions," argued Nelson. "The buck stops here. Now the buck stops in Switzerland. The buck stops in another account. It's a literal buck. What we worship is money.

For a long time, we worshiped lawyers. Lawyers interpreted the law. They were the high priests of society. Now they're shysters; you know, they're chasing ambulances.''

"Now we don't believe in our institutions.''

"It seems that to protect the status quo,'' Nelson went on, "as opposed to the tremendous gains in public participation in what's considered a democracy, the threat to those in charge of the status quo then pushed everything into a 'Me Generation' in the 1970s, which, in effect, destroyed every institution that we had. People don't believe in the Supreme Court. Now it's up to Sandra Day O'Connor; she's going to be the deciding vote. The eight men are split, right, so she's going to cast the deciding vote because she's a woman. She has lots of kids, so she's like a great, great mother of the nation. You know. We don't believe in family. More than fifty percent of marriages fail. We don't believe in government anymore. We had a President on the verge of being impeached. He got a pardon by the next joker, who lowered the speed limit. We had a President who was 'The Great Communicator' who, without his cue cards, was 'The Great Bumbler.' ''

"Who would have stayed in for a third term,'' asked Parker, "if that were possible, though psychologically our country couldn't take it. So what do we have left? And the responsibility you talk about here is a real responsibility. But it's not this incredible burden of responsibility if you don't attach your name to every single thing and if you pick two things, not just randomly or arbitrarily. You know? You say, 'This year I really want to work for the American Civil Liberties Union and I want to work for Amnesty International. And those are my two things. I'm going to read about it and I'm going to meet with the directors of them and I'm going to travel and meet with lawyers or whatever it is—then it's not as huge a responsibility. It's when you throw yourself out there, you know, and leave yourself completely, I mean, you totally put your ass on the line, then it's irresponsibility, but that's just a huge ego, I mean, that's something else entirely. So I don't walk around with this burden of responsibility because I'm not out there like that. I'm out there on things that I'm passionate about, or that concern me, or that I feel need to be looked at. And I feel the majority of Americans feel the way I do, or that people aren't being educated to understand why they don't know. You know what I mean?''

"A hero's job is to symbolize the best in society," I tried again, "to symbolize its values and virtues, in order that others will emulate his example. The Founding Fathers were the richest and most powerful individuals of their day, they were the 'celebrities' of their society. Though they had the most to lose, they risked everything to lead the Revolution, and not just for themselves but for all Americans. Today, celebrities do the opposite. Rather than stand for our nation's principles, work within society's values and rules, and act as examples for others to follow, all too often celebrities take the money and fame and run, and live by their own personal rules, from wearing sneakers in a non-sneaker-type restaurant to chucking everything and moving to a Caribbean island. It seems that many celebrities have abandoned society."

"Did celebrities abandon society," posed Nelson, "or did society abandon them?"

Hmm. What did *that* mean?

"Well," he explained, "if you fly in the face of convention, for the sake of your hypothesis, because you want to be outstanding, you want to make a gesture, because you're the guy who walks around without any shoes on, or do you do it because you say, 'My God, I can't possibly support this anymore. I don't believe in it.' "

"That's the easy way out. That's ensuring the country won't work."

"How about if you believe that the government is in fact not working and that the news is slow."

"But—"

"But sometimes you can't make it better," Nelson insisted. "It's not like there's penicillin or antibiotics that you can shoot in it. Sometimes you have to mess it all up and say, 'Let's take all the building blocks down,' I'm not saying tear it all down, I'm not advocating anarchy. I'm saying the idea of wearing sneakers in a restaurant is not a real issue, it's bogus."

"But is it? Then you would devalue not only the symbolic importance of celebrities, but also the principles and promise those symbols represent."

"Reagan is a perfect example," Nelson said. "Form does not follow content. You know what I mean? Now we are just living on form. And I'm saying what's happened is, maybe what's built on top of the piling is wonderful, but I say the piling is rotten. And that it's better to wipe everything off the pier and it'll look so beautiful. Take a look at the grounding here and the grounding of American society, subsequent to the changes that happened in the 1960s, and I don't think that the country has done a great job of realigning itself when all the dues of the 1960s came forth.''

"Do you think we're an incredibly different society since the 1960s?'' I asked Nelson.

"Yes, I think we are,'' he said. "But I think we're incredibly shortsighted or paranoid.''

"Yes,'' seconded Parker.

"About what?''

"About everything,'' Nelson answered. He recalled how Reagan had branded the Soviet Union "the evil empire'' and then embraced Gorbachev, and how he and Bush had similarly gone back and forth on Marcos and the Phillippines, and Noriega and Panama, all in the name of diplomacy.

"You know,'' he said, "talking about hero types, Charles Barkley, basketball player, was quoted in an interview, when someone said, 'Why aren't you a little more diplomatic when you say your teammates are wimps and they suck?' He said, 'Well, I don't like diplomacy and I think diplomacy is nothing but lies.' ''

"That's okay for basketball but international politics is another story.''

"Unfortunately, I have to believe there is one orthodox religion and it is the worship of the dollar,'' Nelson declared. "It is the reason the Soviet Union is making changes. They cannot support their economy and keep up with the West. So they got a dove from Georgia, very well-spoken. And he is the wonderful, loving guy, cause he comes over here and walks down Times Square. I can't believe he's going to walk down Times Square and we have to close up the whole city so we can afford him the opportunity to show how free and open he is. I'm not anti-Soviet, I'm not pro-Soviet; I'm much more pro-people. You know, people get lost, human beings get lost in the shuffle for power and worship of the dollar.''

"Were any of you invited to the White House during Reagan's Presidency?''

"Oh, continuously!'' claimed Nelson.

Poking through the laughter was Parker's shy, almost sheepish voice. "I was,'' she said.

"Did you go?"

"Didn't you have to have your wisdom teeth taken out through your ears that day?" inquired Nelson.

"No, I went," she said quietly. "I was invited to sing there."

"For what?" Nelson asked.

"For Easter," Parker said, "1981. Back then, I was very ambivalent about it. It was a very difficult decision. Sometimes I feel it was really unethical of me to go. Reagan's first year in office, you didn't know as much about him, but I really feel some guilt about the fact that I went and sang. But then again, I look at it like, well, I might never be asked back again—and I was sixteen years old."

I thought about John Randolph talking about the White House being his house and enthusiastically accepting his invitation.

"I think we can attribute part of it to your youth," Nelson said. "You were in the middle of puberty. You probably had acne."

I returned to the idea that a healthy society stimulated men and women to emerge from the populace and give of themselves, serving as standard-bearers of our national character and aspirations.

Downey disagreed. "We're living in an age where looking outside of ourselves for heroes is the only way to change the environment, and change ourselves, and change our perceptions."

"Change the world view," Nelson said.

"And I felt like earlier, by the way . . ." Downey slowed and stopped, and started again. "I want to learn the pros and cons of the issues, but ultimately I have to ask what feels right inside of me, and ultimately that's all there is for everybody. And I know that that's going to be up for scrutiny but, in my perception, the people that will scrutinize that, put that down, are people who have long lost touch, at least seemingly, with those deep-rooted feelings or emotions of what feels right."

"What would happen," I wondered, "if your feelings, your decisions, were going to hurt your career?"

"When it really comes down to it," Downey reflected, "my diet is more important than my career. My career is very lucrative and I enjoy it, but what it really comes down to for me is I'm not in it for ego's sake, for flashes of that. When we were out on the streets of Berkeley registering voters, I felt like in a way that was kind of in vogue and other people were doing it or whatever. But when I got out there, it didn't matter how I got there, I got out there and I knew that I felt like I was doing something that felt good. I realized I was doing it for myself and I don't think our message is trying to change the world, I think we're trying to change ourselves, to try to expand ourselves and get back to that place of going with what feels good, of what feels right for the environment. Just like in terms of the movies I get, when I do what feels right and then in the long run I say, 'God, I shouldn't have done that,' but I don't think that that's true, the validity of the experience is really where it's at. If we've become dollar worshipers, then that's wrong. If you look in the Bible or something, it seems to me that the earth worship, the relationship with earth, was kind of cut out because it seemed paganistic. You know.''

There was a brief pause before Parker spoke. ''And also I cherish the thought that I can say how I feel on an issue and I'm not going to be brought before the House Committee on Un-American Activities, you know what I mean? I refuse to believe that could happen again. It did happen and that's overwhelming and shocking and very disturbing to me, and a lot of people were hurt by that, and a lot of people were responsible that are still alive, and I cannot believe that is going to hurt my career.''

''Are you comfortable doing political things?''

''No, it's not comfortable at all,'' Parker said, shaking her head from side to side. ''I didn't like doing oral reports in high school, talking in front of people. I don't like speaking all the time. It's not comfortable. Risks are not comfortable.''

''I actually feel less comfortable and more Hollywoodesque,'' said Nelson.

''Absolutely,'' Parker agreed. ''It's not comfortable.''

''It's very, very hard to lay it on the line,'' Nelson said. ''I'm a Jew and I'm a little bit, oddly, resentful that I wasn't around in 1938. Whether those dogs are barking at me or that gun is pointed at my head, I'm not going to back down. You can have my head. You know what I mean?''

He bemoaned the lack of great, stark issues of right and wrong and the corresponding lack of needed, great, individual risk-taking. This idea struck a sympathetic nerve with Parker.

''I wish I had grown up in the years where I could have actively participated in the civil rights movement,'' she confessed.

''There are enough great issues today,'' I said.

"My question to myself is," Parked interjected, "as a civilian or as an organized group of actors or people within the entertainment industry, if it were the middle of the Sixties, someplace in Mississippi or wherever, and we were down there to register voters and somebody threw a brick at my head, if I were physically threatened as opposed to my ego being attacked, or even my self-confidence being questioned for myself, would I go back? I mean, I don't face these things and it's frustrating to me. I wish there were more things that I could really put my ass on the line for, that felt more gratifying to me. Not for myself, but for the country."

Downey, who had displayed no joy in talking politics this afternoon, had evidently had enough. He stood and excused himself, saying he had to go upstairs to his office and his secretary and return some phone calls.

After that, the conversation meandered on for a while. We had covered considerable ground. These were seasoned film professionals, intelligent young adults, neophyte political mouthpieces. By their own words, they sometimes set themselves up as stationary targets, as the easiest of marks for anyone who chose to deride their intentions and egos. In the end, however, I viewed their motives and actions more benevolently, for at least they were involved and interested in the future, in our collective futures. It was not difficult to write them off for their naïveté or arrogance or sheer wrongheadedness; however, if such flaws were accepted as the measure of one's fitness to speak on political issues, we would have to eliminate this very moment a host of commentators and reporters and professors and political hacks and, surely to no one's surprise, a cluster of U.S. Representatives, some Senators and even a Vice President.

It was also not fair to compare them to the better educated, vastly more experienced John Randolph, just as it is not reasonable for upwardly mobile parents to compare their own upbringings with those of their more privileged offspring. We have raised actors and show biz people and celebrities above us in measures of money, fame and freedom; to turn around and expect them to behave with the same judicious intelligence and emotional discretion that we might expect from any other individual contradicts every impulse with which we have endowed them.

So we have turned them loose and they have come back to us with ideas and schemes, born out of their unique positions. How far will they go? How far do we want them to go? Is this decision still ours to make?

If celebrity political participation is the result, then the state of the political process must be the cause. It was time to step into that world and examine the extent of the populace's disappointment in our elected and appointed public officials, which has helped create the void which many celebrities are eager to fill.

Chapter 6

New York City

Hope Springs . . . a Leak

Running through the political words and deeds of Hollywood, beyond the brewing intelligence and good works, past the self-indulgence and hypocrisy, was a cynicism shared by many Americans, a failing faith in our institutions and our future.

Every year, the Harris Poll conducts a survey measuring its "Index of Alienation." And just about every year, the results are a little more unsettling for those who search for a restoration of confidence and trust.

In 1966, twenty-six percent of those responding believed that "The rich get richer and the poor get poorer." In 1988, twenty-two years later, fully seventy-two percent replied in the affirmative.

In 1966, thirty-seven percent of those responding contended that "What you think doesn't count very much anymore." Twenty-two years later, that percentage had climbed to fifty-three.

In 1966, only nine percent asserted that "You are left out of things going on around you." In 1988, forty-three percent felt dispossessed.

In 1966, twenty-six percent of Americans concurred that "The people running the country don't really care what happens to you." In 1988, the number had increased to thirty-nine percent.

In 1971 (the question was not posed in '66), thirty-three percent believed that "Most people with power try to take advantage of people like yourself." In 1988, almost two thirds of those responding, sixty-three percent, supported the proposition.

Another Harris Poll tested our confidence in our institutions. The results were predictable.

Proving once again that Americans are naturally imbued with common sense, lawyers occupied the bottom of the list; a measly thirteen percent of respondents said they possessed a great deal of confidence in those in charge of law firms. Actually, the leaders of organized labor tied lawyers at thirteen percent.

The percentages for other professions were almost as distressing. Congress was third with fifteen percent, the executive branch of the federal government was next with sixteen percent, then organized religion and the White House both at seventeen, the press at eighteen, major companies at nineteen, and so on. Medicine did best, weighing in at forty percent, still well under even half of Americans, and down from seventy-two percent in 1966.

Of course, one did not have to analyze the Harris Poll to see the shift in public opinion. Several months before the 1988 Presidential election, I visited two New York City high schools, two very different high schools, to probe the views of youth, the views which will determine this nation's course.

Located on a quiet and clean Upper East Side street, boasting a preponderance of offspring of influential and wealthy parents, the Dalton School is among the foremost institutions of secondary education in the city. It is also an enclave from many of New York's grimmer realities. Not that the children are necessarily more innocent than other big city boys and girls—not by any bet. Kids grow up fast in New York, frighteningly fast, too many of them more at home at a nightclub than at home, more comfortable talking to bartenders and drug dealers than to mom and dad. Smart, sadly sophisticated, strangely cynical—the best and the brightest.

School was almost over for the year and fifteen seniors and juniors in the political science class were presenting their final projects. This day, a student was discussing his study on campaign reform funding. He had done a fine job, interviewing a lot of important people, including Senators Dole, Rockefeller and Sanford. As it had taken me some eight months and the intervention of a very important person to get a hearing with anybody on Dole's staff, never mind the man himself, I had a feeling the boy hadn't picked up the phone and arranged all those appointments on his own. The teacher confirmed my suspicions, explaining that the lad's father was a major contributor; when he flapped his wallet, politicians waved in the breeze. Doors also opened, even for a high school paper.

This type of example, undoubtedly reinforced and repeated by how their elders did business, how they moved in society, how they called for a restaurant reservation, taught children how the world worked, a lesson the class had grasped with enthusiasm.

"There's a certain degree of corruption in everyone," one boy declared. "The scandals arise when these people in high positions try to cover up their little, minor bits of corruption."

I wondered what he considered "minor" corruption.

"Watergate," the boy said quickly, stating that Richard Nixon was one of our greatest Presidents, except for that single "mistake."

The students were split on Nixon, though much less so on the nature of statecraft and politicians. They regarded politics as an exciting profession, though difficult and often treacherous. Their attitudes reflected the certainty of youth and privilege, the confidence of those whose places in life were secure and satisfying.

"Corruption is systemic," another boy said. "It's inherent within the system. There's no real way to prevent it. Most of the politicians who end up corrupt, when they come into politics they don't have bad motives; it's when they get a lot of attention, they're at this high applause level and they're doing what other people, what other businessmen on the same applause level, the Donald Trumps of the world, are doing. But when they come back to their homes and they're practically broke, they're making very little money, they want to live up to that materialistic level, and that means corruption."

"I hate to think that all politicians are corrupt," a girl said. "I don't think that's true, but I think it builds up, I think that corruption breeds cynicism and cynicism breeds corruption. It works in a cycle."

"It's part of human nature," said another student. "When you do a favor for someone, you expect a favor in return. It depends on how you define corruption."

"Corruption actually serves a purpose. Either way, whether you're corrupt or not, you're still working. If you get paid off for doing something, you're still doing it."

"I think if you took any two people in this room and put them in government, you would not begin to have the corruption you see now. I don't think the best educated, the intellectuals, are as prone to it." Now *that* was a proposition which garnered everybody's approval.

"I don't think that the best people are going into politics," a girl said. "I don't know if they ever have. I say now that I want to go into politics, but I can also say that when push comes to shove, I'm not going to want to go through what it takes in the country to get where I want to get."

Her pronouncement struck a responsive chord with her class-mates.

"When a candidate runs for office," a boy said. "he enters into this system where his life is open to scrutiny and that really scares a lot of people. That's really a scary thought. Of course, you're going to have enemies, and of course they're going to find any dirt they can on you. You have to live your life in a way, uh, you can't do anything that can be used against you."

As the students commiserated on the hardships of public services, the discourse wound down to a conclusion.

From the ruling class I proceeded to the ruled.

Also situated on the East Side, only about a mile from Dalton, the Julia Richman School is really a lifetime away. Where Dalton is private, rich and mainly white, Julia Richman is public, poor and overwhelmingly black and Hispanic. Where Dalton has guards to keep trouble out, Richman has guards to keep troublemakers in, to protect the teachers from the students, and the children from one another.

I signed in at the security desk by the front door, a prudent measure at a school ranked one of the three most dangerous in all of New York, and walked upstairs to sit in with a tenth-grade class in criminal justice.

The students were not nearly as enthused as their Dalton counterparts about a political dialogue. In fact, they made quite a collective effort to ignore me. If it weren't for the prodding of their teacher, they would have completely succeeded. However, between the two of us, we cajoled some responses.

I inquired whether they looked forward to voting when they reached the age of eighteen, My query was greeted with a loud, mocking laugh.

"What for?" asked one girl. "They're all crooks."

"A lot of kids don't care," said another girl, who evidently did. "They're more interested in the street, hanging out with their friends."

"Voting isn't so hard," I said. "You only have to do it now and then."

"If they have a choice between voting and hanging out with their friends," she said, "they'll hang out."

Could they name the politicians they liked? There was no response.

I mentioned Reagan, in the last year of his Presidency, and was rewarded with hoots and shouts of "stupid, old man" and "senile."

How about his predecessor, Jimmy Carter?

"I don't know if he was really smart," a boy said, "but he was really naïve."

I tried Jesse Jackson and received a mixed reaction.

"He's a preacher, not a politician," another boy said. "If I want to hear a sermon, I'll go to church. I respect him there, but not when he talks about other things."

"He has to prove he can do the job," a girl said.

A boy said "they" would never let Jackson get that close to power. "White people don't like black people giving them orders."

I pointed out that blacks occupied the mayor's seat in Los Angeles, Chicago, Washington and Atlanta, to name a few major cities. Didn't that mean that minorities could help take charge of their own destinies and the destiny of the country?

The class seemed confused, as though the students weren't aware that black mayors existed.

The teacher urged me to stay for the next class, an advanced group of twelfth graders, most headed for college.

Whatever their prospects, their comments sounded familiar: Politicians are dishonest, everything is screwed up, everybody is on the take.

"There is a ruthless quality about politicians," asserted one girl. "There is a ruthless quality about politicians," asserted one girl. "Everybody wants to be on top," a boy said. "Everybody wants power."

"They make you do crazy things, against your principles."

"If you're in the government, you're going to be bribed, going to help your friends, put some money in their pockets."

So who wants to go into politics? I had no takers.

The president of the student government stopped by to make a few announcements to his constituents. I asked him if he was considering a political career.

He shook his head no. "I like to work with people I can trust and in politics, you never know, you never know who's working behind your back. There are students now I'm working with who are corrupt."

"Who? Who?" cried out the other students.

The president held up his hands to calm his crowd. "I'm not naming any names, but she's sabotaging things."

"She, she!" The class exploded in laughter as the bell rang, ending the period.

Julia Richman and Dalton—two schools, two very different slices of American society, different experiences and attitudes and expectations. Even with all that, both groups of students met at dead center in their disdain for politicians and the political process. Both rejected out of hand the traditional beliefs that we, and every successful society, automatically hold to be true: that public service is honorable and important, that our leaders are decent, sometimes noble individuals, worthy of not only respect but emulation, that love of country demands that the bravest and best among us volunteer and rise to the call of duty.

These basic values forge the national character and goals, goals which must, at times, transcend personal ambitions. When this unspoken consensus crumbles, the society loses the ability, the will, to withstand internal doubt and external assault.

From the highly visible to the highborn to the highly disadvantaged, cynicism, corrupting and corrosive, was taking root in the national soul with the speed and tenacity of a medieval plague. Did

celebrities simply reflect our societal dismay or did they promote or
set it?

In attempting to explain the true cause of the Napoleonic invasion
of Russia in 1812, Tolstoy wrote in *War and Peace*:

> Historians, with simple-hearted conviction, tell us that the causes of
> this event were the insult offered to the Duke of Oldenburg, the
> failure to maintain the continental system, the ambition of Napoleon,
> the firmness of Alexander, the mistakes of the diplomatists, and so
> on.

But that was only the surface. What of the millions of men and
women who propped up the rulers and fought their wars and died in
service to their ambitions?

> . . . then again we remember the readiness or the reluctance of the
> first chance French corporal to serve on a second campaign; for had
> he been unwilling to serve, and a second and a third, and thousands
> of corporals and soldiers who shared that reluctance, Napoleon's
> army would have been short of so many men, and the war could not
> have taken place.
> If Napoleon had not taken offence at the request to withdraw
> beyond the Vistula, and had not commanded his troops to advance,
> there would have been no war. But if all the sergeants had been
> unwilling to serve on another campaign, there could have been no
> war either.
> . . . The historian, who says that Napoleon went to Moscow
> because he wanted to, and was ruined because Alexander desired his
> ruin, will be just as right and as wrong as the man who says that the
> mountain of millions of tons, tottering and undermined, has been
> felled by the last stroke of the last workingman's pickaxe.

Down and down the spiral wound. Where did it end? Where was
the bottom?

Chapter 7

Philadelphia

Life in the Big City

The bottom lurked just around the corner. Well, it would be hard to say this constituted the absolute, final, blackest bottom, for there is black and then there is blacker. Anyway, this was close enough.

It's pretty clear that faith in politicians has faded across the board across the country. Now we shall see the faith from the other side, how a certain not inconsiderable group of politicians regards its position and purpose. I sought out a couple of political bad apples to better understand the origins of our failing confidence.

The street was broad and relatively quiet, lined with shops, bars and fast food joints generously spaced apart, a common vista in the smaller, often struggling cities of the Northeast. The restaurant was a neighborhood place, a place to go for a drink or a discussion or dinner at the red and white checkered tablecloths.

This summer midday, a handful of regulars were clustered about the bar, sipping beers and arguing about the Philadelphia Phillies baseball game on the television.

Michael (Ozzie) Myers was waiting at one of the tables, bottle of beer in hand.

"My whole career in politics was very, very successful," he said. "I never had any problems, I never had any problems getting

113

votes. The people always supported me, because I was a hard worker.''

Ozzie Myers was raised in the Italian neighborhood of South Philly, familiar to movie audiences as the home of Rocky Balboa of *Rocky*. He left school in the ninth grade and went to work as a longshoreman on the waterfront. After thirteen years, the local bosses picked him to manage the campaign of a candidate for the Pennsylvania House of Representatives. The job did not require much effort; the outcome had been arranged in advance, the Democrats' candidate assigned to lie down for his opponent, the son of a Republican judge. In return, the judge was to guarantee Republican support for a certain Democratic leader as well as a cash payment. Events proceeded according to plan and, as a kind of reward, the bosses chose Ozzie to be the sacrificial lamb in 1970.

But the smooth hum of the machinery was disrupted by duplicity and the machinery angrily clanked back in revenge. The Democratic Party decided that the judge was a crook and was about to double-cross his Democratic pals; in response, the magistrate's offspring was relieved of his legislative post. In fact, when the votes were tallied, Myers had lost—but that was more an inconvenience than an impediment, justice unerringly capable of finding its own path. One week after the election, the Democratic chairman of the City Commission certified the corrected vote and Ozzie Myers was a member of the legislature by two hundred ballots.

Myers's new career was not highlighted by stirring speeches and innovative legislation. No bills carried his name or imprint. He remained the dutiful soldier, quietly voting the party line during six years in Harrisburg.

This is not to say that he did not perform any special services. After the 1972 Democratic Presidential primary, party bosses were accused of engendering a voting fraud, in the course of which poll watchers were beaten. Myers was ordered to South Philly to procure two signatures on affidavits supporting the party leaders' innocence in the attack. However, his proffered documentation neither satisfied nor stopped the federal inquiry when it was discovered that one John Hancock belonged to a gentleman who lacked fingers and hence could not write. Ah well, it is important to remember that politics is not a science, but an art.

Since 1949, Philadelphia's first district had been represented in the U.S. House of Representatives by William Barrett. Described by *The Almanac of American Politics 1980* as "an unobtrusive figure in Washington," the Congressman was "best known for his red hairpiece and for his practice of returning home to Philadelphia every night and holding office hours from 9 to 1." Myers's succession upon Representative Barrett's death was engineered by Mayor Frank Rizzo, State Senator Henry Cianfrani and City Councilman James Tayoun.

Ozzie generated excitement of a singular sort immediately upon his arrival in Washington. A gorilla mask adorned his face at his Capitol swearing-in ceremony. Afterwards, Myers became involved in a scrap which concluded with the new Representative pleading "no contest" to charges of assaulting a waitress and a security guard at a party at an Arlington, Virginia, motel.

On the floor of the House, Myers's behavior was a model of decorum, as he maintained his tradition of introducing neither legislation nor debate.

Ozzie gives a boyish appearance younger than his forty-odd years, brown hair curling over his ears and round, open face. He was fairly stocky and arms were adorned with tattoos. I could not make out the designs except for the number thirteen printed below a pattern on his left bicep. The former ward leader, former state representative, former United States Congressman, spoke in the blunt tones of South Philadelphia about a subject he knew very well, about how things got done in big city politics.

"I think that the way you got to look at a ward leader is that an effective ward leader in this city—and probably in any major city where you have either ward heelers, ward leaders, whatever you want to call them—is the guy who knows the job, the job that can get things done."

"They don't get paid, right?"

"No, you don't get paid."

"How do they make money?"

"Well, a ward leader usually has a good job that he obtained through politics. Most of your ward leaders in this city, and in every other major city, usually has some kind of a good job. He's either a deputy register of wills or, in lots of cases, elected officials. A lot of ward leaders are elected officials. But those that don't want a job, for whatever reasons, I mean they got a good job on their own, or they have their business. A lot of them don't want jobs. And the effectiveness of a ward leader, let me tell you, it ain't in dollars and cents *directly,* but indirectly it is. It's what he can bring back to that community, in service, in jobs. That's an effective ward leader," Myers said.

"An example is a judge. Somebody's going to run for a judge. All right. Well, someone that's running for a judge in a primary, and they look at a ward like this, a very productive ward in a primary, can produce big numbers, where a lot of other wards may be productive in the general [election] but not so productive in the primary. If you get nominated in the primary in the Democratic Party, normally you're a winner come November. You normally win your election in the primary here, even though you have to get elected officially in November. Well, a judge will come to me and say, 'Listen, I really need you to go all out for me and I need you to run me hot as you can down there.' I'll do anything I can to help, you know, as far as the ward committee getting the vote out or I'll speak at your dinner or attend functions. I'll do whatever is necessary. So I may say to you, 'Well look, you know, after you get elected, you're going to have a personal tipstaff assigned to you by the court: What's it gonna be?' "

"A what?"

"A personal tipstaff," he explained. "Each judge has a person that is assigned to him to help him with his functions of running the court. Now that's a good paying job and it's got good benefits, and we go after stuff like that. Now I would say to the judge, 'All right, judge, we're going to run you hard. I don't want anything. After you get elected, I want you to keep in mind one of my people for that job.' Now, you know, maybe he'll be honest and say, 'Look, I can't make you no commitments, but I already spoke to other people about this too, and I'm gonna sit everybody down and try to come up with something that will be beneficial to me and yet I wanna help some of you that helped me, too.' So I would go after that job. If this judge does real well in my area and he gets elected, it don't mean I'm gonna get it, but I have a good shot at it. And lots of times they come through. And every other elected office like that, that's the way they work . . . And that's what a good ward leader does. A good ward leader knows every job that's coming down. If five jobs are being given out on the turnpike commission

John Randolph

Charlton Heston

Edward Asner

Sarah Jessica Parker

Judd Nelson

Robert Downey Jr.

Bruce Babbitt

Sam Donaldson

Robert Squier

Michael Murphy

William Atherton

Michael Myers

John Jenrette

Jack Tanner '88

Jack Tanner '88

Ronald Reagan

Jane Fonda

Fred Grandy

Abortion Rally

or in his area, he wants all five. But he'll settle for three, he'll settle for two, whatever he can get. . . .

"You've got to also realize that a real good strong ward leader can usually, in a primary or even a general, be very, very influential in the outcome of that election. The way he lays out his strategy, the way he lays his workers out, his committee people and what they're instructed to do. Like normally, I won my own ward two-and-a-half to one in 1980, but I was a ward leader. Normally, okay, I'd win it eight or ten to one, so because of the conviction and the expulsion it had some effect, obviously. Normally, I'd win it ten to one, not two-and-a-half to one, ten to one—that would be a normal election. And you know, in the county board of elections, of course, there's proof of these facts, this can be documented."

"Why are the ward leaders so strong?"

"Well, because I think it has a lot to do with old school-type politics. This is a neighborhood where you still do favors for people. You know, the average constituent is looking for getting a little favor, once in a while. And it could be the most simplest thing in the world, but there's that personal contact that I think is so important.

"In other words," Myers continued, "today, the electorate only gets an opportunity to see most high elected officials through the media or what they read about, either the printed or televised media. Other than that, they don't never. Around here, this kind of a neighborhood, you grow up, you get to meet the people, first of all your committeeman, you get to meet your ward leader. And your elected officials participate in a lot of activities that take place. So they're always involved. And I think that people that really benefit are obviously the people in the community. They get a shot to really get to know their elected officials. So they benefit, probably."

Whether the people really benefited in this arrangement was open to question, but it was true that, politically, Myers lived by these ideas and, for a long time, prospered.

"I think I did a lot of favors. As far as in Washington, I didn't do a lot. But I was new. See, I had learned enough about politics that in your first term you don't go to Washington and try to set the world on fire, like you're going to change the whole system and become a very influential member of Congress with two years under your belt. I had learned that in the statehouse long before I got to

Washington in the way I was taught politics, the way I had learned this business, that it don't work that way. So I didn't get overly excited about trying to go down there and beat drums to change the system. My theory was to build up a strong home base, using the power of that office to do that, through the various favors that can be done. You know, many doors become open to a member of Congress. So I used to commute quite a bit, I had office hours three nights a week. My predecessor, Bill Barrett, he was a legend in his own time, was not ever very active in Congress, but he was so powerful in this area that no one could ever defeat him. The way I got to succeed him was through his death."

"And after he died, he actually still won."

"Yeah," Ozzie said. "He was nominated in that primary. I think it was May 1976, he was nominated posthumously and he got forty some thousand votes and his closest opponent got ten. Four, four-and-a-half, to one."

"Why did he win?"

"He won because of the strength of the ward leaders."

"Why did they want him to win?"

"They wanted him to win," explained Myers, "because then, under the party rules—at that time, there were seventeen ward leaders in that congressional district—so at that time, after the election was over we got together. The chairman of the Democratic city committee called a special meeting of the caucus for the First Congressional District for the purpose of selecting someone to run as the Democratic candidate in lieu of Barrett because of the death, and that's where I came into the picture. I was selected by seventeen ward leaders. That's what happened, and that was the reason behind it."

So Ozzie Myers went to Congress. That was the beginning, of course, of his greatest glory, his greatest greed, and, of course, his end.

"When you were in Congress, what particular area interested you?"

"Well," Ozzie said, "I was on the labor committee and, of course, I had a labor background. But I was moving to get on the Appropriations Committee. The Abscam story broke on Saturday. It was February 4. Well, that Monday, okay, that Monday, I was scheduled to go on the Appropriations Committee. If you remember at the time, Dan Flood, from northeastern Pennsylvania, he had been on the Appropriations Committee and he had his problems and he resigned. And, of course, a vacancy was created.''

Representative Flood was accused of selling his influence and pleaded guilty to conspiracy.

"I had the support of our regional delegation, that was Pennsylvania, Ohio, West Virginia . . . I was ready to go on Monday.''

But Monday never arrived for his appointment for, as Myers said, "the Abscam story'' came first.

Astonishingly few people remember Abscam today. The scandal erupted not all that long ago—1980—and as the sordid facts tumbled into public view, they made front page news, day after day. But we live in a world where a tale of corruption is not some rare, isolated event, but merely one more drop in a tidal wave of shame.

To briefly summarize: Operation Arab Scam began as an FBI undercover operation to recover stolen securities and paintings in the suburbs of Long Island, New York. Mel Weinberg, a convicted stock swindler, helped the government in the scheme in exchange for a recommendation of a reduced sentence. Upon the successful completion of that investigation, Weinberg offered to go after bigger game for the Bureau. So it came to pass that Abdul Enterprises and Sheik Kambir Abdul Rahman—FBI creations invented to entice crooked pols by claiming to offer money for help around the immigration laws and investment opportunities for the make-believe sheik's infinite millions—went to work. And so the FBI went after many government officials.

Abscam's promise of easy cash, however tainted, first attracted Camden Mayor and New Jersey State Senator Angelo Errichetti, who unwittingly led the Bureau to Kenneth MacDonald, vice-chairman of the Casino Control Commission, then to New Jersey lawyer Alexander Feinberg, then New Jersey Senator Harrison Williams.

On and on the string unraveled, until the FBI simply ran out of funds for the investigation. Several (usually anonymous) politicians speculated that the inquiry's termination was just as well, for the supply of eager, outstretched hands only appeared to be increasing, and increasingly distinguished. A federal prosecutor commented, "Everybody was laughing at what was happening. It was like guys were coming out of the bush, saying, 'Hey, give me some of the money.' They'd pay one guy and the next day five guys would be calling them, guys they didn't know. The tapes were hilarious.''

Eventually, Abscam required twenty-three months, $800,000 and one hundred federal agents. The haul included one United States Senator, seven Representatives and two dozen state and local officials: thirty-one public servants in all, hailing from Congress, the New Jersey legislature, New Jersey's Casino Control Commission, and the Philadelphia city council.

Ozzie Myers was indicted by a federal grand jury on charges of bribery, conspiracy to defraud the United States, and interstate travel to aid racketeering. When the trial closed, the jury required just one day to find Myers guilty. Approximately one month later, the House of Representatives voted 376 to 30 to expel Congressman Myers, the first member removed since three Representatives were cast out in 1861 for supporting the Confederacy. Eventually, he was to spend some twenty-one months in prison.

This was not the end of the Ozzie Myers saga, for the suddenly former congressman was a candidate for a suddenly unoccupied congressional seat.

Myers had won the voters' blessing in the primary held in April, three months after Abscam broke, four months before his conviction. His comfortable victory was not much of a surprise; after all, the party was behind him. Vincent Fumo, South Philly ward leader and state senator, walked the neighborhood primary voting day on behalf of Myers.

"How's Ozzie doing?" Fumo asked his constituents. "Do me a favor, vote for Ozzie."

The ward leader's rationale for assisting the troubled congressman spoke volumes about urban politics. "The code of loyalty that exists down here in Philadelphia is what makes South Philadelphia such a great place," he proclaimed. "If we had more of that in this country, we'd be in a lot better shape."

Fumo would find himself in a lot worse shape six months later, when he was convicted on mail-fraud charges arising from a plot to use the state payroll as a Democratic Party payroll.

With the nomination in his pocket, convicted felon Myers sought to win back his seat. If Myers triumphed, Congress would have no legal recourse but to seat him; the House would have to decide whether it wished to commence a new expulsion process.

Philadelphia Mayor William Green led the fight to rid the city of Myers. "When the Democratic ticket is crooked, the straight lever is not the answer," the Democratic mayor said, announcing his support for independent Thomas Foglietta.

Not all party officials concurred with the mayor.

"I'll deliver the vote for Ozzie," ward committeeman Matthew Cianciulli said. "I'll deliver it for Ozzie just like I did for Barrett after he was dead." Cianciulli was available to work for Myers because he was free pending appeal after a conviction for vote fraud.

City councilman James Tayoun offered his personal vision of sin as he explained his backing of Myers. "It's heresy to tell Democrats to split their vote."

November 4, 1980, proved to be a most unsatisfying day for Myers. The Supreme Court rejected, without comment, his appeal for a review of his conviction. Also on that Tuesday, the country, including South Philadelphia, went to the polls. Myers was a loser in a three-man race to Independent Foglietta. The Democrat didn't do badly; far from it, emerging with 35.65 percent of the vote to Foglietta's 38.95 percent. In fact, Myers beat Republican challenger Robert Burke by 10.23 percentage points.

Nevertheless, for the first time in a very long time, the Democratic candidate would not be representing Pennsylvania's first district. This astounding circumstance did not mean that South Philly would be without a Democrat in the House, for shortly before the general election, Foglietta, a former Republican city councilman, officially joined the Democratic fold.

Of course, how many remember any of this? Abscam was one stop along a rocky road, sandwiched between Watergate and the unprecedented moral, ethical and legal laxity of the Reagan Administration. Who has time to reminisce about Ozzie Myers and company when new scandals are always unfolding, like the mismanagement and fraud at the Department of Housing and Urban Development which, to this date, totals $4 billion of taxpayer money and counting, involving scores of Reagan appointees and government officials, reaching right into the Cabinet? According to the latest issue of the *Statistical Abstract of the United States,* published by the Bureau of the Census, 1,192 men and women were indicted for public corruption in 1986 and 1,192 federal, state and local officials were prosecuted in violation of Federal Criminal Statutes. Of these, 1,027 were convicted and 246 still await trial. Confronted by all this, who has time to remember Abscam and Ozzie Myers?

Despite his distant, diminished significance, Ozzie Myers had more to say that was worth hearing. He viewed the political system as a symbiotic process, politicians seeing that their friends and constituents got their share of the bacon so their friends and constituents would see that the politicians got their share of the fat. To Myers, it was a system that made sense, a system that worked, a system that the reformers and amateurs and outsiders misunderstood and hated and constantly tried to destroy.

"Was the old system better?"

"In my opinion," Ozzie said, "without a doubt. I think that where you have a chain of command, where you have a person on that street, where they can pick up a phone and they can reach a committeeman, and that committeeman's at the house giving them house-to-house service, and that committeeman has access to the Congressman, the councilman, the mayor. And that kind of a system keeps the whole community involved, and more gets done, because you're dealing in a bloc. If the committeeman goes in there and he's a good committeeman—I don't care if he's Republican or Democrat—if he's a good committeeman, if he can produce numbers on election day—he only has to work two days a year and that's primary and general—if he can produce the right numbers on those two days, he's recognized as a meaningful factor in the political realm. He's going to get a favor. If he asks somebody for something, they're going to want to do this guy, they're going to want to help him. Now he ain't normally asking for himself, he don't have nine hundred kids he's gotta take care of, he's asking for his division."

"But doesn't this system inevitably lead to corruption?" I asked Myers. "No competition, no accountability—corruption."

"I don't think that that's necessarily true," he replied. "I think no matter where you go, there's corruption. Put two guys in one office, they can breed corruption. All I'm saying, I think the competition in the Philadelphia scene, for example, was within the Democratic Party. The opposition wasn't, unless they had a super candidate on occasion, the Republicans didn't mean too much. But the opposition was really within the one party system. There was always opposition vying for places—"

"But inside the party it's quiet, it's not public. The ward leaders decide."

"People still have to vote," Ozzie said. "But I mean, yes, they're influenced by people that's doing them favors. There's no question about that. And you ain't going to change that system. I mean, as long as I can do something for you, you're going to come back. It's that simple."

Myers's arms swept about the room. "You come in here to eat and every other day you get a free lunch, you're going to be back. You'll be a steady customer. If I can do something for you, you're going to return. It's that simple. And, you know, you get involved with all these congressional campaign committees and even U.S. Senate and of course the Presidential campaign committees, all these volunteers are out there—well, let me tell you something about these volunteers: There's a certain percentage of them that are true volunteers, who just believe they're doing something to help this country move forward—and I do believe that—but the majority of them volunteers have an ultimate motive behind in their minds somewhere. They got a motive where they want to be in this job, they want that job, they're looking for something. They're not volunteering because they want to see the Statue of Liberty shining. They're volunteering for other purposes. They want a job, they want something down the road. And you'll find that with volunteers. So you got someone who's supposed to be volunteering because this is the American way, but yet, in the back of their mind, they're looking for something. If it ain't for them, it's for their husband or wife, girlfriend, whatever. They got some reason they're doing this."

"Do you like politics?"

"Yeah," Ozzie responded with enthusiasm. "I like politics. I had a lot of fun at it. Yes, I did. I met a lot of great people in it and I think the greatest thing I ever learned in politics was how to say no. And the thicker your skin gets, the better off you are. You gotta be like a duck, you gotta let the water roll off your back. Because there are so many little things that happen, on a daily basis, if you ever tried to take them all seriously you'd get a straitjacket after about two months. You'd go batty. I was an elected official for over ten years, counting the statehouse and the U.S. House, and I was a ward leader for longer than that and involved through the ranks of the ward system, I was the ward chairman, I was first vice chairman, I worked my way up—you learn that a certain percentage of politics is total bullshit. I mean, *total*.

"But you learn to sort through that, you learn to see right through it. You can tell the fakers from the real people, once you get a little experience at this business. The fakers stand out, they almost glow. It's like seeing a rotten tomato in a bushel, you know where it's at, you pick it out, you throw it away. There's sincere, dedicated people that really are true volunteers, that's what I'm saying to you. But you'll find the majority of those people are not."

I asked Myers whether politics attracted dishonest people.

"No," he said. "I don't necessarily think it attracts corrupt people. But what I think what happens in politics, you learn to cut corners. And sometimes that gets dangerous. And then you get a lot of basically greedy business people and so on, that are always looking to force money down your throat to do 'em a favor. It's common. They're not giving out of their heart, like these volunteers I talk about. If somebody's giving you a big donation, they got some ulterior motive."

"So you'd say politics is not a corrupt business, but it's a very cynical business."

"Well," Myers said, "it's cynical to the degree, that there's a lot of greed involved. Not necessarily on the members' part. The member gets manipulated in many ways."

Considering Ozzie's formidable experience in Philadelphia politics, I noted that he must know about a host of activities that, if not illegal, must be judged unethical.

"There's many, many things that are unethical," Myers responded. "I found that it was to my best advantage to mind my own business. There were members that would womanize, there were members that were alcoholics, there were members that were gamblers. And every vice that you could imagine, members of Congress had. And no different from the general public. Yes, there's faggots in there. Certain percentage of them are gay. I mean, that's been proven. But what percentage of the overall population is gay? I mean, that's a part of it, I don't think you're ever going to change that."

"But I don't mean that kind of behavior, I mean—"

"Well, but I mean, I don't think it's too ethical for a member of Congress to be out laying drunk in a car four o'clock in the morning with some whore, do you? That don't bother me none, as long as it ain't my wife or my daughter."

Myers gave a brief laugh. "You follow what I'm saying? It ain't gonna bother me none. But to some people, that would be reasons for high treason or tar and feather him immediately. Me, I could care less what he does at four o'clock in the morning."

I asked Myers if after working his way up from the bottom, didn't he have to make so many deals and compromises that even if he wasn't personally corrupt, he would have to become corrupt as part of the corrupt system?

"Well, I can't agree with that," Ozzie said, shaking his head. "I really can't. People get exposed and manipulated a lot when you get into higher elected office. You get exposed to more, let's say, unethical-type deals. Okay, things that are not so kosher that you get involved with because some good friend has got a friend that's a lawyer for this firm, and you get involved with things that you didn't go there to get involved with, but somehow you get involved with. Whether it's campaign contributions or whatever, when it comes down to actually doing something illegal, you got to say no. I always found if someone came to me with a proposal, I would refer them to whoever I thought could help them in that area. You know, because I was far from an expert in many of those areas, like, uh, uh . . . Well, I was never considered an expert in any area. Other than how to get elected."

Myers laughed again, louder.

Once more into the breach: I started on the spirit theme. What effect did Abscam and other scandals have on the faith of the people in politics and politicians?

"Well," Myers answered, "If you put politicians on a scale one to ten and included other professions, probably the only ones that would rank lower right now would be lawyers. 'Cause everyone looks at a lawyer as a thief. Next to the lawyer would be a politician; probably number eight would be doctors. They look at them as thieves, too—the general public. The real heroes today are the sports figures and, of course, clergymen, and things along that area."

"How could politicians up their rating?" I wondered.

"Well, I would think that they could up their rating by spending more time back in the districts, instead of trying to be high falutin' Washingtonians, once they get elected. I think they ought to have to go back and meet and face their electorate. They ought to cut down the scheduling. They spend entirely too much time in Washington. And I think that breeds problems."

I inquired about Myers's future. "You ever think about politics?"

"Well, I've always thought about politics," he said. "I was in a situation where there wasn't too much I could do about it."

"Ray Lederer is a ward leader." Lederer also lost his Congressional seat in Abscam, was also convicted and served time in prison.

"Yeah, I may run for ward leader again," Myers said. "Because, right now, the councilman who just got convicted is the ward leader here. Did you know that? He's getting sentenced on Wednesday."

The more things change, the more they stay the same.

"He would have to give up his city council seat once he's sentenced," Myers explained. "See, it's predicated upon being sentenced. In other words, in a ward structure, as far as the Democratic city committee rules for this city and county, he would not have to step down."

"He wouldn't be too effective from jail."

"Well, that's the point," he said. "He's not necessarily going to jail. You know what I mean? Once he's sentenced Wednesday, he would probably appeal. He has made several appeals to the judge that he was tried in front of, but the judge has denied them. Now I would think he would appeal those denials to the circuit, the third circuit here, and may possibly take them to the Supreme Court. If everything went against him, if he ran the regular appeal process on his case, he probably has nine months. So if he's sentenced Wednesday or whatever, I don't see him stepping down on Thursday. And I ain't looking, you know, to drive no stakes into his heart. I will let nature take its course and see what happens. But in Philly, Harry Jannotti never stepped down from ward leader when he went to jail."

"Don't you think he should have?"

"Well, not necessarily. I think, uh . . ."

I found all this a bit extraordinary. Is enough never enough?

"He went to *jail,*" I said.

"Well, Myers began, "but he was only in jail for a couple of months. He only performed once in jail—"

"I wasn't talking about how long. Somebody in jail shouldn't be serving as one of the people's representatives."

"I don't necessarily think that's true," demurred Myers. "If you were going for an extended period of time, a year, two years, three years, something like that—then yes. I would say the ward leader himself should step down. Because he couldn't be effective."

So that's how the game sometimes works, and how some politicians think. Is it any wonder that some Americans have stopped listening to politicians and started listening to somebody else, anybody else—celebrities, for instance?

I tried the inspiration angle one last time. "It's not exactly a good example for children—the ward leader in jail. It reminds me of those old movies, with the crime boss in Sing Sing, getting his nails manicured and running his business from his cell."

Myers grinned. "Yeah, but you gotta realize, children can't vote."

His smile widened and then he laughed, loud and long.

Chapter 8

Florence, South Carolina

Southern Hospitality

A small item in a magazine revealed that former Congressman John Jenrette was considering another run for the House. The article stated that Jenrette's appeal in his South Carolina district was "undiminished."

It appeared I had found a place where a lot of people weren't mad about the state of politics at all.

"A group of friends are putting together the money to do a poll," Jenrette said over the phone, "to give a better consensus of what the real feelings about John Jenrette are."

Why a poll?

"I, we, got a situation," he replied in his unvarnished drawl, "where a person might be for John Jenrette with their heart, but when they go to vote their head might say, 'He's got too much baggage.' I've got to really look at that; it's a situation I've never been in before, naturally, and I won't know how far it carries over, and that's why I'm spending the money, or authorizing expenditure of the money, to do the poll, so that I'll know if I'm getting heart feelings that are not head feelings."

Ozzie Myers had shown me how the corrupt politico viewed his position and his constituency. I had come to South Carolina to turn that around, to see how the constituency viewed its chosen, corrupted public servant. I saw how the lowered expectations of the public towards politics, and the diminished aspirations of politicos towards their profession, act on one another. Nothing abstract or theoretical here, no Harris Polls or interviews with celebs or students, but a hard reality, situated in a place of pain and hardship, a place where the people awoke to discover their champion was a two-bit criminal.

Jenrette said the poll would cost about $20,000.

I asked if politics was worth it—and I didn't mean the money.

"I miss it and I would like to run," Jenrette said. "That's the bottom line. But I'm not going to do it unless there's a reasonable—and I certainly don't expect an assurance but even a reasonable—chance that people would forgive me and support me."

The people of South Carolina had a lot to forgive. Like Ozzie Myers, John Jenrette had been caught in the Abscam trap—caught, convicted, jailed.

"I have larceny in my blood," Jenrette informed the FBI undercover agents, a secretly taped statement which became famous. Nowadays, naturally, more people remember Jenrette's ex-wife better than they remember Jenrette or anything he said. Rita Jenrette, after fleeing the sinking ship, went from dutiful wife to mini-celebrity, facilitated by her book in which she described how she and her husband had sex on the steps of the Capitol, bared almost all for a *Playboy* pictorial spread, and appeared in a film improbably entitled *Zombie Island Massacre.*

"You're welcome down," responded Jenrette. "I'd be happy to talk with you. I don't know what you could glean from my limited knowledge."

I said I could learn quite a lot.

A short time later, I found myself riding in the passenger seat beside ex-congressman and local legend John Jenrette, fuzzbuster beeping, on the lookout for old friends and new voters. We sped from one small town to another—there were only small towns in these parts—pulling into hardware stores, dry cleaners, diners, pausing to greet anybody Jenrette recognized, conversing in between stops.

"When you speak of morality in Congress, you're dealing with five hundred and thirty-five prima donnas with big egos," Jenrette said. "It's difficult, is what. And I dare say that if you look at corporate America, the dealings between corporate leaders and all would be just as dubious, and you would find just as many flaws as you would by looking into the morals of members of Congress. Now there's a difference to the extent that we're elected to do the laws, but what about a corporate president who has hundreds of thousands of stockholders? Now I know there's a difference, but . . ."

South Carolina's Sixth District was a red and brown quilt, a place of tobacco farms and textile mills inland and lovely beaches on the coast. It was also a place of poverty. This had once been plantation country and the history showed in the landscape—driving along, we passed one large, handsome house after another, ringed by manicured lawns and then agricultural fields and then clumps of shacks, obviously without electricity or plumbing. Too many blacks, constituting forty-one percent of the local population, along with a lot of whites, lived in intolerable conditions with little opportunity for change or improvement.

At the same time, the people were remarkably courteous and a buffet dinner at the Thunderbird, with all the trimmings, cost six dollars, tax included.

John McMillan had represented the Sixth District in the House since 1938 and conducted business the old-fashioned way, catering to tobacco interests via his seat on the Agriculture Committee and neglecting his black constituents. Passage of the Voting Rights Act of 1965 altered the certain measure of power. A young attorney named John Jenrette recognized that McMillan's electoral days were numbered and challenged him in the 1972 Democratic primary. Although only thirty-six years old, Jenrette had already served for eight years in the state legislature, where he had gained a reputation as a liberal. Rallying black support about him, Jenrette defeated the incumbent but lost the general election to his Republican opponent, swept into office on the Nixon-Agnew landslide. Two years later, the natural order was corrected as local Carolina politics reverted to Democratic control, and John Jenrette went to Congress.

"We're gonna stop here," Jenrette announced, pulling off the road and into a parking lot before a very large building. "You can't come all the way from New York and not see a tobacco auction."

The warehouse was a huge structure, open, dark and damp, 210,000 square feet inside, packed with fifty-four rows of tobacco, ninety-five piles to a row. Federal inspectors moved through the narrow lanes, grading each pile. Buyers from the cigarette companies followed an auctioneer in single file, along both sides of each row, like baby ducks trailing behind the mother. The auctioneer walked along, continually rattling off the price of each bundle of tobacco, not pausing even for the purchasers' bids, which were duly noted by a clerk. Forklifts plowed around the floor, restacking the piles as they were bought and sold.

Jenrette knew his way around the warehouse. He told me how he had grown up on a farm which had raised tobacco, among other crops. More exactly, Jenrette came from a poor family, of the kind called dirt farmers. His hands were large and rough and strong, the hands of a man who had worked in the fields. His face was ruggedly handsome and creased from the sun, though his sandy, longish hair afforded him a boyish mien.

Jenrette put on a big smile and approached a man who was busy checking figures on his notepad.

"Nice to see you," Jenrette said. "How's it going?"

The man was wiry and old and he looked at Jenrette and smiled broadly. "Well, I'll be," he said. "How've *you* been?"

They shook hands and the older man asked if he could take Jenrette around.

"That'd be mighty kind of you, sir," Jenrette replied.

Jenrette introduced me to our volunteer host, a supervisor in the warehouse, and implied I had flown down from the big city to find out about tobacco. I supposed he imagined it was easier than going into an explanation.

In any case, the supervisor, who had spent fifty-two years in the tobacco business, was pleased. "Well, good for you, good for you," he said. "And if you learn anything about tobacco, for God's sake, tell us."

"Could I introduce you as our next congressman," the man inquired with a twinkle in his eye, "or should I not say anything?"

"Naw," Jenrette said. "You don't believe that."

"Are you gonna run?"

"I don't know," Jenrette said.

"Oh, yes, you do," the man replied.

"No," Jenrette said. "I don't know neither."

If Jenrette really didn't know if he would run, then he was the only one with any doubts in all of South Carolina. The newspapers had been writing about his prospects, and the editorials I had read were not too thrilled with the notion.

The Sun News, published out of Myrtle Beach, summed up the prevailing sentiment, at least among intellectuals and the establishment set:

> As we noted during the last congressional race, if Mr. Jenrette ran from prison, he'd have to be given some odds of winning. His support, we think, lies among the large body of voters, but his support among the large money-givers remains weak . . .
>
> Lest any reader get the idea we are encouraging Mr. Jenrette's candidacy, allow us to disabuse you of the notion. Mr. Jenrette may have technically paid for his crime against laws, but he has yet to pay for his social crime against the voters who elected him and the constituents who trusted him . . .
>
> Mr. Jenrette rubbed his constituents' noses in his misdeeds and ill will in Washington. On many of us, the scars still show.

The supervisor waved a couple of men over. "You keeping busy?" he asked Jenrette while we waited for the others to join us.

"Oh yeah."

"Good, good."

The two fellows recognized Jenrette and eagerly shook his hand.

"How you getting along?" one asked.

"Fine, just fine," Jenrette responded. "Can't complain."

"Mr. Sherman," the supervisor said, "he's down here learning about tobacco. I told him when he learned it to come and see and tell us."

One man queried Jenrette as to whether he was campaigning for Congress. As usual, Jenrette stated that he was simply looking around, trying to decide.

"Wait a minute," the supervisor said. "If you're ahead and you don't run, who will?"

The tobacco men discussed several other prospective candidates, who were quickly dismissed for various inadequacies.

"The damndest thing I ever heard yet," the supervisor declared, "was this farmer said, 'Hell, we ain't got a damn congressman.' "

The others nodded in agreement.

The auction line trod nearby. Jenrette scanned the dozen men for a friendly or familiar face. Through the entire visit, he had appeared nervous and unsure about his reception, obviously concerned about rejection. But it was more than the ordinary candidate's reflex to appeal to voters, it was clearly a personal rather than political need to be accepted, to be *liked,* for God's sake. Jenrette's hunger was so plain, so undisguised, so tinged with guilt, that it was a painful performance to watch.

"How you doin'?" he tried rather tentatively.

One individual glanced up from his perusal of the tobacco piles and responded with some distraction. "All right, all right."

The line kept progressing, with the constant stream of price quotations punctuated by the shouts of buyers, leaving Jenrette behind in the wake. The supervisor took matters into his own hands and nimbly leapt forward and corralled a fellow from the end of the procession, physically pulling him away.

"You know John Jenrette, don't ya?"

It took a second but then the middle-aged man's features lit up. "Oh yeah!" he said, smiling. "How you gettin' on?"

"How you doin'?" Jenrette countered. "Nice to see you again. Been a while. Things going well?"

"Good," the man said, glancing at the slowly vanishing auctioneer. "I met you about ten years ago."

"You're getting younger, I'm getting older," Jenrette said and the man shook hands again and hurried back to work.

The supervisor brought Jenrette around to greet several other people and then the three of us adjourned to his office for a rest. He began telling me about the problems of tobacco price supports when Jenrette quietly interrupted, his voice an intense whisper.

"Should I run?" he asked the supervisor, with the deference due a supplicant before the Dalai Lama.

The supervisor ruffled his brow, giving the question appropriate consideration. He was more than a spry old fellow, he was sharp and well-fixed and influential with an awful lot of people. His opinion counted and any smart politico had better ask for it before asking for anything else.

"I'll tell ya," he said. "Here's what I think. If a man now runs, it'll cost him several hundred thousand dollars. You get a two-year job, you get about $79,000 per year. If you get in debt, you can't pay out. Hell, they ought to make the term of congressman six years and senator eight, and not let him run, say, but two terms. And it would make it economically worthwhile."

He glanced through the window onto the warehouse floor, checking the activity.

"I will tell you this," he said. "You go to the country—and I believe I go to the country more than anybody in the building—and everywhere I've been, there are two things. If you call John on a Friday, he'd either have a letter to you Monday morning on your mail route, or else he'd call you up. And you go to the farmers, and I'll bet you seventy-five percent of the farmers have told me, 'I would vote for John Jenrette.' Now I'm not in politics and you say, 'Well, you don't bring it up.' Hell no, you go a crossroad to drink your Coca-Cola, they'll bring it up. The other thing, the preponderance is that the colored people, the black folk, would vote for him today. And he was a good congressman."

Jenrette sadly shook his head. "I just don't know if people would."

"All right," stated the supervisor. "It's like the man said: 'I went to this place and there was the envelope.' They said, 'Give the man,' and I said, 'I ain't taking a damn thing.' That was Senator Thurmond. They handed you the envelope and they said, 'Do this, you do that.' And here we are."

A brief pause ensued while all considered the regrettable past, Jenrette with head bowed.

The supervisor spoke again, on a sprightly note. "I got a report on the contributions by the political action committees. You ought to see it, it's just hard to believe!"

Jenrette leaned his head back and yelped. "Whoa!"

"Now don't you know darn well," the supervisor said, "that if you farm out ten thousand dollars to ten people, and you get that, you're obligated. That man's got a right to expect something."

"Sure," concurred Jenrette.

"What they ought to do is finance it just the way they do the Presidential election, and not let a man spend so much."

"We ought to have public financing," Jenrette said, nodding. "In my opinion."

"Well, that's what I'm talking about!" the supervisor insisted. "That's it!"

"Listen," Jenrette said quietly. "I'll send you a note and tell you where to send my contribution. All right?"

"All right."

"You can raise me a couple of grand," said Jenrette. "I know that's right."

Jenrette was ready to depart, and the supervisor put his hand on the politician's shoulder.

"I still say you did a good job in Congress. I'm not in politics, but I thought you certainly served the public. And I went to any farmer with a filling station, you didn't have to bring it up, they brought it up."

I wasn't sure, but I thought I saw Jenrette's eyes mist over.

"That means a lot to me," he said. "Really."

John Jenrette was the only congressman a lot of people ever had. That was the phrase I heard again and again. The first elected official who could be called on the phone, who listened to a problem, who tried to do something about it. The first official who cared.

The last day Jenrette spent in jail was also the opening day of the local tobacco market, and the opening of the Democratic political season. Tobacco still being king, a South Carolina politician would not miss opening day any more than his New York counterpart would decline to march down Fifth Avenue in the Columbus Day Parade. Everybody was there, from the governor to congressional candidates, magistrates to mayors. With a line-up like that, Jenrette's homing instincts could not be denied. He walked straight out the front gates of the Atlanta Federal Penitentiary and back into action.

"Ah, well," Jenrette admitted. "I have difficulty in looking on myself as a criminal for one, I guess. And it had been six years since I had been involved in any way and I thought six years was adequate to have tested my, uh—if you believe in the system, I had every right to be there. But it's not easy. And for a long time, five or six months, I kept looking over my shoulder, wondering what people were saying."

"He did right by his constituents," a black man said. "He took care of his people. He cared about us. He was the people's congressman."

"What about his going to jail?"

"Hell," he laughed. "Everybody gets in trouble."

"Not everybody gets in trouble with the FBI."

"I don't know anything about the FBI."

"What about the federal government?"

The man laughed again. "I don't know anything about the federal government," he said. "And I don't trust the federal government."

I was surprised by his attitude. Wasn't Washington responsible for most of the legal and social progress initiated in the south?

He smiled and shook his head. "You might be talkin' about a city like Charleston or Columbia, but down here, change comes a little slower."

All he knew for sure, just like everybody else knew, was if a sick child required medical attention or a store owner had a zoning problem, Jenrette was the man who would help. And help like that was no casual matter, not when some people were always on top, while others were always, endlessly, on bottom.

"John don't think race," the man affirmed. "He don't know about race."

"And the rest doesn't matter?"

"If they want you," the man said, "they'll get you, and they wanted John and they got him. Look at this Iranscam stuff; somebody did something bad, but nobody's doin' no time."

"But what about—"

"Just another show," the man said. "I don't understand it anyway, and I don't want to."

Jenrette and I drove up to a General Motors dealership. Jenrette jumped out and pushed open the glass door, looking for the owner, an old pal. He was not in sight, so Jenrette visited with a waiting customer, a rather prim woman of about forty, gray hair piled high and starched in place.

"How you doin'?" he said, striding across the room, hand outstretched. "John Jenrette."

"Fine," she replied, recognition dawning. "Fine."

"You here to buy a new car?"

"No," she said, hands folding back across the lap of her light blue pants suit. "I'm having mine serviced."

"They treating you right?"

"Fine, fine, fine," she said. "If they didn't, I wouldn't be here."

Jenrette put his hands in his pants' pockets and rocked on his heels. "My parents used to drive all the way over here to buy. From Lawrence."

"Is that right?"

"Yes," he nodded. "It is."

They both laughed and then the owner walked in from the garage. Jenrette said his piece, then greeted every employee in the shop, constantly fending off questions about his political prospects. As we started to leave, the woman with the ailing auto hurried over to Jenrette, took his hands in hers, and whispered in his ear.

"I appreciate it a lot," Jenrette said, holding onto her grasp. "Thank you a lot."

"God bless you," she responded.

"God bless you," Jenrette said. "I'll be talking to you."

As we drove off to Jenrette's next engagement, I asked him what the woman had whispered.

"She and her church had been praying for me," he said, "and wanted me to run, and had been reminding people that we all make mistakes. She was gonna tell her pastor that she knew that my life was meant to help people."

"It's amazing to me that the American people are so quick to condemn somebody when they're in office—for anything—and so willing to forgive, too."

"Well," Jenrette said, "I've been out eight years. I've got a whole new identity thing if I decide to run."

"Do you find a lot of people who, under no circumstances, would accept you?"

"I don't, but they're there." And then Jenrette became uncharacteristically quiet.

Aside from his efforts on behalf of his constituents, Jenrette had been a controversial figure long before his Abscam conviction. He had been investigated for questionable land deals, he was a recovering alcoholic and he was a womanizer. Indeed, was he ever a womanizer—in his first divorce, twenty-three women were mentioned in the complaint. Jenrette freely admitted the list could have been longer.

The Florence Morning News conducted one of those inquiring photographer features, asking people whether Jenrette should run and if they would vote for him. The answers were, as usual, split.

A middle-aged white woman said, "I think he should run and I would vote for him. I think he made a good congressman. We're all human—we all make mistakes. I think he got tricked." A woman same race and similar age disagreed: "It's his decision. I would not vote for him. The man has no morals."

A black man was very supportive. "I certainly hope he does. I would support him. He was a very good congressman while he was in office. He was a people's man and he helped the poor. We need more congressmen like him. I've always believed Abscam was a set-up and I don't believe he did anything more than other congressmen."

Jenrette was an effective U.S. Representative of a type; he was not a national leader, an ideological trailblazer, a man whose name was destined to become a rallying cry for a cause. Jenrette was the sort who was good for his district, who knew how to bring home the bacon to his constituents: in other words, a more benevolent version of Ozzie Myers. Actually, though South Philadelphia no longer resembled a 19th-century offshoot of Tammany Hall and South Carolina's Sixth District had left behind its class system and racist regulations, South Philly and Horry County still had more in common with their pasts than either might care to admit.

To some, Jenrette must have seemed a modern Don Quixote, tilting against the windmills of privilege and entrenched power, against the establishment which ruled these rural lands from generation to generation, economics and tradition uniting to become unbending fact. So it was that Jenrette had found a niche, an opening; simply by foregoing old prejudices, by believing that every person, black or white, should be allowed his due, his chance at the American dream, he had earned the respect and support of a sizable segment of the community. The truth was, Jenrette's heart, or at least a part of it, was in the right place. But was semi-sincerity enough to merit election as a United States Representative?

Evidently it was in South Carolina's Sixth District. Not that his constituents had any illusions about John Jenrette. They had heard all the stories about Jenrette's drunken behavior, how he had been virtually unable to function for the last year of his last term, how his aides had to cover for him continually—they knew it all. At the end, they knew he was a crook. Many despised him for his sins but many others forgave him, even excused him.

If the people were willing to accept these transgressions from an official, then of course they would not mind the public and private transgressions of preachers and business leaders, let alone actors or athletes. Then, of course, celebrities can lay claim to occupy center stage, politically speaking, because all expectations and aspirations on all sides have been lowered and diminished.

Eventually, though I do not know the reasons, Jenrette decided not to run. He did continue to make the news, however: several months later, Jenrette was arrested and convicted for shoplifting in a Washington, D.C., store.

Jenrette's comeback had come close. Maybe next time he would make it all the way. Why had the Sixth District voters permitted him back into the political hunt? Were the people so cynical about the electoral process that they were willing to settle for a felon?

Riding along the highway, Jenrette suddenly turned to me. "I expect you are condemning politics pretty well, aren't you?"

"Me? I like politics."

Jenrette smiled to himself. "How do you feel the system can be fixed so we won't have some of these things?"

"You mean corruption?"

"Yeah."

"I don't think it can be," I replied. "I think politics is essentially a business of people, not laws, and you can't fix human nature with laws."

"Well," Jenrette said, eyes on the road. "You might be right."

Chapter 9

Washington, D.C.

Hardball

Robert D. Squier understands celebrities, politics and the use of celebrities for political purposes. Squier/Eskew Communications, appropriately located in a townhouse a few blocks from the Capitol, is one of the top political consulting firms in the country. In the course of reaching the top of a very competitive profession, Bob Squier has advised dozens of state and national candidates, more often than not successfully, on how to gain and keep public office. Like most consultants, Squier works only one side of the street; in his case, the Democratic side.

Actually, Squier is something of a media celebrity himself, handsome and articulate, a political commentator on *Today,* a regular on the talk show circuit. I imagined there wouldn't be much talk about how bright or fresh or well-intentioned stars are from this sophisticated professional.

"You have to divide the use of celebrities and celebrity involvement before and after campaign reform," Squier said. "After campaign reform, you had to basically retail the money raising. And that meant having big events, or events where you really had to have a draw. The days of five guys who were each going to pony up $500,000 were gone forever.

"Now, the Republicans are very good at doing direct mail to address that," Squier continued, "the Democrats not as good at direct mail but better at finding somebody who is a draw. So a celebrity is, by definition, perfect. If you are a person who can draw a thousand people to a room by your name, then you are valuable to a campaign. So, in a sense, they've gone from a group status right down to the center of the process, where the money is. If you are involved in providing money for a campaign, that is the very center of what is going on."

I asked him, "Is it more useful when the celebrities raise the money themselves or when you use them by bringing them into your campaign?"

"That's hard to say," Squier replied. "You could certainly point to the instances where they have come to an event and the event has literally made the difference in the campaign. You go as far back as Dick Lamm's first campaign for Governor of Colorado in 1974. We did that campaign, and we were struggling for money. The people didn't know all that much about him. We were not reaching the center of the electorate. John Denver agreed to do one concert for him and that one concert basically elected him governor, because it was over $200,000 in profit to the campaign and it was *bang!* Instant. So in a way, these people could be the big rollers in politics if they wanted to, they could take it to the next step and say, 'I'll do a concert for you and it'll be worth a million dollars.' So, in effect, they can give something that can be worth a million dollars, when it comes to their fans, who they can still retail. The financing of politics is now wholesale because of campaign reform laws, very little retail, and yet celebrities still have the power, if they want to do it, to inject big hunks of money into campaigns, either through their own celebrity as a draw or through what they do, as a bigger draw."

That all made perfect sense; since the election reform laws had limited the amount any one person could contribute to a campaign (a maximum of $1,000 to a Presidential candidate, for example), politicians could no longer rely on fat cats to open their wallets and let the money flow directly—the "retail" way of doing business. Celebs, however, could perform at a concert, for example, and have thousands of fans pay twenty dollars, twenty-five dollars, whatever, and have it go to the campaign—"wholesale" fundraising.

"Isn't there's a difference between you bringing them into a concert arranged by your campaign, and having to send your candidate before the HWPC, for instance, and have him submit to grilling by the members?" I repeated the story of a visit to the HWPC by a prominent northeastern U.S. Senator, told to me by his campaign's financial director. It seemed this senator sat with growing irritation as he was peppered with not necessarily coherent or concise questions from an aggressive committee representing the group; as his short replies expressed his displeasure, the inquisitors were also less than satisfied. Finally, no longer able to hide his emotions, the distinguished senator informed the committee members that they were, and I quote, "full of shit." To his surprise, this did it; for some reason, the questioners were happy, and the senator received his campaign contribution.

Squier laughed and nodded knowingly, having heard variations on the theme before.

Having to choose between the two methods of celebrity fundraising, individual or group, I assumed the former instance was still the overwhelming preference.

"Sure," Squier responded. "I think it's fair to say that the Hollywood Women's Political Committee is just like any other political action committee. You try to do the retail side of fundraising before you ever go to a political action committee, because there's a penalty to be paid every time you go to a PAC of any kind. Most PACs have some kind of aura about them, that you have to deal with their politics. And if you're a candidate running in the center of the Democratic Party in the center of America and you go to the Hollywood Women's Political Committee, your opponent is likely to try to make a case against you by saying you have gone someplace that is further left than your constituency in order to get the money."

Whether the show biz groups wielded any real power was not the issue to Squier. What counted was how their participation was viewed by the media and public.

"We work in a different world," Squier said. "We don't work in a world of reality, we work in a world of the *perception* of reality. And the only reality we can deal with is how people turn things around to use them. So you're always looking at the world in a very defensive posture. 'I take this dollar, what will it cost me?' It might cost you access, it might cost you work; in that case, politicians might ought not to take it. It might cost you something in a campaign, and there are PACs, not just HWPC, but PACs all over the country, that lend themselves to a perception that can be used against the candidates they support.''

"Leaving the perception of reality behind, do you believe any of the show biz groups wield any real power, considering their lack of any single issue, economic or ideological, which dominates their attention and directs their actions?''

"Yes,'' Squier answered.

"What is their real power then?''

"The power is money,'' Squier replied. "Money equals power.''

Now that was a professional pol talking. But how do they use the money?

"By choosing,'' responded Squier. "By helping some people and not others, and thereby affecting the result. But in terms of after that takes place, there is no real interest. They have power, but they don't exercise it for any purpose other than the pure exercise of power. I assume they are like most other political actions committees in the sense they are at their most powerful when they leverage themselves. And that is a case of going before the committee, doing your dance, then getting your five grand. If you had really impressed them and your opponent is really impressive, you could leverage that operation through its members into hundreds of thousands of dollars, by getting people to show up at events, by getting them involved in your campaign.''

"In that case,'' I suggested, "only real celebs count, eliminating any depth to the group's structure, limiting its power. After all, another PAC—one representing a union, for example—can not only raise money but can mobilize hundreds of volunteers, essential to any campaign, making the group itself, not just its stars, interested and important.''

"Oh, yeah,'' Squier concurred. "That's why I say the future of celebrities, if they really want to make use of it, is in being able to involve themselves into a campaign. Gary Hart was in a very tough race in 1980 and called on his friend Warren Beatty to come in and help him out. And Beatty gave him a day, basically two events. The first event was a traditional fundraiser, out at the country club where, you know, people who already have given come and get to see Beatty, and some more people come and give, one of those kind of events, and it did very well. The other event—I don't know who thought of it—was a one hundred dollar nonpolitical fundraiser. They just made it a hundred bucks at the door and advertised on the radio, 'Come and see Warren Beatty.' I went to both of the fund-raisers. The second one was the most fascinating event I've ever seen in my life. It was a room entirely full of women, who had paid one hundred dollars to see, have their picture taken with, shake hands with Warren Beatty. There weren't four men in the room! And those women had no interest in politics at all.''

I told Squier how I had seen Warren Beatty at a New York political fundraiser a couple of years ago, and the reaction was rather different. In fact, standing amongst the mainly female crowd, I heard a lot of disdainful muttering about thinning hair, crinkles around the eyes, weight gain.

"New York's a bad place," Squier observed. "Where these people are most valuable is when you get farther and farther from the cities, primarily New York and Los Angeles, where they can be seen on the street."

"Can they get their fans to vote the way they want them to?"

"No," Squier said emphatically. "Getting their fans to vote the way they want would be very, very difficult. Some people have an impact on candidates in special cases; Gary Hart was very much influenced by Warren Beatty, as far as communications and what to do in his campaign went."

"And lifestyle."

"I have a theory about the two of them," Squier said. "It's actually my theory, though you've heard many versions of it. My theory is that Warren wanted to be Gary, and Gary wanted to be Warren."

"That was a very good theory," I complimented him.

"Thank you."

"Aside from that particular and peculiar instance, can you think of another case where a celebrity had a real impact on a candidate or campaign?"

"No," Squier answered. "They might be able to get themselves elected, but that's a matter of name identification. Even that con-verts to money. If you're a celebrity and extremely well-known, and the personality that you're known for, especially on television, is very positive, the people have a kind of warm feeling about you and know your name. In a lot of places, that's worth a million dollars. I mean, suppose you're running in a state like New Jersey; it costs three million dollars to get known there. So just celebrity itself has a certain currency in politics.''

"From your standpoint, how did all these intermingling of show biz and politics occur?'' I asked.

"That's hard to figure,'' Squier said. ''In 1968, we did a telethon for Humphrey, and we had the stage packed with stars, just packed with stars, so that it would give a certain interest to the program. Paul Newman was the co-host. And what we were clearly saying with our celebrities was, 'He must be very special because all these people you think are very special have come here to be with him.'

"There's always been this fascination of actors for politicians and politicians for actors,'' he continued. ''I introduced Paul Newman to Hubert Humphrey, and I was with each of them at separate times just before they met each other. And they were both absolutely fastened on the idea of meeting the other. Newman was very self-conscious about what he was going to wear, and so was Humphrey. And I had the horrible feeling that Newman would show up in a three-piece blue suit and Hubert would have a shirt unbuttoned open to his navel and a gold chain around his neck. Just as though they were trying to figure out what the other one would expect and then each would do the other thing, and it was so complicated, it was wonderful.''

I talked about how strange it seemed that politicians would summon celebrities to address committees on the country's problems, as though the stars were going to proffer solutions. One example that received wide media attention was the joint appearance of Sissy Spacek, Jane Fonda and Jessica Lange before the House Democratic Task Force on Agriculture in May 1985. The actresses had all starred in movies that dealt with the plight of farmers. As a result, both the actresses and the politicos believed that the stars could contribute to Congress's understanding of the complex problems and issues facing the American farmer.

Fonda attested as to her fitness for testifying: ''Perhaps I felt at home with these people because, as far back as I can remember, my father had loved to plow the fields and plant and grow things,'' she noted. ''While he was never a farmer by profession, as you know, he always felt a kinship with rural America, and maybe that was why, of all he loved Thom Joad in *Grapes of Wrath* the most. . . . Maybe that's the most wonderful part of our profession, is that it exposes us to these realities and allows us to be affected. That's why I am here today.''

Representative Thomas Daschle of South Dakota, an organizer of the event, said the actresses ''did not pretend to be farm experts, but were simply trying to educate America.''

''That's more complicated than what we've been talking about,'' Squier said. ''You see, when politicians invite celebrities to come to a hearing and speak, and then are uncomfortable with the relationship they have established, it is because they feel they can't draw the cameras themselves. So the politicians need the celebrities, and they would try to maneuver and make use of them. So there's some very interesting interplay going on.''

''In your experience, do the celebrities know why they're there?''

''Oh, yeah,'' Squier said. ''Absolutely.''

''If they understand, why don't they feel like idiots?''

''That's not the actor's problem,'' Squier replied. ''That's a casting problem.''

That was clever but not clever enough to pass as a real answer, and Squier knew it.

''It's very simple,'' Squier said. ''Some people are draws and others aren't, and you coddle the people who will draw audiences for you and you beat up on the rest.''

Viewed from a certain perspective, what had changed with the increased role of celebrities in politics was a matter of technique, not philosophy or politics. Federal campaign reform had demanded a partial shift in tactics, away from the fat donors with the big cigars who negotiate for ambassadorships in smoke-filled rooms, and towards the sleek celebs with their own publicity flacks who seek to impress their ideologies on politicos in front of amphitheaters filled with fans. So what? Once the adjustment was made, did the difference make a difference, as far as the result went? On the other hand, did it alter everything, did the means become the ends? Were professional politics and philosophical politics separable?

Viewed from a certain perspective, Bob Squier was right; it *was* simple.

I visited with a six-term U.S. Representative, a Democrat who, by virtue of his liberal leanings, had had his share of celebrity encounters. I had offered to attribute any of his remarks which might damage his relationship with the Hollywood community to an anonymous source, and he had accepted. After perusing the transcript of the interview, I decided that discretion required blanket anonymity.

The representative recalled a visit by singer Carole King.

"She has a home in Idaho and came here to lobby on behalf of the Idaho River bill, which is still pending in Congress," he said.

"Did that have any impact on you?"

"Yes," the representative quickly replied. "It had a negative impact."

"Why?"

"Because I thought she was silly and kind of sanctimonious."

"But you saw her because she was Carole King, famous singer?"

"I saw her because she asked to see me," he said, "and I certainly had heard of her, and I liked her as a performer. But then I called her later on, because I got into a very tough race at home, and I got a lot of help from environmentalists around the country, who contributed a lot of money. They really helped a lot. So I called her and asked if she thought she could help me, do a concert for me or something. And she said, 'Well, I can't help raise you money, but I can help raise your consciousness.' "

The congressman groaned, then laughed. "Oil and water," he declared, "the politician and the folk singer. She had no reason to raise me money; if she had said, 'I hope you understand, I just don't do that,' I would have said, 'Fine,' and that would have been fine. But she didn't have to give me that stupid line about 'raising my consciousness.' Pete Seeger did a concert for me and raised a lot of money. He was great. Very nice. Raised a lot of money, because of my work in environmental issues. He didn't tell me he could raise my consciousness. So I don't deal with her anymore. Not that she wouldn't raise money; because she's a pain in the ass."

"Deal with any other celebrities?"

"Yeah," he said. "The other guy from 'M*A*S*H,' Mike Farrell, has come in—very nice guy. The guy who's on that TV show about policemen, 'Barney Miller'—Hal Linden."

"They're all interested in the environment?"

"Peace in Central America, the environment, liberal causes," the representative said. "We've had a lot of people come in. They attract people. They sell tickets. You have Hal Linden, he's going to do a thing, twenty-five dollars a head, fifty dollars a head. Oh, Eli Wallach campaigned for me. People will come. Celebrities have been very helpful."

"Well, now they're more organized. They have their own PACs, in order to accumulate power. I mean, I assume that's why you form a group."

"Right," the congressman concurred.

"Have you dealt with any of those groups?"

"Yeah, the Hollywood Women's Political Caucus. Is that what it's called? They talked to me," the representative said. "They were upset because I did not vote to eliminate the MX missile entirely. I voted to wipe out a lot of the money but keep some modest research going. They went on and on about how they couldn't help me because I supported that. I think they finally helped, but it got to be ridiculous."

"Did you go out to Los Angeles and meet with them?"

"No," he said without hesitation. "They went on with this big thing, and I met with them at the convention in Atlanta. Very nice women, but silly."

I told him my story about the distinguished senator and HWPC, and about the interrogation.

"Yeah, yeah," the congressman nodded. "They can keep their money. Stick their check in their ear."

"But they liked the senator's attitude and gave him money."

"Yeah," he said, "and they gave me money too. I argued with them. I said I'm against MX, blah, blah, blah, but we did a lot of research and we ought to keep it going. You know. They can be difficult for a politician to deal with, but I guess you should have to deal with that, just like we have to deal with a lot of groups. I don't know. I think a lot of these celebrities and their groups are regarded as pains in the neck. But some of the people who came in to help me couldn't have been nicer."

"What is their basic agenda?"

"A liberal agenda," he answered, "at least the ones I have dealt with, like the Hollywood Women's one. They don't have one specific issue that is determinative. Of course, they get it down to one issue, in a negative sense. I mean, I have a one hundred percent rating from ADA (Americans for Democratic Action), one hundred percent COPE (Committee on Political Education, AFL-CIO), one hundred percent ACLU; if I lose, they'll never get another Democrat from that district. I mean, it's unbelievable! I've cast thirty thousand votes in twelve years in Congress and they found a vote they didn't like. That's the kind of thing that drives people right up the wall.''

"How did this notion of celebrities speaking before congressional committees get started?"

The politician shrugged at the obviousness of it all. "TV's there. That's the only reason to do it. Unless, of course, it's about an issue that concerns them, like colorization of films. That makes sense.''

"Well, what about when they have celebrities come in and speak about on the farm issue because they starred in a movie about farms?"

"Well, what do you think?" he asked in a way that didn't require an answer.

"Okay. Well, what do you think it does to the public perception of Congress?"

"Nothing. You raise awareness of the issue. You get the American people to care about it, you bring attention to it, you get TV, you get the press; there's nothing wrong with that. Now, I wouldn't just take testimony from movie stars, but for publicity, it's okay. Look, when the members get together privately to write a bill, I don't think they sit around saying, 'Well wait, Sissy Spacek said . . .' Give me a break. They're just trying to get on TV, and that's the only way to get on TV. Because the public likes Sissy Spacek. They like celebrities.''

"More than they like Congress?"

"Sure," the congressman said. "They hate politicians. You know that.''

We all know that. Putting this in perspective, let us remember that for over two hundred years we have hated politicians. It is the natural distrust of a free people, or perhaps any people, towards those who seek to lead them to that shining light that sometimes, truly or falsely, the leaders alone see. Yet, while we proudly proclaim our dislike of our elected officials as a group, we just as proudly assert our affection for our particular representatives, as proved by a ninety percent re-election rate for the House. A senate seat is less safe, the Presidency less so again, this decreasing job security as we move higher on the power scale the result of intensified competition for the posts, and also greater unfulfilled expectations for more powerful positions. We expect our representatives to be interested in issues close to home, and we complain to them about broken streets or ask them to get a nephew a job, as I learned from Ozzie Myers and John Jenrette. From our senators and Presidents we expect more, we expect a national vision, even a global vision. We expect, we want, we need a vision larger than our own, greater than this moment. And we are disappointed.

Recently, we were all treated to a view of the birthday party Malcolm Forbes threw for himself, spending over two million dollars to fly some seven hundred guests to Morocco for a few days of self-indulgence and self-promotion. Naturally, Malcolm and his friends did not frolic unobserved; the media was invited to the circus and participated with gusto. Not only did the rags cover it, but seemingly everyone and every information outlet had a story on the event; "Crossfire" and "Nightline," two of our most serious news programs, devoted shows to both celebrate and denounce Forbes.

Is this good? Is an invitation to such a blowout the goal for which we are all supposed to strive? One might think so from the guest list. Not only were the usual Hollywood types like Elizabeth Taylor there, and the usual society types like the Trumps, but also politicians like Governor Thomas Kean of New Jersey, statesmen like former Secretary of State Henry Kissinger, journalists like Walter Cronkite, as well as an announced three hundred major corporate CEOs. At the top, whether politicians or anchormen or corporate raiders, celebrities are more comfortable with each other than with any of us. At the top, they are a club, a separate society. Never mind the Hollywood types and the society types. Is this why one should want to succeed in business, journalism or politics?

If politicians persist in being crooks or fools or playmates for the rich, then how are they acting any differently than the celebrities we read about in the tabloids? If politicians continue to pander to the polls and cameras, then how are they performing any differently than the celebrities we watch on sitcoms and soap operas? Celebrities did not force their way into politics—politicians, aided by the media, opened the doors and invited them in.

Actually, sometimes it seems that between the celebrities and the politician, not to mention the media and assorted other power players, the only people left on the outside are, well, the people.

Chapter 10

New York City

Fiction for Real

At the bottom line, which is where these matters inevitably end up, the show was done for entertainment, for fun, you might say. Nothing to get excited about. It was only television, and cable, at that.

Yet there stood Robert Dole, looking distinctly uncomfortable. March in New Hampshire was as cold as advertised, and the two Presidential caravans slowly lumbered towards each another. Their respective standard-bearers marched at the fore, accompanied, surrounded, engulfed, by hordes of aides and journalists and supporters and tourists. Such confrontations were inevitable on the campaign trail.

"Hey, Jack, how're you doing?" Dole greeted the other candidate with feigned interest.

Jack Tanner, former congressman from Michigan and longshot contender for the Democratic Party nomination, gave a wide smile and warmly congratulated Dole on his energetic race for the Republican nomination.

"You're really something," Tanner said. "You're really doing it."

Dole attempted a lighthearted chuckle and failed. "Well, we got them on the run," he replied, and mumbled a half-phrase: "Beating the bushes." Then Dole tried that off-key laugh again.

Now this was strange. Why would Robert Dole, Senate Minority Leader and one of the smartest, toughest and most powerful individuals in the government, a man known to relish rassling with everyone from ward heelers to Presidents, appear at a loss bantering with a relative political nobody? Because the political nobody was no politico but an actor, and this was no chance encounter, but a scene being filmed for "Tanner '88," the Home Box Office series conceived by director Robert Altman and writer (and "Doonesbury" creator) Garry Trudeau, documenting the sincere and doomed Presidential campaign of a liberal dark horse, from the first primary in New Hampshire through the Democratic convention in Atlanta in July, five months later.

Actor Michael Murphy portrayed Jack Tanner as a politico in the John Kennedy mold, lean and handsome, mature though unfailingly youthful, more emotionally than intellectually stimulating.

Murphy, best known for his roles in *An Unmarried Woman,* *M*A*S*H* and *Manhattan,* leaned back in a booth in a Manhattan diner the spring after the election—a year after Tanner's meeting with Bob Dole—and agreed that the senior Senator from Kansas had trouble relating to playing a part in a television show.

"Yes, I think that's true," Murphy conceded. "Dole's sort of a kick-ass kind of guy. He was always that way, he was that way with us, and if you look at the footage, I think it's clear he's a lot more comfortable twisting arms in the back room than trying to do p.r."

I reminded Murphy of how the Dole bit ended. As the two candidates moved off, attended by their handmaidens and eunuchs, Tanner's daughter handed Dole a souvenir "Tanner '88" button. In a seamless motion as graceful as Fred Astaire catching and passing off Ginger Rogers, Dole accepted the button with a smile and tossed it to a waiting assistant.

"You see, there again, it's exactly like it is in show business," Murphy said. "You know, you want to get Emmy Awards, so you get an Emmy consultant who helps you get your award. None of it is particularly honest. Everybody goes through the motions, and then gets up there and acts surprised, when it's something that's bought and paid for. In both cases—I mean, he's a pretty straightforward guy, you know, we're playing the scene: 'Here, let me give you a button.' "

Murphy affected an extremely unimpressed expression and tone, imitating Dole: " 'Oh, yeah, great,' and he gives it to somebody else. That's the way he feels, he does not have time for that shit. And I think he's sort of Goldwateresque in that way, they're both to the right of Genghis Khan, but there's a certain sympathetic thing about them because they don't seem like they're up there being slick and lying to you. He may step in it four times a day, but he's saying what's on his mind. Like Goldwater, people perceive him as dangerous; he'd get mad at the Russians and drop the bomb. That's where the camera doesn't work for Bob Dole. But I'd much prefer that to this, 'One more for the Gipper' stuff."

Murphy's unique perspective during the filming of "Tanner '88" had given him a chance to observe some quirks in real presidential campaigns. For example, one day, Tanner had crossed Gary Hart's path as Hart was leaving a television studio. The ex-Senator from Colorado strode neatly into his acting role. "So how's it going?" Hart had asked Tanner, clasping his hand. "I gave you a plug in there, so get going."

"It was strange," Michael Murphy said to me. "We met Gary Hart the day he came back into the campaign, and I'd been reading all he'd been through, the scandal and everything, and we called and asked him if he wanted to appear and he said sure. And I remember vividly, I met him down in the lobby of the local ABC station. And the doors of the elevator opened and I thought, 'My God, there's Gary Hart!' I mean, I've been around actors and those bullshit artists all my life, but this guy was a serious player who just had it all pulled out from under him. And I'll tell you, I had this very emotional response to the guy, he was wandering around there in the snows of New Hampshire by himself—well, with one helper left. His entire group left him, and there was a lot of talk around Washington that he was self-destructive. All these guys were out of jobs now, they were down on him, and I saw this enormously vulnerable guy.

"Smart man, you know, who made some bad moves, and the chickens had come home to roost," Murphy continued. "You could see, plainly, the pain. So he did the show, and if you look at the footage, you see this vulnerable guy out there. I mean, one of our guys said, 'We'll call you later,' and he said, 'Uh, I don't know if I've got anything to say.' It was a very tough time for him. And then he sort of gained back some momentum; not that his campaign picked up steam, but he seemed to get his confidence back. And I know what that's all about; when you're playing a character—it's worse, obviously, when it's your life—it's all about confidence, you know, you stand up there and do your work. And if you have your confidence taken away from you, you're in trouble. And that's what people see on that camera when they're looking at politicians.''

The champ of the politician walk-ons had to be Pat Robertson. The quickest smile and loudest laugh in the race, the Reverend was ready when Tanner met him on the steps of the courthouse and commented, ''You sure are tearing them up in my home state.''

''Well, Michigan is a strong one for me,'' Robertson chortled. ''You know that, Jack.''

Robertson wished Tanner the best and then started to shove off in search of political converts, when a reporter standing behind the actor called out a question about ''Christian hardball,'' referring to Robertson's exhortation to his troops to fight as hard as their secular opponents.

Without missing a beat, the Reverend grinned at the stranger and launched into a story about his youthful exploits as a boxer and wrestler. This had evidently prepared him for his new career, where he was ''playing for keeps, playing serious, but not dirty.'' That done, everybody said their thank you's and farewells and Robertson was gone, smile on high.

I asked Murphy if he had rehearsed the scene with Robertson.

''No,'' Murphy replied, ''I just kind of yelled down at him. He knew we were going to do it. I said, 'It's Jack Tanner,' and he said, 'Oh, okay, all right.' And we just did it.''

''He was good,'' I said. ''A natural.''

''We had an interesting thing happen,'' Murphy continued. ''I was traveling with a bunch of guys, a lot of them were actors, and we also had the local press, and we also had the networks, when Robertson came in with all these people. So suddenly there we were, in this deluge on the courthouse steps in New Hampshire and you didn't really know who was a real press guy and who was an actor playing a member of the press. So there was this crush of people, and one of the actors who was playing a reporter stuck his head out, after I had done the banalities, and said, 'What about this

Christian hardball?' That had been in the news, and you could see Robertson sort of respond to it. But then he got his act together and answered it, and I could just see the wheels turning, like I've seen with a zillion performers. So he was good at it, in that kind of slick way. He comes from all that Christian broadcasting, and hawking into that camera with all that fake sincerity. So I compare him with a guy like Bruce Babbitt and I like Babbitt better, I like Dole better, I like these guys who are not quite so good at it. And I think it's a big problem in this country, when you look at people like Reagan and Robertson and people who are at home with that camera and you buy it, because that's not what running this country is about."

Despite Michael Murphy's insight, his view was that of an outsider peering into the political process. To see the world from the other side, I tracked down Charles Todd, administrative assistant to the Speaker of the Tennessee House. During the 1988 campaign, Todd had received a phone call from the state film commission asking his assistance in arranging a political fundraiser for a television character.

"I said, 'You're kidding,' " Todd recalled over the telephone in his soft Tennessee drawl. "Then I thought, 'Well, sounds like fun.' " So Todd went to work.

"There was no script," Todd said. "The whole thing was impromptu. A lot of the TV guys said they enjoyed making ours more than any of the others. The whole thing was set up like a political fundraiser that you would do, giving money to a Presidential candidate, with entertainment. And they did need people who were used to doing that sort of thing."

In Todd and friends they had found the right people to throw a grade A party, with country music star Waylon Jennings headlining, state politicians lined up to endorse Tanner for President, local television personalities covering the gala, and a room full of people drinking, singing and raising hell. In short, politics at its most convivial.

I asked Todd if any of the pols were hesitant to appear on the program.

"There was a bit of, 'What'd you say?' " Todd said. "A lot of that. Basically, we went through the routine, gave them the outline of the program, what it was about. You know, that it was a political satire, getting a message across, and the guy, the director, Altman, did have his beliefs.''

"Did it worry any of the pols that this mixing of fact and fiction would make people say, 'God, I always knew politicians were just actors?' ''

"Well, now," laughed Todd, "you know, basically that mold was broken in 1980 when Ronald Reagan came to office. And I figured we'd do two things, we'd help the political image and we'd also help the acting profession.''

Besides, the pols knew they could depend on Charles Todd, for one very good reason. "I assured them all they wouldn't be embarrassed," Todd said. "That was one basic assurance that went down and with that assurance, everybody become comfortable. And they believed what I was saying, cause if I steered them in the wrong way, they'd grill my ass.''

The politicos had to stand up and say something nice about Tanner for the cameras, and Todd hit on a surefire way of animating their creativity. It turned out there was another Tanner, a John Tanner, the real item, running for Congress from Tennessee, and Todd borrowed him and his reputation.

"So instead of John Tanner," Todd said, "it was easy to say Jack Tanner in '88, and we're for him all the way. And you don't necessarily dabble in the Presidential thing, you just give the basic issues, whatever areas of expertise the different representatives preferred, and expound on that. The guy's running for President, use the national issues and go with it. And have fun. And act like you normally do at these things. And that's how it went.''

From the look of the pols, fun was the key thought. One by one, they fairly gushed into the camera.

"I've known Jack Tanner for many years," claimed Speaker of the Tennessee House Ed Murray, "and I feel that he can represent the views of the people of the United States better than any other candidate.''

"Jack Tanner has a very exciting philosophy," averred State Representative Thomas C. Wheeler. "He has views on nuclear waste that all the people in this group can envelop. He's just the kind of candidate we can be for.''

State Representative Lois DeBerry was not to be outdone. "I

think he's young, he's energetic, and I think that he's the kind of President that can lead us into the year 2000.''

Naturally, there was a joker in the pack. "I'm for Al Gore!" shouted State Representative Robert S. Stallings.

I asked Charles Todd to talk about the difference between politics and show biz in presentation.

"Well, where they correlate is presentation," Todd said. "Packaging. I guess when you're putting on a political event, it's just like show biz, to a certain extent. You know, you have sound, you have lights, you have a script, you have people, you have a message you're trying to get across and you're trying to make everybody leave like they're wanting more. What you provide is the candidate, and you give him a forum, the proper forum, and you try to generate something newsworthy, something you get a news bite out of.''

"I guess that's why the show biz people were so good at putting on a political event and the political people were so good at pretending to be in show biz," I said.

"Yeah," agreed Todd. "Show business is often cutthroat. Politics is too. Politics, you got to keep on doing it. Elvis had to sign autographs, but we have to take calls if somebody needs a road fixed or if their brother-in-law's out of a job, or somebody broke his leg and can't work for three days or three months. If you go into your home district, you're going to end up with somebody needing something. That's why when I go on vacation I go up in the woods or to the beach.''

"Tanner '88" could not neglect Hollywood, so the candidate was dispatched West for a fundraising party around the pool. Tanner was introduced to actress Rebecca deMornay, who played herself, or at least a version of herself, and the actress questioned him in most forceful fashion.

"The bottom line is," she said, "how do I know that you're not just another liar, you know, that we get on TV? I mean, how do I know I can trust you?''

Graciously ignoring the presumptuous tone of the query, Tanner attempted to reply. "It's a very difficult question. You know, I often think it's a little bit like falling in love, Rebecca. You know, it's like you have to have an intellectual approach, you have to look at the issues, but at the same time you've got to have a visceral response to the guy that you're—''

DeMornay cut the candidate off by waving her hands in front of his face and shaking her head no. "I mean, there no TV screen there. Can you talk to me honestly? Can you?"

Noting the lack of communication and clearly feeling this was a permanent condition, Tanner excused himself, to the actress' evident disdain.

"That was a good idea," Murphy said. "I kind of got into that, 'cause I wanted to show how politicians aren't really tuned into what these guys are thinking."

Murphy had become rather friendly with Bruce Babbitt, and spoke about the time he accompanied the former Governor of Arizona and Democratic Presidential candidate to an authentic Hollywood meeting.

"I went one day to a thing with Babbitt, where he spoke to these high-level Hollywood-types, a small gathering of about twenty people. The thing I remember most of all is how while he was up there giving a speech, talking to them about what he thought, and they were all—I remember the body language—they were all sort of lying back"—and Murphy slumped deep in the booth, hooding his eyes with absolute boredom, throwing out a fast question with the same attitude—" 'Well, what do you think about this?' " Murphy sat back up. "I mean, it was just a complete lack of respect for the man. The ego in that town." He shook his head. "I stood there and thought to myself, 'God Almighty.' "

I asked Murphy if, as an actor, he understood politics—the public presentation, not the issues.

"Yeah," Murphy said. "And a lot of the issues." He laughed and shifted his seat. "Yeah, I felt I understood the presentation very well. Very well. Sure. That was what we set out to do with the show, we really wanted to show the process, by which a guy who was a decent man gets involved with all this, and exactly what he has to go through, the degradations as well as the high times."

Murphy talked about his own style of Presidential campaigning.

"We would hit a shopping mall," he mused, "and I would go around saying, 'Hi, I'm Jack Tanner, I'm running for President,' and I'd be followed by this entourage of cameras. And these people were used to that. We'd be up in New Hampshire and I'd be standing in front of a factory and they'd been shaking hands with fifteen guys who wanted something from them, and I was just

another one of those guys. When it started out, in the very beginning, I would explain what we were doing, and Bob Altman would
say, 'Just forget all that, just tell them you're running for President,
cause we got to get this shot.' And sure enough, within twenty
minutes, it was very easy, and I would say, 'Hi, I'm Jack Tanner,
I'm running for President,' and they'd say, 'Good luck' or 'Yeah,
yeah, yeah, I just want to get to work.' ''

Charles Todd also experienced this crossover between the show
and real politics. ''Very few people kept up with the whole series.
You know, they would be flipping channels and see it, and not
really know. I had instances of people calling up and saying, 'Well,
I thought you were with Al Gore. Here you are endorsing some guy
named Tanner.' And questions like that, and that was at the local
truck stops and coffee stops, when I went back in my home area.
And then you have to say, 'Well, it was just an act.' But you know
when it first came out, I never thought about that, but it happened.''

''By the time I got to the convention I was very comfortable,''
Murphy said. ''And when I walked out on that floor, thousands of
people were screaming 'Tanner!' It was a very different sort of
character than I had ever played. And then, apropos of this, and
apropos of what you are writing about, I would be down there and
I'd see all these actors kind of standing around, who were used to a
lot of attention and who were getting a very different kind of
attention.''

Murphy paused to chuckle, shaking his head. ''And it all seemed
very lightweight to me.''

''Celebrities were certainly out in force in Atlanta.''

''Tom Hayden had this thing all organized,'' Murphy said. ''He
had all these young guys and he took them all down there . . . I
don't know why. They all seem to want to gravitate to the spotlight.
It's an ego thing.''

''They want to be taken seriously.''

''Well, why should you take Rob Lowe seriously?'' Murphy
answered. ''Where they miss the boat is that you're taken a lot more
seriously if you keep your mouth shut and do good work.''

''I suppose when you make a lot of money fast and young,
perhaps it's easy to lay back and bask in the spotlight.''

''It's not a good life, it's not a good way to live,'' said Murphy.
''You can't focus everything on yourself and go stomping through

life and expect to be a happy person. That's why a lot of these people wind up the way they do. I won't spend my time worrying about my celebrity status, I want to be able to focus on getting into what I'm doing. That's the pleasure of it. That's what's truly satisfying: the work. It isn't about going out there and grabbing attention. And I saw so much of that, I saw it at the convention, I'd see these kids swagger around in their oversized suits, doing their fake modest stuff. You know, I said, 'Please.' But they're young, in their defense.''

I asked Charles Todd whether the real John Tanner, the authentic political candidate, had benefited by collecting ''Tanner '88'' buttons and recycling them to service his own campaign.

''Well, we got buttons, but I kept mine as a souvenir,'' Todd laughed. ''It was really great. I mean, they had the bumper stickers and the buttons and then John, he sat with Michael Murphy at the front table there. So the real John Tanner sat beside the fictional Jack Tanner. And John went on to win.''

Though I have no information as to what brought John Tanner victory in Tennessee, it is certain that ''Tanner '88'' emerged a winner because the series was fiction in fine form: clear, biting, funny, real. And though it dealt with factual events, mixing characters and candidates into a fascinating, rich brew, ''Tanner '88'' never tried to be more than it was, never crossed into that unmarked but distinct territory where television becomes confused and pretentious and preachy and, ultimately, destructive.

TV can be good, but it's not good enough to leap up from entertainment and act as the Oracle of Delphi, as the keeper of wisdom, the dispenser of truth. It's an old story—you work your way up from the bottom, make a fortune, buy a big house, drive a big car, achieve all your dreams, and find yourself still unfulfilled, find you want more, find you need to count, crave respectability and significance and, finally, power. The streets are littered with the egos of the wealthy who have sought to transform their financial or social status into something deeper, broader, greater. This campaign season in New York, we witnessed the embarrassing spectacle of cosmetics heir Ronald Lauder spending $14 million of his own money to gain the Republican nomination for Mayor, a pathetic, distasteful attempt to buy his way into office. What would have rendered this absolutely obscene is if this effort had worked, as it too often does.

In the matter of television, a similar thought explains why the medium, the most powerful of all communication mediums, can't let news be news and entertainment stay just and only that. In the hands of the best, as in the case of those involved with "Tanner '88" it can work. In the hands of the rest—and television is overflowing with the rest—it can be a disaster.

But so what? Television is our citizenry's prime link with the world, it selects and shows and explains and, thus, decides. The machine rolls on, the images overwhelm and television chooses its own fate.

The problem is, its fate is also ours.

Chapter 11

New York City

Non-Fiction for Reel

A new group was formed not long ago in Los Angeles. Entertainment lawyer Bonnie Reiss left her practice to establish Earth Communications Office, with the avowed goal of influencing humanity to protect the environment by influencing Hollywood.

"Our job is to target the few thousand people in this industry who affect a few hundred million," Reiss stated in *The Hollywood Reporter*. "One mention about energy conservation on 'The Cosby Show' could have enormous impact." With donated office space by Ron Howard and Brian Glazer's Imagine Films and taped public service messages by Mel Gibson and Goldie Hawn, among others, and boasting a long list of show biz luminaries on the board, ECO is well on its way to making an impact.

"We're saying, 'Forget your money. You people in Hollywood influence the masses. You can help wake them up.' " Therein lies the core of Reiss's intent, to get show biz to focus on environmental issues. Her effort appears to be taking hold; it was reported that David Zucker is planning to set his film *The Naked Gun II* around the theme of solar energy, the writers of the TV series "ALF" have pledged to include environmental concerns into their scripts, and Pee-wee Herman has also promised to alert his youthful audience.

"This industry is a microphone to the masses," Reiss said. "It's able to globally communicate a message which can help bring about an effective response."

Writers have always used the issues of the day as settings for their stories and plays. Given the contemporary business of mass entertainment, it is now not necessarily writers—who occupy a low rung of the show business ladder in prestige and power—but producers and directors and stars, who look to the headlines for subject matter for movies and television shows. However, screen and video communications have become so enveloping and overpowering, such an invasive, pounding constant in our lives, that the media's ability to promote messages is unparalleled and unequaled by any other bureaucracy or institution. Thus, the responsibility of those who decide what will be seen by the public, particularly on television, has mushroomed to incalculable proportions.

More than once, I have heard people who grew up during the Depression explain that though their families were poor, everybody else was in the same boat, so they were never aware of just how impoverished they actually were. Observers have often noted that this possibly fortuitous isolation no longer exists, that the TV sets and magazines of rich and poor alike convey the idea, especially through advertising, that we are each entitled to a satisfying, well-paying job, a gorgeous, concerned spouse, hordes of caring pals, an expensive foreign car, a big house situated on a manicured spread, and plenty of cold beer to go around: For all you do, this Bud's for you! The ads proclaim that Rolex watches and Mercedes sedans and Armani suits are the things that make life worthwhile. For many people, these displays serve as a mocking commentary that they are so far removed from achieving these badges of immediate societal significance as to render them cut off from the larger community. In response, a small percentage seek to acquire these material symbols through illicit means; consequently, in an inversion of what is supposed to be intended for the "good" people, drug dealers and those of similar ilk have adopted the Rolexes and Mercedes and Armanis as their overt markings of success.

Let us briefly examine several instances where the media increasingly influences our communal outlook on our political system. For the first example, I have selected a show which painted a disturbing picture of American life, while the other examples blur the actual lines between fact and fiction in potentially distressing ways.

"Miami Vice," the series about two daring and dashing South Florida police officers, was one of the most popular programs during its five-year run, which ended recently. Not only did the show, with its rock score and pastel hues, alter the very style of much of television, the Italian clothes worn by detectives Sonny Crockett and Ricardo Tubbs launched a fashion trend adopted wherever the series aired.

"Miami Vice" accomplished one other thing. It furthered the concept of a corrupt America, of a decaying civilization; week after week, Crockett and Tubbs wearily contended with crooked pols, crooked judges, crooked lawyers, crooked cops, crooked bankers, crooked business leaders, crooked journalists, crooked preachers—in short, crooks under every rock and behind every desk. Thrust into this decadent stew, the detectives fought back with their separate moral code, and chose which laws needed obeying and when.

The final two-hour episode of "Miami Vice" neatly sums up its long-standing attitude. Dispatched to Central America to bring back a Noriega-type dictator who, threatened at home, has agreed to provide the U.S. with evidence of the international drug conspiracy, the detectives return with their dubious prize to discover that the United States government is allied with this scum and fully intends to return him to power. Having seen just about all they could stand in five years on the job, they can stomach no more and shoot the dictator's plane out of the sky before it can send him home.

The chief American federal agent is furious at the detectives for destroying his plan. "Take a look at the map, Crockett," the fed states. "Real estate's turning red all over this hemisphere. Your brand of law-and-order went out with Wyatt Earp. There's only two things that count: American interests and anything that's counter to them."

"You're what's counter to it," Tubbs responds. "You and all those slick, deal-making lawyers."

"I don't make policy," the fed sneers. "I enforce it."

"And cover it up when it goes wrong," Crockett says.

"That's right," the fed agrees. "And I got carte blanche, babe. I could shoot you, right now, easy. No one's ever going to ask any questions."

The fed's obvious lack of virtue also ensures a lack of the nerve necessary to carry out his threat. Regardless, Crockett and Tubbs quit the police force on the spot. In the course of their partnership, each has suffered various outrages, including being beaten, shot and blown up on land and on the water, but this is really the last straw: being yelled at by a fed. A man can only take so much.

So what do we learn? We learn that the American government is not merely cynical and corrupt but morally bankrupt. We learn that might triumphs over right, except in those cases when right employs the methodology of might and annihilates anyone within sight, after which the natural order reverts and might returns to triumph again. We learn that hope is a joke and the future full of despair, and that those imbued with dignity and courage have no honorable option but to turn their backs on this whole damn mess and flee.

Stated once, the message flies past. Stated once a week for five years, and then forever in reruns, and then more or less duplicated by show after show on television and in the movies, the message takes on another meaning entirely. How many programs and films promote the idea that the smartest move a fellow can make is to earn or steal a pile of money and then relocate to that desert island with the native girls before civilization catches up? The movies used to require that bad guys who wanted to go straight had to suffer some horrific penalty first, balancing the scales by paying for their sinfully derived profits. But those were the old movies and the old ideas; nowadays, gratification must be immediate on film as well as in real life—real life as known by celebrities, that is.

But that is not the essential problem. The problem is the contempt in which films hold the basic institutions which form the core of our system. It is not just comic book action adventures like the motion picture *Die Hard,* which show the authorities to be incompetent and cruel; nor is it only films like *Power,* which purport to reveal the rotten reality of politics; nor the catalogue of moronic conspiratorial features spawned by the Kennedy assassinations, such as *The Parallax View, Executive Action* and *Flashpoint,* which attempt to explain such tragic events by naming official agencies as the murdering instruments.

Rather, the contagion can infect the most mindless escapist fare.

The Blob was a harmless movie produced in 1958 about a huge jello creature from outer space, which devoured its human victims in extremely neat fashion. Some thirty-one years later, a remake had transformed the original, simple space monster into an uncontrollably vicious germ spawned by a government plot to concoct a new type of biological weapon. Instead of assisting the inhabitants of the beleaguered town, the screenwriters had the government dispatch the military to cover up the embarrassing error by eliminating the populace of this small piece of America.

This receding faith in the fundamental good will of the representatives who constitute the government inspired even the happy, hugely popular science fiction film *E.T.* Only the children (and selected adults when properly instructed by the kids) could be trusted to demonstrate any decency and common sense. The antagonists were the adults, authorities and scientists who descended from the federal monster to ruin everything. And why were the adults interfering? All because of some evidently silly notions about curiosity and progress. While the audience inevitably cheered at the triumph of the children, I wonder how many would seek out the counsel of their kids instead of dialing 911 if little green men landed in their own backyard.

Let us go one step further into the blur. Fiction is, after all, fiction. But what happens when fiction and fact meet?

Celebrities are frequently employed for their special touch of "credibility," whatever that might be, for a variety of serious programs, from news documentaries to political shows. Sometimes the celebrity even knows what he or she is talking about.

Medical Aid for El Salvador, the group Ed Asner helped start, regularly sends small delegations of American citizens, often from Los Angeles and often from show biz, to El Salvador to promote its point of view and its work. The group uses a video (partially sponsored by Medical Aid though produced by an independent company) to interest people in traveling on future delegations.

The film was shot in November 1988, when a contingent of Hollywood types flew to El Salvador, accompanied by a video crew. As usual, the visitors were shuttled around the capital and introduced to a variety of Salvadoran officials and civilians, who pressed their beliefs on their guests. As expected, judging by the video, the Salvadorans were mainly opposed to their government's policies, and U.S. support of those policies.

Not surprisingly, the Americans who were eager to journey to Central America were pretty much convinced that the U.S. was wrong for backing President Napoleon Duarte and his administration. Thus, regardless of their knowledge or experiences, they easily accepted any anti-government messages, and were happy to pass them on as unimpeachable fact.

The video began with a series of shots showing scenes of war, suffering and refugees, as well as Presidents Reagan and Duarte. Interspersed between the carnage and the grief were placards presenting selected slices of history, which laid the blame for the country's troubles on the government and military, theirs and ours, without once mentioning the guerrillas or their communist supply-masters. Shortly thereafter, the celebrities appeared to explain their presence.

Actress Cynthia Gibb, who appeared in Oliver Stone's *Salvador*, a film which struck a distinctly anti-U.S. policy pose, spoke first. "During my involvement with the film *Salvador*, my interest was really piqued in the country. I found myself to have a real empathy for the people of the country, and I felt as an American that I owed them something. I feel like Americans have butted their nose in the country's business." (It seems worth noting that the movie was shot in Mexico, not El Salvador.)

Hart Bochner, star of the mini-series *War and Remembrance*, had his own reasons. "I went down as a U.S. taxpayer concerned about the fact that two million dollars a day over the last eight years had been going in aid to a country that I essentially knew nothing about."

Charles Matthau, film director and son of actor Walter Matthau, left no doubt as to his geopolitical outlook. "Let's face it, we have an image problem in the world of being the 'Yankee imperialists.' And to go down there as listeners and not dictators and directors is valuable, I think."

The film showed the Americans busing and walking around San Salvador, meeting and greeting those high and low. The group spent an hour talking with an army colonel, identified as the head of the chiefs of staff of the Salvadoran Armed Forces. The colonel evidently impressed his visitors in a distinct way. As one young American, identified as a "film distributor" recalled: "I just sat back and I go, 'This is the head of all armed forces, a man who is supposedly more powerful then President Duarte?' The man was attractive, you know, he was well-groomed, he was charming, he spoke well, and it was really scary, because he's kind of like a snake coming out of a little barrel, you know, like hypnotic, kind of hypnotizes the crowd." As the film distributor's voice broke into a laugh at her description of the soldier, the colonel himself popped up on the screen, talking to the Americans. And my goodness, she was right: he was well-groomed!

The colonel said that his government was fighting communism and trying to support a democratic system. Then, over more images of death and destruction, the film distributor related how the visitors asked him a lot of questions the soldier did not answer to their satisfaction.

"Maybe he really did think that he was fighting off communists," the distributor allowed. "Though every word he said did not match with what I saw. It's when you look at someone, you say, 'You know, I want to believe you, you look like a nice fellow, but you know what? It's not true! Why don't you come with me, look what these people think of you and the government that you are trying to support.' "

The collective wisdom garnered by the Yankee imperialists was all the more impressive because they did so in just a one-week trip, with two days traveling to and from Central America, three days in the capital city of San Salvador and two days in the countryside.

This would seem like pretty harmless stuff, given the absurdity of the whole scenario. One would have to accept the underlying premise of the film, that the celebrities are not only intelligent but knowledgeable, reliable observers, intellectually capable of jousting with the reputed head of the armed forces.

Even so, this kind of video documentary can be found in the arsenal of many political organizations, and is ordinarily utilized as a fundraising tool. Medical Aid's experience explains why—a representative from the group, personally unimpressed by the film and the celebs, acknowledged that the video was quite effective in stimulating interest in Medical Aid.

And if that was effective, well, what about when fact and fiction do not simply meet but cross over with the intention of confusing the point?

Linda Ellerbee is, or was, a television journalist who made a career partly out of debunking hypocrisy and pomposity. Recently, Ellerbee showed up one morning on a spot on "Today," seated on a chair in the middle of a typical news commentator setting, the room done in soothing tones of blue and grayish white, conveniently matching her own outfit. But something was amiss, for where a map adorned one wall, the logo "America Prefers Maxwell House" was emblazoned on the other. And then Ellerbee smiled at the camera and spoke: "I'm Linda Ellerbee. In a national test, people said Maxwell House coffee is better than Folger's coffee. They said it tastes rich. Willard Scott is out seeing if other people agree. Willard? What is going on there?"

The camera cut to Willard Scott, "Today's" weatherman, standing amidst people in cowboy attire. "You haven't had fun, Linda," Scott said, "until you take up clogging. . . ." While the cloggers clogged around the room, Scott interviewed satisfied Maxwell House customers and then he and Ellerbee finished hawking the coffee.

It was stunning that Ellerbee would trade on her credibility to shill for a product and that "Today" would accept a series of commercials that starred a former news correspondent.

Ellerbee shrugged off the suggestion that the audience might be confused by her employing her journalistic standing to sell coffee. "Americans aren't babies," she told *Newsweek*. "They're not too stupid to know the difference between news and commercials."

Why then, *Newsweek* asked, was she hired? "They wanted me because I have credibility from my news work."

We proceed another step forward, or backward, and watch the blur become complete. An episode on last season's "A Different World," a television sitcom set at Hillman, a black college, opens with Dewayne Wayne, a program star, engaged in a race for president of the student body. His opponent is an unethical woman who would promise anything to get votes.

Meanwhile, it turns out that an administrator of the college, an Army colonel, and Jesse Jackson were boyhood friends, and the

Reverend stops by for a visit. When Jackson strolls onto the set, the studio audience cheers. Wayne, also present at the moment of Jackson's arrival, displays a comparably excited reaction.

"I worked for you!" Wayne sputters. "I voted for you!"

The colonel informs Jackson that Wayne is running for office, and the Reverend replies that he occupied a similar position in his university days.

"It's a good thing I didn't have to run against him," Wayne says.

Wayne's exhilaration at the encounter cannot be contained. As Jackson walks away to wash up, Wayne shouts after him, "Keep hope alive! Keep hope alive!"

Wayne's campaign proceeds badly, faltering in the face of his opponent's flashy gimmicks. Thoroughly discouraged, he is ready to retire from politics. "I'm out. Nobody on this campus cares about anything important. It's the Me Generation. So I'm going to take care of me."

In order to reverse Wayne's fortunes, his best friend and campaign manager "borrows" Jackson's photo for a poster, which implies that the Reverend endorses Wayne. The legend reads, "He is somebody!" playing on Jackson's oft-repeated phrase, "I am somebody!"

A contrite Wayne goes off to the colonel's house to apologize to Jackson for the poster. While the colonel is outraged, Jackson is singularly patient. In fact, this is a hallmark of the show; throughout the half-hour, the Reverend is repeatedly accosted by a stream of invariably awed and tongue-tied admirers, and he always displays impressive understanding and good cheer.

Wayne tells Jackson he is dropping out of the race. "Only a fool would keep taking these beatings."

Jackson responds that he knows the feeling, garnering a chuckle from the audience.

"But you're Jesse Jackson," objects Wayne. "People listen to you."

"That's because I wouldn't give up," Jackson says. "I was not a chump, I would not surrender, I stood up. And you must stand up."

"Nobody cares," Wayne replies, "if I try to set up a scholarship fund or save student activities. No one else is thinking about the future."

"So why should you?" Jackson interjects. "You want to be a leader? If you can't take the heat, get out of the kitchen. You can't cook with cold grease. You've got to stand up to be a leader."

"Reverend, I've tried," Wayne concedes. "It's not my fault. No one is listening to me!"

"You've got to stand up," Jackson says and puts his arms on Wayne's shoulders. "You can't surrender. A man can't be heard if he stops talking. Stand up."

In the last major scene, Jackson speaks before the student body, introduced by the colonel as a "world leader."

"Ladies and gentlemen," the Colonel begins, his voice rising to a crescendo, "my friend and yours, Reverend Jesse Jackson!"

Naturally, Jackson receives a standing ovation from the crowd, one of several. His speech addresses the dilemma of the depressed Wayne, referring to an anonymous person who felt he could not make a difference in his life.

However, Jackson continues, shifting his sights to the larger stage, look at the monumental changes that have occurred in this country during the past thirty years. "The changes did not come from Wall Street or the White House or the Congress or the courts," claims Jackson, but always by one young person who believed he could make a difference, from Rosa Parks to Dr. Martin Luther King to Goodman, Chaney and Schwerner.

"One person can make a difference!" he declares.

Jackson prods the young people to register to vote. "You have the power!" Jackson shouts, receiving another standing ovation.

The epilogue reveals that Wayne does not give up the race, though he eventually loses. That's not what really counts, Wayne insists. "Look," he avers, "it's not important whether I won or lost, the important thing is I had something to say and I said it, and I'm going to keep on saying it." He pauses for a moment. "I wish I'd won," he admits with a frustrated grimace—the cute kind of grimace, of course, which causes the studio audience to laugh appreciatively.

This was hardly the first instance of a politician appearing on a television show. However, there is a tremendous difference between a cameo appearance by Gerald Ford and Henry Kissinger on

"Dynasty," (*Hello, Alexis,* a Teutonic voice woodenly grumbles), and the extraordinary event I had just witnessed, a free half-hour commercial for Jackson on network television. I wanted to know if the powers behind "A Different World," viewed this episode in a similar light, and if they intended to serve as propagandists for Jackson's ambitions. I spoke by phone to Thad Mumford, co-executive producer of the series.

"Did you envision the show as having true political content?" I asked.

"Really, no," Mumford answered. "We thought of this less as a political statement and more of a way of showing the students reacting to Jesse Jackson, and being touched by his message; being touched by the message of, one, the importance of voting, and, two, just the impact of a person of his stature would have on the students, and most of the audience. It was not meant to proselytize for political purposes at all."

"This is the first time," I said, "I have ever seen a politician not in a passive, benign, cameo setting, but in an active, political setting. You don't think there was a political impact in the way he performed on your show?"

"It was not meant that way," averred Mumford. "People will take it the way they can. You know, Jesse Jackson is more than a politician, Jesse Jackson is a minister, he is a diplomat, he is a citizen of the world, who has very important things to say to black people. He is a leader, yes, but he is not just a politician. And I think it sort of limits him; I mean, we didn't have to go to equal time, because he is not just a politician. If he were a candidate, we probably couldn't have done the show we did."

I was unconvinced. "An underlying premise of the show was not just that he was a smart, charismatic guy, but that he was right, fundamentally right."

"Well," Mumford said, "I don't know how you say no to the message that people should vote."

"But that was really just in his speech at the end. After all, Dewayne said he worked for him, voted for him, etc. He and the other characters tripped over themselves in their adoration of him, they said and acted with the idea that he was right, not on that issue, but as a political figure."

"That they tripped over themselves had more to do with the fact that he is this very impressive person," Mumford responded, "who just happened to run for the Presidency twice. It wasn't just a reaction to a candidate or to dogma or a point of view, it was to the man. The kids would have had the same reaction to Mickey Mantle."

"But do you think somebody else, let's say Governor Cuomo, who is also a man as well as a politician—"

"But Governor Cuomo," Mumford interrupted, beginning to sound agitated, "and I like Governor Cuomo, is not as charismatic as Jesse Jackson. And his appeal . . . he is not a black leader. I mean, a black person of substance is going to be much more appealing to a black school than Governor Cuomo is, and that's just a fact of life."

"I agree with that, but I was asking, is Governor Cuomo more of a politician than Jesse Jackson?"

"You're missing my point," Mumford said. He was definitely irritated now. "The reaction was not just to the politician, it was to the man. We did not cast Jesse Jackson the politician, we cast Jesse Jackson the man. The reverend, the diplomat, the black leader. We didn't cast the politician."

"I'm not trying to pick on this, but it's a distinction I don't get. I think of somebody who's perpetually involved in politics, and perpetually running for office, as a politician."

Mumford's tone made it clear he did not concur. "It's a platform for his ideas, yes, but he does much more than that. And he is a man who came from the community, still lives in the community."

"You would separate Jackson from any of the other presidential candidates, as far as appearing on your show? If you had a show based at a white college, you would have put on a white politician?"

"No, because white politicians don't do as many things as Jesse Jackson does. You're missing the whole point! He's not just a politician! And, yes, it is very different in that it's a black world. We don't have as many people from our community who've done what Jesse Jackson has done. White people have many people, so it's not as special."

I didn't know how much longer Mumford was going to indulge me, but I pressed forward. "So you would say that if he ran for

Mayor of Washington and won, it would be different?'' Talk had Jackson considering standing for the Mayor's job.

"It would be a little different,'' Mumford said, "because he would have an actual office.''

"So then you would treat him a little differently on the show.''

"It would be a little different, but it still wouldn't mean we couldn't have him on, as a person of the world. But yes, if he beat Marion Barry, then it would be a little different.''

"Or if he were just running, you wouldn't put him on.''

"No, we wouldn't,'' Mumford said, "because that is endorsing a candidate.''

Mumford's tolerance shortly expired and the conversation ended.

Not all of this made sense. It was ludicrous to claim that Jackson is not a politician; one might argue that he is merely a pol who has yet to win an election, or, if one prefers, a more devious or more saintly practitioner of the art, but the argument has to stay within the bounds of reality. And once we acknowledge reality, then it is obvious why Jackson did the show. Was it simply to promote voter registration or inspire black students or seek a new career as a TV actor?

I spoke to a representative from Jesse Jackson's Rainbow Coalition, who affirmed the gist of Mumford's assertions, that Jackson was interested in spurring voter registration, particularly among black youth, a prime audience for "A Different World." The spokesman agreed that Jackson was perceived as more than just a politician, but "also as a celebrity," and that the portrayal of his character was "realistic."

However, the representative did not hold with Mumford's view that Jackson's appearance did not serve the Reverend's political goals.

"Well, of course it did,'' he said. "Why do it if it didn't?''

Why, indeed? This was a case of situation comedy as platform for a politician, his ideology and his ambitions. If it is true that history is written by the winners, then in our society, history is being written, or edited, by those who control the airwaves. The blurring between reality and fiction progresses, entertainment and fact become combined, human drama becomes melodrama. Once the divisions are no longer set and absolute, then we must rely on individuals to decide what is okay and what isn't. Jackson is all right but

Cuomo isn't—who will decide? Who can we trust? Why must this overlapping and melding and mixing go on?

I don't know about the other questions, but the answer to the last is certain: this goes on because it works.

When it comes to politics, show biz knows better, if not best.

Chapter 12

Phoenix

A View From the Top

Christa Severns, special assistant to Governor Bruce Babbitt, summed up the state of the weather in town by claiming that if Venus had oxygen and a couple of retirement communities, it would be a dead ringer for Phoenix in the summer. She definitely had a point, because there is hot, there is hotter, and then there is August in Arizona.

Arizona is a rugged, gorgeous land, a fantastic vista that inspires anyone capable of inspiration. This was the real West, and it bred a large measure of strength and resolve in its natives, qualities found in its crop of nationally renowned politicians, from the conservative Barry Goldwater to the liberal Bruce Babbitt.

Babbitt, former Governor of Arizona, ran for the Democratic nomination for President during the 1988 season. He did not do very well with the voters, but he was a hit with the media. It is no exaggeration to state that he was one of the very few candidates who emerged from the race with his public character intact, enhanced actually, by not only his intelligence and wit, but also his consistent good humor in the face of the daily small and large humiliations inherent in standing for electoral office in today's United States.

Bruce Babbitt is a smart guy and a nice guy, but not very smooth on television, which certainly did not boost his Presidential chances. He knew a lot about celebrities: They're like a herd of antelope. They crowd together, sniffing, listening, then sprint to one place. At first, they were with Gary Hart. And then they briefly sprinted to Joe Biden. Then even more briefly to Paul Simon. And then they sort of lost interest and disappeared, mainly because Michael Dukakis wouldn't give them the time of day.''

He also knew a lot about the media.

"So how is the media changing?" Babbitt began. "A whole variety of things are happening, particularly on television. One factor that must not be underestimated is the splintering of the television spectrum, which has forced the networks into a kind of downward spiral. For a long time, the monopoly, or 'triopoly,' acted as a kind of restraining influence. That's all gone now, and all you have do is watch the Fox Network, as my kids do, to understand what's happening.'' Babbitt's laugh suggested he did not think too highly of the programs offered by the Fox Network.

I asked him what he thought of the television talk shows which feature a politico one day and a celeb the next, and the difference in how each is treated. Consider: how often we have seen the politician grilled with a skepticism bordering on outright distrust, his motives or fundamental honesty doubted as a matter of course, both by host and audience members, while the celebrity can spew forth the most astonishing nonsense, such as blathering on about having been Cleopatra in a previous life, to an applauding, approving crowd. While it is not unreasonable to question our public servants briskly, it is also not unreasonable to expect that they will be treated with something approaching the same basic respect as a movie actor.

However, precisely the opposite frequently happens. Everyone looks the same on TV, squeezed into the same box, seated on the same stage, in the same chair, talking to the same interviewer— congressman following crooner following senator following shepherd. On talk shows, every guest is essentially the same, except the politicos are accorded harsher treatment. The message to the viewer is obvious: Who is more important, who is truly worthy of your attention, your respect, your love? Who is better?

"That's interesting," Babbitt said, nodding. "I never thought about that. I think you're probably right. But I'll tell you, as long as it's straight news, or a straight news show, I have always felt that the skepticism and combative tone of interviews was pretty fair game. That's part of the American cultural tradition. The problem is, there's not even much of that anymore, politicians aren't even on the news unless they're being disgraced or caught *in flagrante delicto* or something."

"You don't sound impressed with the media."

"The fragmentation of television has really interesting effects," Babbitt replied. "For those who really care, television has never been better. The rise of C-SPAN [Cable-Satellite Public Affairs Network, broadcasting congressional and public interest forums and, foremost, activity from the floors of Congress] and CNN has provided extraordinary access. Watching C-SPAN is really unbelievable. Turn on ESPN and and watch mudball—oh, some great sporting events, too, but it's like this." Babbitt waved his hand up and down to signify the unreliable quality of the sports channel's programming.

"C-SPAN is uniformly good," Babbitt continued, "If somebody is a recluse or a shut-in, or living in the Texas Panhandle or northwest Arizona, the available TV political content is better than it's ever been. But it's only the five percent who access that at all. The large broadcast media is sliding."

"Do you see the media as either liberal or conservative?"

"Neither," Babbitt said. "I've got to tell you, the national press is very good. They really are. They are extraordinarily competent people. You know, they have egos; everyone in their game has an ego, and they're part of the game, and the egos bring the usual problem. But they are enormously professional, competent people."

"I've found that liberals often claim the press is conservative, and the conservatives claim vice versa."

"The press is establishment," Babbitt replied. "There is no question about that. Establishment is a kind of cultural point of view, which starts out with certain premises, which relate to kind of a subtle view of the existing order and not a lot of interest in the things that are taking place on the fringes."

I asked Babbitt how he felt about all this personally, since the media had helped put to rest his comatose presidential campaign.

"I don't object to the techniques of TV," Babbitt said. "We have to use them, and adjust to them. In 1860, you needed a barrel-chested baritone, so people could hear you a quarter-mile away. Today, you have cameras and makeup and consultants. I might have not used television successfully, but that's the way it is nowadays. Not that you want to take it too far, or you'll end up like Ronald Reagan. Everything he knew and believed he learned in Hollywood. He was the product of that world, he understood it, he embraced it.''

As Babbitt noted, Reagans' show biz background provided him with an especially keen appreciation of the importance of the media. All roads lead to the media, as far as celebrities go, for without the shows and interviews and articles there would be no celebrities. Of course, there would be a bunch of actors and singers and whatnot with a lot more privacy, if a little poorer and quieter. In short, it would be more like the old days, the really old days, when gladiators or court jesters or carnival sideshows were summoned to perform for the king's pleasure or the public's amusement, and then sent off when it was time for the serious people to get serious again.

Since precious few performers would wish to return to those times, a love-hate relationship has developed between the watchers and the watched. Each needs the other to flourish and, according to the available evidence, the celebrities infrequently enjoy the dependence.

"People detest the press," Bill Atherton had told me, "because the press does not have good will for people in terms of quoting them accurately. Anybody who says they like the press is a liar. Nobody trusts the press.''

Interviewed in *Esquire*, Robin Williams explained the relationship a little differently. "It's like two lepers doing a tango: *Uh-oh, you walked away with an arm! Ohhh, look!* It's difficult with journalists because they come in thinking, 'Well, I've got to find something,' and we know. It's like a Bergman film where you're playing Parcheesi with Death.''

Barbara Ligeti, theatrical and film producer and former Broadway dancer, provided an example of the relationship in action. "I was part of this sleep-in in Washington two-and-a-half years ago,'' she said. "to support and dramatize a bill to help the homeless. So we slept out in the street overnight—a hideous experience, I have to tell you. Dennis Quaid slept out, and so did Brian Dennehy, and also Martin Sheen, who actually organized this. All these high visibility people were needed for a very simple reason and Brian Dennehy, who is a Columbia University graduate, stepped up and actually said to a CNN reporter, who had asked why he was there, 'Because if *I* weren't here, *you* wouldn't be here. If Dennis Quaid weren't here, if Marty Sheen weren't here, you wouldn't be here with your cameras, not just for a bunch of nice, concerned citizens.' And that was the point. And that really says it all.''

Though many people consider the press as left-leaning, a charge Ronald Reagan used to his advantage during his Presidency, liberal celebs have as many complaints as conservatives about the media, Ed Asner being a prime example.

Three overriding problems exist. One, the media is perceived as arrogant, fat and comfortable, basking in its power, determined to make and live by its own rules, whether or not those rules step outside societal standards. Frequently sheltered under the ethical umbrella of "the public's right to know," the media can be quite abusive. We have all witnessed the pack of reporters hounding the distraught mother to reveal to the world what it's like to have one's daughter kidnapped by an axe murderer. Similarly, anything goes when it comes to celebs—get that picture or story at any cost, whether one has to employ a telephoto lens or rent a helicopter or bribe the maid—unless, of course, the star in question is *so* important or beloved that the media deems it necessary to cover up his misleads or eccentricities.

This idea of above-and-beyond-the-rules has somehow become so accepted in America that it is surely one of the prime attractions of the profession. I first learned of this phenomenon almost ten years ago while taking a seminar under the joint aegis of my university's law and journalism schools. As I recall, the question was posed that if terrorists had seized a nuclear plant and threatened to blow it up and release the radiation, resulting in perhaps millions of deaths, and only you, the famous reporter, were to be permitted inside for an interview, would you help the FBI and police get in and save the day?

Though the law students agreed as one that rescuing millions from death was the obvious priority, virtually every fledgling journalist stated that the outcome, however regrettable, was not the concern of the fourth estate, that the reporter's loyalty was not to

God, country or people, but to the *truth*—whatever that means. I note that working journalists were also participating in the seminar and their collective attitude was vastly more sensible than that of their future colleagues, stimulated by a yearning not only for the truth but also a yearning to survive. Though the untried students had taken the media's fidelity to its higher calling, this *truth* thing, a few yards too far, they had adopted the right feeling, that *truth* above all counts. Of course, there is God's truth and science's truth and then man's truth, a far lower order of truth indeed, but that is a discussion for another day.

This media's second basic problem is its insatiable need to find something new to push, promote, report. The media does not deal in novels or art, artifacts to be carefully, lovingly examined and reviewed and enjoyed; the media trades in facts and photos, in immediate images, in action and result. When so many tales, so many personalities, are needed to constantly feed the media machine, then everything and everyone becomes news, and is accorded their fifteen minutes of fame. There can be no bystanders, no out-of-bounds, because once the camera shows something, it is instantly transformed into old news and the perpetual search for the next topper, the next greatest or most awful or most exciting or most frightening rolls forward. In this exhausting war, no one is better suited for cannon fodder than celebrities, celebs who seem to lead daring, or at least different lives, celebs who act and sing and dance and drink and divorce and lie and cheat and talk, talk, talk. A perfect fit.

The third problem grows out of the second. I have been using the terms "press" and "media" interchangeably, though the former means the gathering of news while the latter refers to any instrument of communication. However, in our world, the two are rapidly turning into one and the same. What is news? What is journalism? *The New York Times* qualifies as a news organ, yet what about *People* magazine, which focuses on personalities rather than stories? We count the network evening news shows, yet where do we put the local shows, which devote as much time to personality and feature pieces as to hard news? Never mind the local news—what do we do with "Entertainment Tonight", which chronicles show biz "news," or "A Current Affair" and other offerings of tabloid television, which specialize in tales of money, mayhem and sex?

What about the talk shows in their myriad formats, from one-on-one to panel discussions to studio audience participation to a juggling act between host, guests, studio audience and home viewers? Do they present news or gossip, facts or rumors, do they add to the general knowledge or distort and obscure it?

Flipping the perspective from politician to journalist, I traveled from Bruce Babbitt to Sam Donaldson, another fellow who knows more than a little about the media and politics. Donaldson earned his position as one of America's most respected journalists during his tenure as ABC's White House correspondent, and is now co-hosting the network's latest news program, "Prime Time Live."

The new show is broadcast out of ABC's studio on the New York's West Side, and we sat and talked in his relatively small office on the fourth floor. Donaldson began by saying he didn't think he could be of much help to my inquiry, since he was a hard news reporter and knew nothing about celebrities and show biz. The phone rang and Donaldson spoke to somebody "in the field" detailed to keep an eye on Boris Yeltsin, the Soviet political maverick who was then on a lecture tour of the United States.

"It's interesting about someone like Yeltsin," Donaldson said after hanging up the phone. "On one side, he's an important political figure and a news individual in the pure sense of the word. On the other side, he's a celebrity, in that sense of the word, without using the strict dictionary definition, or maybe in this case applying it.

"Yeltsin has become a little larger than life now," Donaldson continued, "he's the man of the hour, the toast of the town, use any cliche that you want—so where do you find him? You find him on the front page of today's paper , and you find him in *The Washington Post*'s style section, as they chronicle that he put away a pint and a half of Jack Daniel's the day before yesterday. And they're very kind; what clearly happened was he made his way around drunk on his feet, smooching around, and mumbling and what have you."

"That's intriguing because being a celebrity here won't protect him back home."

"Back home they're drunk all the time!" Donaldson exclaimed in that unmistakable assertive style.

"I didn't mean that part," I said. "In the U.S., being a celebrity insulates you from criticism."

"It either insulates you or it magnifies the criticism," he responded. "Think about it; of course, you can point out that if you're not a celebrity, nobody gives a damn about your views, so you're not subject to criticism. However, if you are a celebrity, and then you can't say anything spontaneously or anything outrageous, without having to pay the piper."

"What's the payment?"

"What's the guy's name," Donaldson said, furrowing his brow and thinking. "Very liberal—"

It was easy. "Ed Asner?"

"That's right," Donaldson said. "I think, to some extent, his career suffered because of his politics."

"He would agree with you. In fact, that's the guy everybody comes up with when trying to think of somebody who's been affected by his political acts." I gave my Shirley MacLaine example, where she chats about reincarnation and other issues of "higher consciousness" to the acclaim of the adoring host and audience, while the poor politico is set upon with sharpened teeth. I recalled a discussion I once had with Lawrence Eagleburger, currently Deputy Secretary of State, where he described battling his way through the skeptical thicket during an appearance on "The Donahue Show."

"How interesting," Donaldson asserted, "because if I had interviewed the two of them, I'm certain that for all my attempts to play the devil's advocate, or to be a reporter, I would have treated Eagleburger with more respect. Let me choose my words—I don't mean respect in the sense of a human being, but I would have put him on a different and higher plane than Shirley MacLaine. To me, Shirley MacLaine is a dingbat. I mean, that's fine, I don't mean to be pejorative, but I wouldn't take her seriously. I take Larry Eagleburger seriously, although I disagree with him; any Kissinger disciple has got in me an adversary. But you're saying most shows are just the other way?"

"Well, you don't have celebs on to interrogate them, if you ever want them to come back. On the other hand, a politician is on to be interrogated."

"See," Donaldson said, "that's why I don't think I can help you much, because I don't know much about that."

"That's okay," I countered. "Now this scenario I have been describing is on TV every day, and you see it just like everyone else."

"I'm just like any other casual observer," Donaldson noted. "I have no expertise. I have expertise as a reporter, interviewing subjects who are news subjects. I have interviewed very few celebrities, and always because they have come into the hard news field in one way or another.

"Warren Beatty started it in the sixties," he continued. "Well, he may not have started it, but he was clearly one of the early Hollywood types who went to work for a national candidate. Not just his name, but also his participation. Now it's just accepted fact. I covered Michael Dukakis this past summer and fall for ABC, and there was this succession of so-called celebrities coming around. I don't remember them all, because frankly I don't know them. I had to learn who Daryl Hannah was. Let's see, there was a young man, very famous—oh, Michael Fox!—I kind of know who he is. So if you're asking the question, the answer obviously is from the standpoint of a political reporter, I have been more and more aware since the sixties that the so-called celebrities are involved in the system."

"How do you think this has affected the process?"

"I don't think it has affected anything," Donaldson said. "By affecting the process, do you mean, change votes by the fact that they are either present and have lent their draw power or given their imprimatur, I don't think it's transferable. I don't think the fact that Daryl Hannah has a following helped Michael Dukakis. I guess it didn't hurt him, but I don't think it helped him."

"But if the first step is working for other candidates then the second is running for office. And whether Ronald Reagan—"

"I think Ronald Reagan is such an anomaly," interjected Donaldson.

"Why?"

"I think you cannot say he is forerunner of a succession of successful celebrity politicians," he said. "I'm not saying there's not going to be another. I know Clint Eastwood and Sonny Bono were elected mayors of small towns."

"Forget them. What about Bill Bradley and Jack Kemp?"

"But I don't think their political careers are solely based on something, their celebrityhood, which they then simply traded on,"

Donaldson said. "You would argue—correctly—that Bill Bradley might not have gotten to be the senatorial candidate in New Jersey if he had not been the sports star he was. I guess maybe what I'm reflecting is my opinion that somehow serious sports figures are on a little different plane than Hollywood actors. I'm just reflecting my prejudice, I suppose. I guess I don't see Bill Bradley as your typical celebrity who suddenly wants to dabble in politics, and thinks he is going to be elected because he is a great box office draw."

"What about Congressman Fred Grandy?"

"You can pick out individual examples," Donaldson insisted. "I don't think Ronald Reagan is going to be the first in a long line of Hollywood Presidents. So maybe I guess I'm saying, I would take it case by case."

I suggested to Donaldson that celebrities have a leg up on other political aspirants. Where entry and advancement in politics used to be vertical—one started at the bottom and worked his way up—today, politics is more and more frequently a horizontal game, in which someone makes his or her name in another field and moves over to politics at a correspondingly high level. I wondered whether Donaldson felt that this change in political career advancement had changed the nature of the people involved in politics.

"Well, I was amused by something I heard over the weekend," Donaldson said with a grin. "I was listening to the radio and some professor somewhere was being interviewed because he had written a book, and the thesis was, startlingly, that it is often more important how you say something than what you say." Donaldson paused for effect and laughed.

"I mean, we all understand that," he noted. "I'm falling back on familiar ground now. I maintain that if television had been present for the Lincoln-Douglas debates, Abraham Lincoln would still probably have won. Believe it or not, I read at one time all the debates, and it seemed that Douglas's reasoning was often well-knit and Lincoln's was not as well-knit. Nonetheless, it was clear to me that Lincoln came across as the more interesting person. His choice of words was more interesting. Television would have picked this up. So—has celebrityhood changed the process? If a celebrity knows how to simply be a presenter in a far more interesting way; and this was Reagan; that is some sort of an advantage. But that doesn't war with my thesis, which is Ronald Reagan is not the first of a great wave of celebrities, and Charlton Heston will be our next President, and after him Clint Eastwood.''

''Though Heston has been asked to run for the Senate by both parties.''

''Yeah, yeah,'' Donaldson replied. ''I've certainly been asked to run, in the sense that having seen what they can do with Reagan, think what you can do if you had someone—though I don't know much about Charlton Heston—''

''Who's a better actor.''

''Who's not only a better actor, perhaps, but has a better mind,'' Donaldson added. ''But I shouldn't say that, because I don't know Charlton Heston. Now, Reagan wasn't a mindless twit. Ronald Reagan is Ronald Reagan. He believes what he says. I never believed he was deviously sitting in the Oval Office, saying 'Okay, Ollie North, we're going to put this one over on the American public.' He was not interested in details, he listened to his advisors, but he knew enough to know what he wanted to accomplish.''

Speaking of politicians, I said that I had recently interviewed Bruce Babbit, who was awful on TV but loved by the media.

''Yeah,'' Donaldson said quickly, ''but the so-called media loved him for various reasons. We love losers, for some reason. But that's not bad. Another one of my thesis is that the loser, whether in life or in politics, really needs a platform a lot more than the winner, because the winner can always get a platform. I never paid any attention to all those people who said we never gave Ronald Reagan a fair shake to get out his message. Christ, he got out his message in huge waves! It was this guy over here who never got out his message. So if Babbitt got a little attention, that's okay. But if you notice, a person comes in at a certain point because he's lost. Then we discover him, and he becomes a champion, he gets on the cover of *Newsweek*, and we say, 'Oh, if only we'd discovered him earlier. . .' But if Babbitt had come up in the polls, we'd have savaged him.''

''What do you think about legitimate news shows having celebrities on to discuss political issues?'' I brought up ''Nightline'' hosting Charlton Heston and Paul Newman for a debate on a nuclear freeze.

''That to me is disturbing,'' Donaldson responded with a frown. ''It seems to me that you have two kinds of people commenting on things. The people who know something about the subject gain a platform by virtue of their experience, their expertise, their position, and by position I mean one we would recognize as a legitimate position on that subject because they are working in the field. And the second type of person is the man on the street. 'Hey, what's your opinion?' 'Well, I think this and this.'

"Okay. The disturbing thing is that we take celebrities in another field and, because they have a legitimate platform and position in that field, as celebrities, we try to transfer it to something else, something political perhaps. If Paul Newman and Charlton Heston are indeed working very hard in the field of a nuclear freeze, I guess they're legitimate. I won't pass on that. But I've seen and you've seen many interviews in which you take a celebrity and put him or her in a position to comment in a serious way on a subject, but it's not like the man on the street. 'Okay, we're going to get eighteen opinions and here is Cher's and hers is as good as anyone else's, and what do you think?' No. Now, it's different. Now, there's a glorification and a magnification. I told you earlier I don't think the audience pays any attention in the sense of, 'Oh, if Cher is for someone, so am I.' But it takes valuable time and valuable space.

"Which makes it important," I asserted. "By virtue of showing that opinion, by virtue of using up that valuable time and space, the media is giving it a legitimacy."

"Whether we want to or not," Donaldson said, "it gives these people a legitimacy beyond just the man on the street. There's a legitimacy of expertise, when in fact there may be no expertise whatever."

"When you watch television or read magazines, you get the idea that famous people like other famous people. Even if they don't know one another, even if they're in different fields, celebrities seem to naturally gravitate to other celebrities. They're happier and more comfortable with one another. They're somehow all the same. We just saw that Walter Cronkite and Henry Kissinger attended Malcolm Forbes's birthday party in Morocco."

Donaldson shook his head mournfully and mumbled, really to himself: "I don't like that Walter went." Then, in a louder voice, he added, "I could see a lot of those other people going."

Donaldson was back up to speed. "Jack Kent Cooke is the

Washington Redskins' owner. Several years ago, I got on his list to get into his box. It was clear the only reason I got on his list was that he apparently saw me as what I suppose you would define as a celebrity.''

"A useful one."

"Well, that's right," nodded Donaldson. "If I thought that Jack Kent Cooke really admired the work that I did, and thought, I don't know. . . I had no personal relationship with him, there was no. . .'' Donaldson was uncharacteristically hesitant, evidently unhappy, even disconcerted by the celebrity side of his profession.

"I went a couple of times," he said, "and then I turned down every invitation since. Because I just think it's kind of a false. . . What am I doing there? And I'm not going to criticize other reporters who may be in that box. Each one has a different relationship with Cooke, but I had none."

"Or maybe they just want to go to the game."

"That's fine," Donaldson answered. "And I have to confess to you I'm not a great sports fan. I don't kill to go to sports, or I guess I'd have to weigh that in. I felt very uncomfortable, because clearly the only reason I was being invited was because of so-called celebrityhood. And yet I don't look at myself as a celebrity. I don't look on myself as someone who basically says to the public, 'Look Ma, it's me, no hands!' Therefore, I'm going to continue to earn a living because of your reaction to the fact that it's me. I still look on myself, and I hope I always will, as a reporter, a newsman— newsperson, if you will. The news is important and my association with it on television as someone who tells you about it clearly brings me into the public eye; I understand that, I'm not a fool. On the other hand, I don't think people are tuning in to see me, I hope they're tuning in to see me do the news, or the news as done by me, but the news comes first, the story comes first. So for Jack Kent Cooke to invite me into his box doesn't make any sense."

While Donaldson had been his usual energetic self throughout the interview, this topic had really stirred up some extra excitement. "I give speeches," Donaldson continued. "I give more free speeches, if you count every time I go to a journalism class or something, than I give paid speeches, but I give paid speeches to the usual types of groups. Well, now I don't give any speeches, because we're trying to get this show off the ground. But regardless, recently something has happened. Speaking bureaus will call and say, 'Will you accept a date for this group?' But it's not a speech, they just want me to come and mix and mingle. I answer, 'Well, of course not. Of course not.' "

"And they'll pay you the same fee?"

"No, it's a reduced fee," Donaldson said. "But what is this? I'm supposed to show up and just walk around the room, saying hello to people, and pocket a fat check? Now, you see, that's over a line. That's what—I hate to keep using Daryl Hannah, help me think of another celebrity."

"Rob Lowe was a big political celebrity until—"

"Yes, until *that*," laughed Donaldson. 'Other than that, Mrs. Lincoln, how did you enjoy the play?' But you see, that sort of appearance was something a celebrity would do, and would probably be paid good money, and probably the person paying the money would get what he paid for. Everyone would leave the party or the luncheon saying, 'Gosh, Daryl Hannah was here, or someone like that, wow.' But for me to do it, it would be saying, 'Yes! I'm not a reporter, I'm not a newsperson.' You want me to come in and talk about the news? Talk about how Bush's doing? That is legitimate. But to have me just show up because I'm on television and people see me and have opinions about me, which would cause heads to turn and tongues to wag in the room."

"Well, what about Linda Ellerbee?"

"Look at Linda Ellerbee," Donaldson jumped in quickly. "It can be said that Linda Ellerbee was never in the absolute mainstream of on-the-beat journalists, but she certainly has been in the mainstream of journalists who were considered legitimate, part of the craft. Now, in one fell swoop—I only deal in cliches—she's crossed over an invisible line we all understand and she can't come back. She can get work in the business, in the sense she can be on television and talk about news stories, but Linda Ellerbee will never be hired again by one of the mainstream news departments to be a correspondent or an anchor or a commentator."

"Why does it matter that she did a commercial?"

"Because we have to be in the viewer's mind clearly one thing and not be confused with another, so that some element of trust is there up front, without reference to the facts we are presenting. The viewer must know that if Linda tells you something, it will not be based on a private arrangement, in which she will say anything for money, that as a reporter, this is her view. She may be wrong, the facts may ultimately prove that she didn't have all the facts when she made her report, but at least she thought she did, and that's all the public can ask of us.''

''Do you think the way the media presents politics is changing?''

''It's evolving, it's changing,'' Donaldson replied. ''The old role of the so-called impersonal reporter who stood outside and used to measure objectively in poundage or in minutes, or if you presented a spokesman for one view you had to present two other major views with two other spokesmen, I think is changing. We went through a period, a fringe period of so-called advocacy journalism, of which I don't approve. Because as I understand it, in advocacy journalism, you start with a point of view and you then attempt to present that point of view and marshal the evidence to support that point of view.

''But what I see happening now is that more and more reporters, not just commentators or editorial writers, believe it's proper to start without a point of view, to start and find out the facts, but as you find the facts, not to feel a necessity to say, 'Well, I kind of know it's this way but I've got to be objective and, therefore, I will continue to present it as it's six pounds of one or six pounds of another and you, ladies and gentlemen of the television audience, can now make up your minds now that I've presented all of these facts; you will see through the ersatz six pounds and you will understand.' I think, and I think more and more people in the business think this, that the obligation of the reporter is to find the facts where they are and present them that way. And then, in effect, you say, 'We looked at it and found that this didn't hold water, for the following reasons, and this did, and therefore we think it's this way.' ''

We talked a little more about this and that, and then Donaldson had to get back to tracking Boris Yeltsin and similar matters. It had been a worthwhile conversation, and the same went for my discussion with Babbitt. In several ways, the views of the politician and the journalist intersected. Each denied—no, more—each *disdained* the idea of knowing at least as much as the average American about celebrities. Each professed admiration for the practitioners of the other's occupation. Each was the sort of person who took his professional obligations very seriously and very personally.

Both men also shared a clear grasp of the realities of the media, and how a politician had to understand it to survive and succeed. While Babbitt was more dismissive of Reagan, both talked about how the techniques of television were politically manageable, not awfully frightening or mysterious to the professional politico, just another method to be mastered. Interestingly, both referred to the Lincoln era, Babbitt when he spoke about the barrel-chested orator, and Donaldson when he asserted that the extraordinary character of Mr. Lincoln would have emerged triumphant even in this electronic age.

Others have publicly disagreed with this last assessment, the line going around that if Lincoln had lived in this era of nine second television bites, he would have said, "Read my lips—no more slavery," in imitation of George Bush's no new tax pledge, which was of course in imitation of Clint Eastwood's Dirty Harry snarl, "Make my day." It is a glib sentiment, a cynical and superficial argument.

Yet while the great can rise above any technique or technology, what of the lesser politicians? What of the public? Perhaps because Babbitt and Donaldson, singularly intelligent, intellectual, committed individuals, both discern their responsibilities and goals with such keen sight, it is easy for them to dismiss the influence of celebrities on the system. However, we are not speaking with the elite to investigate the habits of the elite; rather, we are concerned with the flow of this nation, with the mass movement of faith and hope and values. In this regard, it is not a question of how honorably and wisely Bruce Babbitt and Sam Donaldson follow their personal and professional ethical standards; for though they, and many others, undoubtedly maintain the highest standards, this does not stop the failure of our system to promote true heroes and instead push forward celebrities as substitutes. This does not slow the blurring of all those famous people into one big stew, this does not halt the confused message of what qualities are really solid and good and deserving of our support and emulation.

Who is ultimately responsible? If not the Babbitts and the Don-aldsons, then who? It is a Tolstoyan dilemma—who pushed whom into history, Napoleon or the corporal, the leader or the led? Who created whom, the politicians or the public, the celebrities or the media?

There is surely credit enough for all.

Chapter 13

New York City

Rock Rules

Though the focus of this book is firmly on the American arena, and also on Hollywood and actors, the special world of contemporary music cannot be ignored, for it has taken a singular turn, veering into involvement in a number of international political issues.

Rock and roll began as the sound of rebellion, a sound and a style, shocking parents and thrilling kids. As rock became bigger, more acceptable, more profitable—as rock became an industry—it lost that initial, essentially innocent fire and joined the mainstream. Nevertheless, musicians frequently struck out on a different political course than performers in other entertainment fields.

Music has long played a part on the American political scene, exemplified by folk singers Woody Guthrie and Pete Seeger. Writer of over a thousand songs, perhaps the best known of which is "This Land Is Your Land," Guthrie began by alerting America to the plight of the migrants from the dust bowl during the Depression. Seeger, who wrote "If I Had a Hammer," met Guthrie in 1940, and together and separately the left-wing artists sang, marched and spoke on behalf of a multitude of causes for the better part of this century. They supported a variety of striking unions, opposed American backing of England at the start of the Second World War on the grounds that it was anti-Soviet, later taking up the fight against Hitler when we entered the battle.

In the 1950s, Seeger would find himself listed in the pages of that scurrilous journal, *Red Channels*, called before the House Un-American Activities Committee, and blacklisted. After a ruinous stretch, Seeger was able to put the McCarthy era behind him and go on to another roll call of causes, protesting apartheid, nuclear power, segregation and other abuses. More than fifteen years ago, growing up in a small town along New York's Hudson River, I watched Seeger, a neighbor a handful of villages up the line, sing about cleaning the river, still one of his prime concerns.

In some ways, the activism of such artists, including both their accomplishments and mistakes, presaged the story of rock and roll. But of all the ways rock would differ from folk, the most obvious and most critical would be the scope of rock's reach and influence. Rock and roll, in its first forms, was born in the United States in the fifties and then swiftly swept across the world, emerging as the truly international culture. Homegrown musicians and stars went global, their songs played and loved from Moscow to Tokyo to Lagos to Rio.

American political rock took center stage during the 1960s, fueled by the passions of the Vietnam War and the civil rights movement. The participation of John Lennon, New York City resident, typified the contradictions of the era, as meticulously documented in Robin Denselow's book, *When the Music's Over*. The Beatles' 1968 single, "Revolution," written by Lennon, in the year of the Tet offense, the assassinations of Robert Kennedy and Martin Luther King, and riots in the inner cities, spoke against violence:

> But if you want money for people with minds that hate
> All I can tell you is, brother, you have to wait.
>
> But if you go carrying pictures of Chairman Mao
> You ain't gonna make it with anyone, anyhow.

Criticism from the radical left in both America and England perhaps prompted Lennon to alter one line when the song appeared on the *White Album* two months later. After singing, "When you talk

about destruction, Don't you know that you can count me out,''
Lennon quietly added the word "in." In his attempt to have it both
ways, Lennon of course negated the effect of either sentiment.

So it continued; while Lennon's "Give Peace a Chance" became
an anthem of the anti-war movement, repeatedly chanted by half a
million people in Washington, D.C., on Vietnam Moratorium Day
in November 1969, his "bed-in" with bride Yoko Ono that same
year in the name of sponsoring peace scaled the dizzying height of
egotism. Day after day, the pajama-clad couple lay under the covers
in their suite in the Amsterdam Hilton, spouting about peace to the
amusement, amazement and disgust of the worldwide audience kept
informed by media summoned to the bedroom. As related by
Denselow, when the Lennons repeated their exhibition in Canada,
Yoko explained to cartoonist Al Capp that she and her bed could
have halted Adolph Hitler and the evil he wrought. "If I was a
Jewish girl in Hitler's day," she said, "I would become his girl
friend. After ten days in bed, he would come to my way of
thinking."

Self-indulgence, thy name is rock star. Even more than movie or
television celebrities, musicians have insistently led lives of rampant selfishness. Perhaps part of the reason lies in the makeup of the
respective businesses; where actors have to attempt to get along
with producers, directors, casting agents and sometimes other actors
in order to procure work, rock stars are professionally self-
sufficient, an autonomy which can bleed over and develop into
ruinous emotional isolation. Money, sex, drugs, and rock and roll—
every man-child's favorite thrilling nightmare come true, and the
real (sometime short) life story of many a musician.

I have known David Krebs for a long time, have worked with him
on occasion, and consider his history to be an indicator of the
movement of entertainment figures into politics. Not that anyone
would consider Krebs the typical rock insider, imbued with the
typical rocker's background or outlook: a man with degrees from
both the Columbia Law and Business Schools, Krebs left the William Morris Talent Agency to develop and manage some of the
biggest rock acts of the past twenty years, including Aerosmith,
AC/DC, Ted Nugent, The Scorpions and Def Leppard. Among his
other successes, Krebs co-produced the international theatrical hit

Beatlemania, and created the Texas World Music Festival, perhaps the only annual American rock and roll festival, surviving twelve years at the Cotton Bowl in Dallas.

So Krebs knows rock and roll. But sometime around the start of this decade, he decided that wasn't enough and started to learn about weightier matters.

"I began to feel a little insecure around 1981, 1982," Krebs recalled, "after *Time* and *Newsweek* both ran big cover stories about America in a recession, and I happened to read *The Economist*, from London, and that talked about America in a depression. I said to myself, 'There's a big difference between recession and depression,' and I began to look and read, and I began to see a change in our society early in the Eighties, I started to see us move away from our previously consistent development of an increasingly prosperous and numerous middle class."

"So what did you do?"

"I moved away from music and I began to spend a lot of my time on things that have nothing to do with making money but have to do with trying to protect democracy from the excesses of capitalism."

I asked Krebs to list the issues he was working on in order to advance this rather imposing goal.

"I'm one of three founders of Music In Action," he replied, "which was formed in response to what we perceived to be a threat to First Amendment freedom of speech, in terms of the ultra-right evangelists and the PMRC (Parents' Music Resource Center) attacking music and calling for an industry-imposed ratings system. We in the industry felt that there's an inherent problem with what is called the 'chill factor,' which means that when once stores at the mall level don't buy records that are rated 'X,' the records are effectively censored. Music In Action presented a petition with fifty thousand signatures to the Attorney General on the two-hundredth anniversary of the signing of the Bill of Rights."

The PMRC, founded by Susan Baker, wife of Reagan Treasury Secretary and Bush Secretary of State James Baker, and Tipper Gore, wife of Tennessee Democratic Senator Albert Gore, has caused enormous distress and upheaval in the rock business, and, in turn, resulted in enormous difficulties for Senator Gore in his 1988 Presidential campaign. But more of that later; Krebs had only begun enumerating his political activities.

On election eve, 1980, Krebs put together a nationwide radio show called "America Live," which starred different artists, who performed and also encouraged young people to vote. Before that, he organized the California World Music Festival, which drew over 100,000 people and, apart from the music, promoted solar energy by highlighting a house run completely on the sun's power. A few years ago, he founded a nonprofit group called Uncommon Sense, dedicated to studying the impact of capitalism on democracy. Sometime in 1990, Krebs will start publishing his own newspaper, *The National Times*, which will compile some of the best political and economic thought from around the world each week—"an upscale *Reader's Digest*," in Krebs's phrase.

"How would you describe your politics?" I asked him.

"I would describe my politics as patriotism," Krebs said with a smile. "Liberal with respect to social issues, conservative with respect to fiscal issues, in the sense that I believe we must achieve a balanced budget, cut and eventually eliminate the interest on the debt, which is a total waste."

Krebs's themes, mainly domestic and international economics— and highly intellectual—are not the bread-and-butter of the average politicized rocker. Instead, musicians have devoted a great deal of energy to the international scene. It was the rock industry, led by English singer Bob Geldof, which set up Live Aid, the remarkable relief effort to help the starving in Ethiopia. To comprehend the reach of this effort, understand that an estimated two billion people around the planet watched the concert broadcast from both Wembley, England, and Philadelphia, Pennsylvania, on August 13, 1985, and over $140 million in aid was dispatched to the stricken country. Other causes took note of this success, and sought to enlist musicians in their ranks. Amnesty International, the human rights organization, sponsored two international rock tours, starring performers such as Bruce Springsteen, Sting, Peter Gabriel and Jackson Browne, and watched as membership and contributions climbed.

The anti-apartheid movement jumped aboard with the Nelson Mandela Seventieth Birthday Tribute on July 11, 1988, also held in Wembley Stadium, an eleven-hour show which featured activists spanning much of contemporary music's history, including Americans, Europeans and Africans, from Harry Belafonte to Dire Straits,

Stevie Wonder to the Eurythmics, as well as once again Jackson Browne, Sting and Peter Gabriel. At the same time, Browne was deeply involved in opposing American policy in El Salvador and Nicaragua. Sting was committed to preserving the Amazon rain forest, he had made the trek south several times, beating a path soon followed by politicians and celebrities of all nationalities and stripes. Gabriel had written a song called "Biko," which spoke about the death of black South African activist Steven Biko at the hands of the state's security forces. "Biko" inspired "Little Steven" van Zandt, formerly of Bruce Springsteen's E Street Band, to pen his song "Sun City," produce a video and album of the same name, all of which attacked Sun City, the South African entertainment center, as well as the institution of apartheid and U.S. policy towards the country. In this last instance, one musician's political gesture generated action by another rocker, a pattern often repeated.

Browne was also on the board of directors of MUSE, Musicians United For Safe Energy, which produced the *No Nukes* triple album and film in 1979. Along with other musicians, he fought for California's Proposition 15, which would have effectively stopped all construction of nuclear power plants in the state, and appeared at protests at nuclear facilities across the country. The participation of rock stars over the course of several years helped direct attention to the issue and raise money for anti-nuclear groups, and the cause achieved the thrust of its aims; though plans for hundreds of new nuclear plants were on the boards in the 1970s, public outcry and governmental response killed virtually all new building. Of course, it would be inaccurate to credit the rock industry's role too highly. The disaster at Pennsylvania's Three Mile Island, almost resulting in a nuclear meltdown, and other major problems at other facilities mightily contributed to frightening America near to apoplexy. In addition, not all of Browne and other activists' goals were achieved; Proposition 15 was defeated, and the nuclear weapons industry, a prime target of anti-nuke protesters, was not affected at all. Regardless, on the broader front, strategy had been formulated, work had been done, and results realized.

Most recently, the Soviet Union has become the favorite destination of rock caravans, promoting peace, nuclear disarmament, alcohol temperance, drug abstinence and, naturally, themselves. In August 1989, heavy metal groups Bon Jovi, Motley Crue and Ozzy

Osbourne, among others, including three Russian bands, performed in Lenin Stadium before 80,000 Soviet fans at something labeled the Moscow Music Peace Festival. According to the introductory speech of an official of the Soviet Committee for the Defense of Peace, as reported in *The New York Times*, the Festival's agenda was expanded from drug prevention to include nuclear disarmament and the end of "nationalism, racism and chauvinism."

Apparently not all the rockers were completely up to speed on the objective of their excursion. The *Times* told how Sebastian Bach, lead singer of the New Jersey-based band Skid Row, "finally got a chance to screech into a microphone after several sedate days of being lionized as a role model for temptation-prone teenagers," explained his *raison d'etre* in other terms. "I think the whole point of this show today is for the East to meet the West and kick some ass!"

The benefit—and most of these expensive Russian journeys are partially funded by raising money based on the idea that they are benefits—was devised by Doc McGhee, manager of four of the bands performing. An undefined amount of the profits derived from the prospective album and MTV documentary were to go to the Make a Difference Foundation, started by McGhee as a condition of his 1987 probation after conviction for participating in a major drug-selling scheme.

It is more intriguing to examine how the other side viewed and used the occasion. For years, the Soviets have officially condemned rock and roll as an expression of Western decadence, yet the communists are now throwing open the doors to every traveling sideshow. The newly capitalistic Soviets clearly recognize a good deal when they see one, and soak up considerable profits at home and publicity overseas by hosting every type of entertainer, from Billy Crystal to Billy Joel.

I asked David Krebs why rockers have concentrated their political efforts on international issues more frequently than their Hollywood counterparts, who have often stayed at home and become involved in local and national politics.

"Because the audience for rock and roll is much younger than the audience that film people can appeal to," Krebs replied. "The basic audience for pop music is people twenty-one and under, who aren't ordinarily interested in the kind of specific, intellectual issues that dominate state or national politics. It's hunger, human rights, the environment; ideas everyone can grasp, in an emotional sense. The younger the audience, the poorer your ability to talk to them specifically about party politics. People under eighteen are not in a position to contribute electorally, and people eighteen to twenty-one, based on statistics I've seen, vote far less frequently than any other age group in the country.''

"And when they do vote," I added, "they've voted more right than left, unlike rock and rollers, who are overwhelmingly left.''

"Well," Krebs said, "these people feel that Carter was a failure and, on the surface, Reagan was a success. Otherwise, it would have been impossible for Bush to have run on the idea that there has been prosperity for the last eight years, which is highly challengeable.''

"But American rock stars don't back international issues because of the age of their fans.''

"Live Aid got its real push out of England," Krebs pointed out, "and that started American rock and rollers on the international road. Most rock and rollers don't keep up with what's happening in politics. They're available to support causes like hunger, raise money for diseases like AIDS, but when it gets down to supporting a specific candidate—particularly the kind of acts with which I've been associated—forget it, because either the act doesn't know anything, or the management tells them to stay out of politics because they think it'll hurt the act's career. Besides, even if the act is political, the audience cannot be turned on in that way. On a certain circus sense, the reality of rock and roll is this infatuation with 'sex, drugs, and rock and roll.' I see the potential contribution of rock in a far different, more philosophical, more patriotic sense of 'God, mother, country, rock and roll,' which is light-years away from 'sex, drugs, and rock and roll.''

"Are rock stars generally an educated lot?''

"I would think," Krebs said, "and I am simply guessing, that there are more educated movie stars than rock stars. I don't think there are many college graduates who are lead singers in rock bands.''

"And once they become rock stars, are they more selfish?''

"Despite the fact that many of the songwriters I know are brilliant," Krebs felt, "I don't know any rock stars who read *The*

Economist or *The New York Times* on a regular basis. It's a question of, where do you get your information? If you don't get enough information, how do you begin to synthesize your political thinking, whereby it makes enough sense for you to take positions that you can back with the information that's necessary to sustain the position? You cannot deal in complex issues such as debt reduction or energy independence and get into them with visceral feelings from the heart, you need to be able to argue intellectually.

"However, I think we will see more and more people in the arts participating in politics, because more and more people will become aware that we don't have real prosperity, and when you do examine the last eight years in context of the history of the country, you see a country that went in the early Sixties from a one percent inflation, a three percent prime, five percent home mortgage loan rate, now going into the Nineties with a five point five percent inflation, ten-point-five percent prime, eleven percent home mortgage, and an accumulation of debt that approaches three trillion dollars, and the interest on the debt in fiscal 1989 being probably higher than the budget deficit."

"You think rockers will understand that?" I wondered.

"I think artists will," Krebs said, displaying more optimism than his own testimony justified. "I think it can be explained to them. I think it can be explained in simple fashion, so they will get it. What is rock and roll but the middle-class, working-class form of entertainment, and who has been most hurt by the last eight years of Republican Administration but the middle and working classes."

"But isn't the nature of rock rebellion to be standing outside the system," I asked. "If rock goes inside the system, doesn't it lose its fire and some of its appeal?"

"No, because we're working inside to push out the ultra-conservatives with their outdated, unworkable ideas," Krebs replied and laughed. "Right?"

"Through Establishment means."

"Some of music's power needs to be pushed in that direction without losing its appeal of semi-rebellion," Krebs said. "But who are they rebelling against? Parents? Remember, every year that goes by, the audience gets older. We are now in our third generation of rock fans. Today, there are important things to rebel against, like living in a society where it should be getting easier, not more difficult, to obtain certain things that were part of the parameters of being a secure member of the middle class, such as owning a house and being able to send your kids to college. Both of these goals are slowly being pushed out of the grasp of the middle class. That is not where society should be headed.

"It is going to take a long time to educate people. But there is no choice, because the only mechanism we have in a democracy is voting. And artists have the ability to raise money. If the nature of politics is that the more liberal the candidate, the less support he will get from the *Fortune* 500 companies and from the richest people in the country, who tend to be more conservative, then one of the few places that provide easy access to money is the rock and roll world."

Though Krebs made a fairly rational case, I had trouble imagining a bunch of rock-and-roll stars seated around a conference table, guitars and groupies quietly stacked in the corner, discussing the microeconomic consequences of International Monetary Fund policies. In any event, I was more interested in straight politics, as exemplified by the Tipper Gore episode.

As has been repeatedly reported, the PMRC was started in 1985 after Tipper Gore bought a copy of Prince's *Purple Rain* album for her eight-year-old daughter and glanced at the lyrics to the song, "Darling Nikki:"

I knew a girl named Nikki
I guess you could say she was a sex fiend
I met her in a hotel lobby
Masturbating with a magazine

The PMRC took off shortly thereafter and swung quickly into action. A letter, signed by the wives of sixteen congressmen, was dispatched to the Recording Industry Association of America (RIAA), demanding self-restraint in the production of records glorifying sex, violence and drugs. The RIAA quickly responded, announcing that the record companies had voluntarily agreed to put labels on albums warning of explicit lyrics.

While musicians resented this self-regulating arrangement, the PMRC pressed further. The group pushed for lyrics to be printed on record sleeves for parental perusal and demanded a more detailed ratings system; most disturbing, the PMRC wanted television and radio stations to refrain from playing controversial songs and videos, and asked companies to reassess the recording contracts of the worst offenders. In short order, Gore and friends moved from a not unreasonable request for some guidance for concerned parents to demands which appeared to be, despite their denials, nothing short of censorship and blacklisting.

In September 1985, the Senate Committee on Commerce, Science and Transportation conducted hearings on pornography in rock music. Not coincidentally, five members of the committee were husbands of PMRC members, including Albert Gore.

The PMRC testified, including Susan Baker and Tipper Gore, and some of the more forthright artists in the music industry fought back. Country singer John Denver spoke out, incongruously seated beside Dee Snider of the heavy metal group Twisted Sister, who made quite an impression on the senators with his introduction: "Thank you for having me here. I do not know if it is morning or afternoon. I will say both. Good morning and good afternoon. My name is Dee Snider. That's S-n-i-d-e-r." Snider went on to claim that his song "Under the Blade" had nothing to do with sado-masochism and rape, as might have been assumed from the lyrics, but actually dealt with the fear of surgery.

Frank Zappa, songwriter, performer and iconoclast, put forward music's best case, furiously and rationally eviscerating the hearings as a clumsy attack on the First Amendment. He reminded his audience that no evidence existed to support the contention that rock and roll was hazardous to the listener, or, in Zappa's words, that it would "damn his soul to hell." "Bad facts make bad law," Zappa said, "and people who write bad law are, in my opinion, more dangerous than songwriters who celebrate sexuality."

Naturally, nobody left satisfied and the warring between the PMRC and the industry raged on, the battleground shifting to the television talk shows and newspaper op-ed pages. Whatever the ultimate effect the sniping and sparring would have on the music industry—and it seems a safe bet that the PMRC's impact will be as permanent as the latest fad diet—the effect on Senator's Gore's career has already been noteworthy.

Gore ran for the Democratic nomination for President in 1988 and, on paper, made an attractive candidate. A prime representative of the "new South," he was thirty-nine years old at the start of the race, a Harvard graduate, a Vietnam vet, an arms expert and an environmentalist, liberal on domestic matters, more conservative in foreign affairs. In the eyes of many political observers, Gore was just the sort of candidate the Democrats needed on the national ticket, a man who could help recapture the South without forfeiting any other section of the country, a handsome young man who could revitalize a perplexed and disorganized national party. Gore was often compared favorably with John Kennedy in style and substance.

Gore was the sort of candidate who should have appealed to the entertainment industry. After all, he exhibited the style Hollywood appreciated, not only as a forceful and effective speaker and debater, but as the only Presidential candidate who had a Beatles song played at his wedding, and one of two (Babbitt being the other) who admitted to having smoked marijuana. On a more substantive level, Gore's basically liberal positions should have garnered him his fair share of entertainment industry backers.

Alas, it was not to be. Tipper Gore's championing of the PMRC poisoned the well long before her husband's campaign reached Los Angeles. "How can I support a Democratic candidate whose wife sounds more like Jimmy Swaggart every day?" asked Danny Goldberg, political activist and head of Gold Mountain Records. When Tipper Gore was scheduled to deliver a speech at the Beverly Wilshire Hotel in March 1988, fliers popped up in L.A. record stores urging people to JUST SAY NO TO TIPPER GORE!

"There is no question that her stand causes very serious problems within the music business and with certain liberals on the west side of Los Angeles," Darry Sragow, a Gore California advisor, acknowledged to *The Los Angeles Times*. "The people involved may be a very small number but they are part of a so-called elite that plays a disproportionate role in the results."

A candidate for any office cannot win if he cannot excite his natural constituency, motivating his supporters to donate time and money. To many consultants, it seemed obvious that Gore, in contrast to the technocrat Dukakis or the Washington insider Gephardt, had to stand out as the youthful, vigorous candidate who could arouse the passions of youth and those who pander to youth, i.e., the entertainment community, in a manner reminiscent of JFK.

The Gores tried to bridge the gap created by the music controversy. Early in the campaign, the couple held a private meeting in L.A. with several entertainment industry heads, including Norman Lear, Irving Azoff and Danny Goldberg, in which the Gores claimed that a great misunderstanding had somehow occurred. Both Gores now turned against the Senate hearings they had respectively pushed and conducted.

"I was not in favor of the hearing," Al Gore told them.

"I understand the hearings frightened the artists community," said Tipper Gore. "If I could rewrite the script, I certainly would."

The meeting was a fiasco, the damage only escalated when a tape or transcript was leaked to the show biz paper *Daily Variety*. Since the PMRC was playing very well in the South, the Gores looked as though they were trying to have it both ways, keeping their crusading credentials intact for conservative supporters while repudiating them for new friends. Once the transcript appeared in print, those who attended the allegedly private meeting rushed to get their criticism on the record.

Danny Goldberg announced he didn't think the Gores "made a good impression on anyone." Miles Copeland, president of I.R.S. Records, informed *Daily Variety* that the Gores' continuing concern with rock lyrics "totally discredits them in my eyes." Charges and counterchargers were traded; the Gores returned to the race, and much of the music industry, as well as the larger show biz community, ended up supporting the Democratic nominee, Governor Michael Dukakis, with neither the candidate nor the entertainers expressing real enthusiasm for the other.

Aside from the effect on Senator Gore's campaign, the controversy revealed much about the entertainment industry, and particularly about its music component. Despite the show biz community's reputed newly-acquired political maturation and sophistication, hysteria overrode all other judgments when regarding Senator and Mrs. Gore. Despite the "bigger picture" that the politically savvy so eagerly embrace, despite Gore's potential as a Presidential or Vice-Presidential candidate, or as simply one more link in the arduous attempt to build a stronger national Democratic Party, the music industry, carrying a sizable segment of the entire entertainment world along, would not place its corporate concerns in a rational context besides other larger issues, would or could not look beyond the trees to see the forest. What about crime, drugs, abortion, the arms race, the environment, the budget, the Middle East, Central America, on and on, all those great issues of the day that entertainers are forever holding benefits to protest or save?

Forget it. Forget it all. When the crunch came—or the imaginary crunch, as in this case—the music business worried about the music business first, music activists cast off their noble sentiments and hunkered down to fight their rapacious foe. In a stunning irony, one of the great triumphs of liberal thought, the ongoing fight to raise women to equal citizenship, came under direct assault. After all, it was Mrs. Gore who led the perceived assault on rock, not her husband. In a profession where the wife is traditionally expected to stand silently beside her man, smile sweetly like a Barbie doll, and never, never cause any trouble, one might think that the Senator was deserving of some applause for supporting his wife's right to air her opinions, regardless of the effect on his career. Instead, Al Gore was blamed for allowing Tipper to skip off and make mischief, as though a man who could not control his own woman could not be trusted to run the country. A writer for *The New Republic* expressed precisely this idea when he wrote that Mrs. Gore was ''unmanning'' her husband and thus imperiling his campaign.

Even after George Bush was elected, the music industry did not forget its disdain for Gore. In late 1989, Senators Gore and Wirth were invited by the Show Coalition to speak at a seminar on the environment. Don Henley, singer-songwriter formerly with the Eagles and active in liberal politics, circulated a letter before the event stating, in effect, that Gore was an environmental fraud just out for political advantage, and urged people to protest his appearance.

Evidently, some in the music business had not grasped the truth of two axioms. One was theoretical: in politics, you let bygones be bygones and live to build a better coalition. The second was practical: which was more damaging to liberal convictions, the PMRC or George Bush's victory?

David Krebs was somewhat involved in the melodrama through his sponsorship of Music In Action and had recently attempted to mend a few fences.

"The Gores have done tremendous damage to what would be one of the most natural audiences for the Senator," Krebs said, "based upon what he represents in most areas, the kind of charisma he has, and the age bracket that he's at. I feel badly that somebody who stood up in a lot of areas was being written off because of this not-so-minor issue. And trying to undo that harm is like entering into a giant minefield."

"So the music business is still angry?"

"Certain artists will hold it against him for his whole career," Krebs found. "I don't know how you turn the industry around."

"It is interesting that the greatest impact the industry might ever have is a negative one, hurting a candidate who seems right up its alley in so many ways."

"But the heart of the rock industry goes to the heart of the First Amendment," Krebs said. "I don't know if you can separate them."

"No one said you should," I replied. "However, the PMRC is a joke, as well as old news. Tipper Gore more or less did what some suggested we do in Vietnam, declare victory and quit. There are bigger issues in this country."

"I totally think that parents have the right to see the lyrics of records," said Krebs. "Unfortunately, once we deal with that, if you rate the records, there are too many store owners who will not stock certain records."

"Is this really more of a practical issue than a Constitutional one?"

"Listen, I have my own feelings," Krebs asserted. "When you talk about obscenities, which is what this was dealing with, I think the biggest obscenity is our national debt and—"

'Wait! Stop! Let's get back to Gore, who was right in so many other areas, according to liberal standards."

"It only takes one wrong move to throw off what would otherwise have been a brilliant campaign," Krebs said and shrugged.

David had scored a bulls-eye there. The Gores' music miscalculation had hardly blown his campaign; other more significant problems had seen to that, such as money, tactics, planning, organization. Nonetheless, the fundraising abilities of rock stars would have helped, and Gore's somewhat stiff image might have undergone a little loosening up, through some media osmosis, by his proximity to entertainers.

And what did the rock industry lose? A chance to have made a difference in the Presidential election. A chance to reach a rapprochement with a politician who, whether the recording industry approves or not, will be an influential voice for years, a politician who is young enough to try for the White House well into the next century. Perhaps most important to many individuals within its ranks, the rock industry forfeited a chance to change the widespread view that its members are unreliable, egocentric, half-baked celebs who can sometimes be useful as fundraisers, and have instead transformed into that most feared political animal, a cool, considerate power bloc.

So what's next? The Gore debacle (a description most rockers would undoubtedly dispute) hardly means the withdrawal of the music industry from partisan politics. However, much of music's energies will continue to be devoted to broader areas, such as hunger and human rights, though the era of spectacular benefits may be sputtering to a close. An unavoidable risk of investing so much emotion and effort in extravaganzas such as Live Aid is the lack of follow-through, of failing to maintain the momentum after the show's over and the house lights go up. The self-congratulatory hype that frequently surrounds this sort of huge event, and similar mini-events, can become suffocating and blinding. The waves of saccharine accolades in which pop stars are ritually washed whenever, for example, they donate a day to record a fundraising song, such as Live Aid's "We Are the World," are more than a bit overdone. In such an atmosphere, it is almost irresistibly easy to feel that the problem, any problem, must yield to this outpouring of love and attention. After all, so much money can be raised in one shot, so much media notice focused, so many people encouraged to sing and shout, that it seems almost impolite to keep harping on the same issue after the anticipation crested and emotions peaked. A perfect resolution: the artist feels good about his contribution, and the audience feels good about helping a worthy cause while having fun, and that should be that. In and out, clean and quick: the attention span of many stars and most of the audience is brief. How many of the thousands of new members Amnesty International signed up during its rock tours will renew their membership next year, when Peter Gabriel and company are not on stage encouraging them to join?

Sadly, few problems are solved in one shot, especially the problems the rock industry has so often chosen to tackle. For every million raised by musicians to combat hunger and the homeless, billions are spent by governments, and the problems still overwhelm the best minds and plans. The conceit that a massive dose of music and money can change the world invariably works against the methodical continuation of effort, the necessary and unglamorous bureaucratization which ensures sustained progress.

From there, we confront another problem, perhaps a greater one. Celebrities collecting money to eradicate hunger or eliminate nuclear weapons often promote the idea that they have gotten involved because the government cannot be trusted. "The people" have to take over, led by their true representatives, the celebs, as though the millions of government employees diligently laboring nine to five are actually aliens from outer space, instead of fellow Americans. While this country was built on the concept of individual and community self-reliance, the Founding Fathers did not intend for us to view our government with contempt. It is always easy to give into that sort of cynicism, as easy as believing the world to be run by a giant evil conspiracy.

So we have events like Hands Across America, a 1986 attempt to find five million Americans who would pay ten dollars each (and a corps of corporations to pay considerably more) to create a 4,000-mile, handholding chain, from Los Angeles to New York, in order to raise $100 million to eradicate hunger and homelessness. We have television host Oprah Winfrey, an immensely wealthy woman, "buying" a mile and declaring, "My mile will be for people who can't afford the ten dollars. No rich people in my mile." We have actress Dyan Cannon announcing, "This is not about any *politics*. This does not have anybody running for office. This doesn't have any of those labels on it. It has nothing but love to it."

So we have an event for the "little people," that consciously disdained politicians and government, though sponsored by corporations like McDonald's and Coca-Cola, both known for selling food, not giving it away. We have President Reagan standing on line, after cutting welfare programs and stating that hunger in

America was a result of the poor's "lack of knowledge" about where to get help. We have an event where over half of the money raised was paid out in salaries and expenses.

In the end, instead of $100 million, some $12 million was collected for charitable distribution, a woeful return for the effort involved, squandering time and personnel which might have been more efficiently employed on more substantial projects.

So it goes in the world of major league celebrity politics; for every Sport Aid, again devised by Bob Geldof, which raised $35 million and engaged twenty million participants in seventy-eight countries, we find a Great Peace March, a walk across the nation for nuclear disarmament, endorsed by singer Madonna and actress Rosanna Arquette, sponsored by a combination of hip companies, budgeted at $20 million, essentially falling apart practically right out of the gate in a flutter of sore feet and bankruptcy.

So it will continue to go, in this strange world of non-political politics, of rock stars and suffering masses, of noble intentions and irresponsible extravagance, of pretentious high-mindedness and global television hook-ups, of arrogance and dedication, of money and more money.

Stop this, save that, all together, after me; well, we shall see.

Chapter 14

Sioux City, Iowa

Gopher Goes to Washington

I had come to Iowa to see the future.

I knew I was no longer in New York before I stepped off the DC-9 in Sioux City. When we landed, nobody made a move to get up until the plane had completely stopped, the seat belt sign had gone off and the stewardess had announced it was okay to stand. While still recovering from that, I found myself ambling about in my rental car, searching for the Hilton. I asked directions at a red light from a guy on a motorcycle, who turned around and had me follow him to the hotel, driving considerably out of his way.

Definitely not New York.

Iowa is an important state politically, for every four years it helps determine who will be the next President by holding the first contest of the national campaign. The Sixth District is farm country, its gentle hills rolling through the northwestern corner of the state, spread out in lush sections of green and gold and brown. According to the last census, conducted in 1980, sixty-six percent of the people in the region were married, and thirty-eight percent had children. The median value of a home was $36,000. Out of a total populace of 485,491, approximately seventy percent, some 348,641, were of voting age. One percent was of Spanish origin; the rest were Irish and German Catholics, Dutch Protestants, Norwegians and English. While these statistics have changed during the past decade, they still serve as a useful guide to comprehending the socio-economic fabric of the area.

Sioux City is the largest city in the district, an old river town along the Missouri, with a population of about 80,000. It is a quiet town.

Iowa's Sixth is Middle America, the mythical heartland that politicians are forever claiming to understand or represent or defend. This is farm country, producing corn, hogs, soybeans, wheat and cattle. Farmers are entrepreneurs, and hostage to the uncertainties of everything from the greenhouse effect to the superpower relations. While recent times have been difficult for Iowans, with the weather playing tricks and farm subsidies on the decline, the region has stabilized in the last couple of years and is on surer footing.

So there we have it; never mind New York and Los Angeles and Washington, with their slick ways and pretensions and scams and false idols; *this* is America.

Which is why I came.

For all its homespun wisdom, its vaunted unblinking common sense, Iowa may have gone Hollywood. Because it was here, in the heart of the heartland, that show biz staked a big claim: Gopher was elected to the U.S. Congress.

Fred Grandy is nobody's fool. A Harvard graduate, Grandy campaigned hard in 1986 as a conservative Republican and gained a narrow victory. Born in the state, Grandy left early to attend prep school in the East, where he roomed with David Eisenhower. After college and a year as an assistant to his local congressman, Grandy headed west to seek his fortune. This is where the story gets interesting, because Grandy became an actor.

Not just any actor, but, after the expected career ups and downs, a regular on the hit prime time television series, "Love Boat." For ten years, and now for eternity in reruns, the big white cruise ship plowed the waters of the Pacific, weekly resolving the romantic dilemmas of all aboard. Millions got to know the mainstays of the crew, including the Captain, the cruise director, the doctor, the bartender and the purser—Purser Beryl Smith, that is, Gopher, to his many friends. The smiling crew comprised one happy extended family, which each assigned a particular role. So while the Captain was the kindly though stern father and the cruise director the sweet, responsible daughter, Gopher was the goofy but lovable youngest son—or maybe nephew, for it would have been understandable if the Captain had wished to put a little extra distance between their bloodlines.

A sweet guy, that Gopher, though hardly John Wayne, never mind Ronald Reagan. But the latter's path was the one Fred Grandy took, jumping ship, so to speak, shedding Gopher's neatly starched short pants and knee socks, and stepping into a dark suit and Iowa politics.

The world, and Iowa, was first informed of Grandy's career change in an exclusive story in *People*; Grandy said his staff had struck a deal with the magazine, allowing it to break the news of his political intentions in the December 10, 1985 edition. The setting seemed appropriate.

"I was the first one to do a story about him actually considering running," said Bruce Miller, managing editor of *The Sioux City Journal*. "He was here for a drug seminar, and he was kind of testing the waters then, and people could not believe that he was actually interested in running, particularly since he had not been here for a long time. I mean, the last time he had lived here he had been twelve years old. Then he went to boarding school and then Harvard and then Hollywood. You would see him on occasion, he would come to a television thing; 'Love Boat' would be promoted on a local channel, the local ABC affiliate, and then he'd come as a local celebrity made good. But really, he had very little interest in the area beyond that, or at least it appeared that way to us. And then here he was at this drug thing, and there was some grumbling about the fact that Gopher was going to run—that Fred Grandy was going to run."

"Since he hadn't lived here in so many years," I asked, "was there any talk about carpetbagging, about Grandy just coming back to use Iowa as a base for his political ambitions?"

"Absolutely," Miller replied. "Clearly, you have to put your time in, except in this instance. People work their way up through the political ranks for years before they earn the right to run for one of these offices. You know, people didn't even know if he was going to run as a Republican or Democrat."

I asked Van Carter, news director of KTIV-TV, the local NBC affiliate, to describe the general reaction to Grandy's announcement.

"Well, I guess I can't really say what most people's reactions were," responded Carter, "but certainly among people I knew it was of mirthful incredulity. In other words, it just didn't make any sense. The word had already been out for some time, had been leaked, probably on purpose. The story was that they were seriously planning to go after Berkley Bedell, who had been a congressman for twelve years and who had been very successful here in what I think might call a more Republican area than Democrat. But Berkley had represented this area and its people so well and with enough dignity that people thought he was fine. They didn't care if he was a Democrat or a Republican, he was just their Representative. So he had actually transcended party lines; he was there forever.

"Nonetheless, the Republicans decided they were going to try to change that," Carter continued, warming to the topic. "Now, I remember hearing an interview many years ago, it was in some Sunday supplement, someone was interviewing Fred Grandy while he was still well-known as Gopher. My wife read it and she was amazed and said, 'Did you know that he was a Harvard graduate, and that he wants to get into politics someday?' At which point we kind of laughed about it, because the character that he was famous for was incongruous with the idea of serious politics. The main reaction of people in this area was, 'This is kind of silly.' They weren't really sure what he was up to. Supposedly, the strategy was to get name recognition out during the first election; this was when they had absolutely no expectations of beating Bedell; then, with name recognition and with him doing whatever he was going to do, they must have had some grand two or three-year plan, then run in the next election, they would make a serious run at Bedell. No one could have written the script any better, as far as Bedell getting some tick bites and contracting Lyme's disease, and announcing he was not going to run again. He was completely debilitated, he had lost his energy and also his enthusiasm. Nobody knew at that time that they were going to figure it out and be able to cure it, and by then the house was sold. No one could have predicted the whole turn of events, and no one could have written a better script for Fred Grandy."

"The big question was if he was going to bridge what we called 'the Gopher gap,' " editor Miller said. "Will we accept him as something other than a bumbling idiot on a television show? And I don't think it hurt him at all, they liked the fact that he was a celebrity."

"But he didn't act like a celebrity when he campaigned."

"Oh, no," *Journal* reporter Mark Reirders interjected. "He always had the glasses on, and a conservative suit, and everything was always very well orchestrated."

"He looked very much like his Harvard beginnings," Miller said, "more so than he ever did in his Gopher days. I remember seeing him at parties out in Los Angeles where he looked very like Los Angeles, as opposed to looking Midwestern. So there was an image change involved."

"Did anyone ask Grandy how his previous career prepared him for politics?" I inquired.

"Public speaking," Miller said.

"That was all part of the basic issue," Reirders added, "certainly in the first two or three months of the campaign."

"Most people who enter politics use their background as a reason," I suggested. "If they were business people, they say they know how to manage money, if they were lawyers, they might say they know about justice and the system, if they were soldiers, they say they know how to organize and motivate people. What does an actor say?"

"But we also had a President who was an actor," Miller said, "and it was real easy for him to say, 'The President was an actor.' "

"Did he make the connection?"

"Oh sure, sure," Miller said.

"Yes," Reirders jumped in. "He could also argue, because he was well-known nationwide, that he would draw more attention to Iowa, and the Sixth District."

"And when he was elected," Miller said, "he was a hot, young congressman to look at, so he carried through on that respect."

"In fact," Reirders added, "there was a lot of national media attention on election night focused on the Sixth, to see whether he would win."

Bedell's aide, Clayton Hodgson, took Bedell's place on the

ballot. Though Hodgson was acknowledged to be extremely competent and a nice fellow, he was not an aggressive candidate— "almost too Iowan," in Carter's words. Grandy won with fifty-one percent of the vote.

"The Democrats did the only appropriate thing, considering the candidate they had," Carter said. "They made the issue of being an Iowan the issue. 'Clayton Hodgson—An Iowan for Iowa.' That was the slogan. And the Gopher thing didn't go away for a long time. However, he had come in early enough to get past that. If he had shown up only six months before the election, there would have been too much Gopher syndrome, and he wouldn't have been able to get past it. But they started almost a year before the election, and so that gave plenty of time for all the Gopher talk to get done, and all the Gopher jokes and the rest. And he got past it."

Grandy's ability to return to the state and be accepted so readily said something for its citizens. "Well, Iowa is not like New England," Carter explained, "where you could live there for a hundred years and your family still doesn't quite belong. Iowans are generally the salt-of-the-earth type of people. I shouldn't say just Iowans, because Nebraskans and South Dakotans are the same way. Midwesterners are extremely forgiving people, and common sense rules. From an Iowan's point of view, you are always willing to give people the benefit of the doubt. It doesn't matter where you've been or what you've been doing, we'll allow people to change. 'Here's a fellow who's decided he's had enough of that Hollywood stuff;' boy, we understand that. 'And he wants to come back to his roots;' we understand that. 'And he cares about what's going on here with the local economy, and he says it well, and he sounds good and he looks good and he's serious. He doesn't crack jokes, he doesn't play his other role at all anymore.' Well, there you have it."

"He was very serious."

"Yes," Carter said. "Extremely. He was in a completely new role. Hopefully, for the forty-nine percent of the people who didn't vote for him, he has taken on the role and isn't simply playing the role."

I requested an interview with Congressman Grandy. He turned me down, uninterested in talking about show biz in any shape or form. Evidently, he had weathered the Gopher storm and did not care to discuss it again. I had already heard about the great "To-

night Show'' controversy, which had the Democrats accusing
Grandy of insulting Iowa on national television: on a 1982 program,
Grandy talked with Johnny Carson about being from "the tough
Sioux City ghetto . . . it's a tough one, not a big one. Last year they
tore it down and put up a Fotomat on the spot.'' Afterwards, a
Democratic Party spokesman responded: "They are not major in-
sults, but I think they'd be classified as minor insults.''

I wasn't surprised that Grandy had declined to talk to me.

Still, the Sixth District's story was worth telling, as was what the
election of its new U.S. Representative might mean.

Grandy is the latest in a line of celebrity politicos. We have Jack
Kemp and Bill Bradley from the world of sports, and also Tom
McMillan, former pro basketball player and two-term Democratic
Representative from Maryland's Fourth District, and Jim Bunning,
former big league pitcher and two-term Republican Representative
from Kentucky's Fourth. Hollywood has given us not only minor
players like Clint Eastwood and Sonny Bono, but also the most
successful of the lot, Ronald Reagan. But that is not all; in 1988,
Georgia's Fourth District elected Democrat Ben Jones, who played
the idiotic Cooter on an idiotic series, "The Dukes of Hazzard.''
(This was his second try, defeating Patrick Swindall, and evangeli-
cal Christian who was on trial and later convicted of accepting
$850,000 in drug money from an undercover agent.) Ronald Rea-
gan hailed from a state that had invented the celebrity politician,
electing song-and-dance man George Murphy to the Senate as a
Republican back in 1964. Murphy was defeated in 1970 after it was
revealed that he had been collecting $20,000 a year from Techni-
color while in office.

On the other hand, California voters rejected the candidacy of
former child star and Republican Shirley Temple Black for the
Twelfth District's seat in 1967. (Black served as Ambassador to
Ghana from 1974 to 1976 and White House Chief of Protocol from
1976 to 1977, and is currently Ambassador to Czechoslovakia.) In
1984, Pennsylvania's Ninth District overwhelmingly denied a
House seat to Democrat Nancy Kulp, who played Miss Hathaway
on "The Beverly Hillbillies.''

A celebrity can have a direct impact on a candidacy even when he
or she is not the contender, as in the case of John Warner and

Elizabeth Taylor. The famed actress had made Warner her seventh husband, and was widely credited with ensuring the election of her spouse to the Senate. The marriage between Taylor and Warner, not exactly regarded as one of the intellectual bright lights of the Washington scene, was not an unalloyed triumph; after a few years, Taylor was publicly calling her husband "Senator Asshole." Separation and divorce followed; whatever else they may have divided in the settlement, Warner retained sole custody of his Senate seat.

Of course, expansion of the criteria by which we judge celebrities opens whole new dimensions for exploration. Though it is often said that this nation has created an untitled nobility to compensate for the Founding Fathers having outlawed the real thing, what we have really done is elevate politicians to the level of celebrities and stars, not barons, or dukes. John Kennedy may have introduced celebrities to the White House and indirectly to politics, but the pollenation went both ways. Whatever one's opinion of their policies, John and Robert Kennedy certainly showed they had the experience and brains to fulfill their elected offices; however, Massachusetts was next presented for the Senate with youngest brother, Edward Moore Kennedy, of whom it was said at the time that if his name had simply been Edward Moore, his candidacy would have been a joke. That was hardly the end of the line, nor perhaps even the most outlandish Kennedy foisted on the compliant voters of Massachusetts, for in 1986, Joe Kennedy II ran for the House from the Eighth District. Joe II won, despite competition from several vastly more qualified challengers, despite having once bragged that he had never finished a book in his life and had no intention of trying, despite having been quoted only a year before his campaign that politics held no interest for him: "It's just not in me to do it. It's such a crummy system." Precisely why the citizens of the Bay State so love their Kennedys is mystifying, but then, can the believer ever explain his devotion to the nonbeliever, be the object of affection a Kennedy or an Elvis?

The Kennedy saga is not ended, for another generation is emerging. Ted Kennedy's son, twenty-one-year-old Patrick Kennedy, a junior at Providence College, felt himself ready for power, and stood for a seat in the Rhode Island State Legislature. The incumbent had faithfully served the area for ten years, and he and the media regarded the boy challenger, who had resided for a total of two years in the state, as an affront to the people. "I thought it might take a bit of the fun out of it if I got involved in Massachusetts," Patrick claimed. Fun might be fun, but his family took no chances, pouring fifty thousand dollars into the race for a part-time job that paid three hundred dollars a year. Young Patrick won out, the voters leaping at the opportunity to acquire a Kennedy of their own. America marches on.

Saturday night is Saturday night, from coast to coast and in Sioux City, too. I went to the hot spot in town, which was not too different from a hot spot in most other places; the music was played as loud, the beer tasted as cold, the men and women circled each other as expectantly and warily as anywhere else. Of course, foreign labels were few and a domestic brew a good three dollars less than most places in New York or L.A.—a reasonable trade-off, by my measure.

A group of young women sat at a long table, laughing and drinking. It was a bachelorette party and they were enjoying themselves. The girls were not thrilled with the idea of being interviewed, however briefly, both because they were having fun and because the citizens of the city were not accustomed to strangers walking up and asking them to offer up opinions. Still, they were good-natured, or at least in good spirits, and they let me ask my questions.

"Did you vote for Fred Grandy in the last election?"

"No," the first girl said after putting down her glass. "I didn't vote for anybody, but I wouldn't have voted for him."

'Why not?"

"He doesn't impress me," she responded and took another drink. "He should have stayed on that ship."

After the women had finished laughing, I asked the girl in the next chair, who also had not voted for Grandy, why she thought he had won.

"I think he was more polished in appearance and the way he spoke," she replied. "And his acting helped because people knew who he was."

The next girl hadn't voted either, but it would not have been for Grandy if she had. She was a sergeant with the 185th Air National Guard and the representative had earned her eternal enmity. "He was talking about the Air National Guard,'' she recalled with disgust, ''and he said something about us being the Army! I still think of him as Gopher.''

''Did you vote for Fred Grandy?''

''Who?'' another woman asked, who had been watching the action swirling around the room instead of paying attention to my investigation.

''Fred Grandy,'' I repeated. ''Your congressman.''

''Gopher,'' her neighbor shouted at her over the noise with mild exasperation. ''Gopher!''

''Oh, yeah,'' she said. ''The guy from 'Love Boat.' ''

''Do you think an actor should be in politics?''

''Sure,'' she answered with a shrug. ''One was President, so why not congressman?''

''I don't know much about politics, but I voted for him,'' grinned another woman, lighting a cigarette.

''Why?''

''Because I know who he is,'' she said, a smile playing on her lips. ''Because of the 'Love Boat.' ''

''So why did you vote for him?''

''Because I wanted to.''

''Because she wants to be on jury duty!'' one of her friends leaned over and laughed.

I spoke to the star of the evening, the intended herself. She too denied voting for Grandy. Every year the number of people who were actually inside Yankee Stadium and saw Mickey Mantle hit his five hundredth home run somehow grows, while every year the number of people who admit to voting for any particular politician somehow decreases.

The bride-to-be contended she knew why Grandy had been victorious. ''Because he was a star,'' she averred. ''He was a well-known name. People here liked him—or liked Gopher—so they voted for him.''

I asked her if she thought more actors would be entering politics.

''No,'' she answered. ''People won't take them seriously.''

''They took Grandy seriously.''

''Yeah,'' she said and frowned. ''I can't understand that.''

Traditionally, pollsters do not seek out clubs or bars in which to conduct their research, and so we can discount some of what was said as the ordinary discontent and disdain of Americans for politicians. Yet why is this ordinary? Americans have always regarded those granted power with a dose of rational skepticism, but that skepticism has grown overwhelming, blotting out hope and trust.

Part of the problem is that we no longer trust the messenger because we can no longer trust the message. Politicians (and the occasional journalist) have sometimes handed over their dignity, and the dignity of their positions, in exchange for a check. Former Speaker of the House Tip O'Neil can currently be seen on television zipping himself out of a suitcase to shill for a budget hotel chain: "Who says a politician can't control spending." At the same time, CBS began offering their viewers a new TV series about the trials of a cute congressman. *New York* magazine summed up the premise in a short preview: "In the latest Stephen J. Cannell production, William Katt is a 36-year-old California congressman who'd really rather surf but ends up fighting Central American drug lords."

Which is more ludicrous, the real thing or the television show? O'Neil is not alone in his debasement of his past, privileged post; Geraldine Ferraro, ex-Representative and Vice-Presidential candidate, hawked diet soda on television, President Gerald Ford spends most of his public time playing in golf tournaments and serving on corporate boards, and President Ronald Reagan, shortly after leaving office, accepted millions for a speaking engagement in Japan; I assume he altered the text from the one he frequently delivered to Americans while President, rallying his fellow citizens to stand up for America against foreign encroachment and capital. How common and contemptible it has become, the politician leaving office and grabbing the gold, from any and all takers. Whom can we believe? Who is for real?

Two names have floated in and out of these pages, like specters symbolizing so much of what we are addressing. Ronald Reagan and Jane Fonda are lightning rods for liberals and conservatives, flash points for anger and arguments and ideological posturing. Yet though each would probably furiously deny it, they share some fundamental characteristics which go to the heart of our issue.

Very late one night a couple of weeks ago, I was sitting with a Vietnam vet, an ex-Navy SEAL seriously wounded in combat, and I asked him what he thought of Jane Fonda.

"All I remember," he said, "is having green and black stuff smeared over my face and laying up to my neck in the mud, waiting for some motherfucker to come by who wants to kill me, and she's sitting there on a North Vietnamese dike, up on an anti-aircraft gun, and telling me I'm a murdering son of a bitch, and I can't forget it."

"If you can't forget, can you forgive?"

"Forgive?" he responded and motioned to the bartender for another round of drinks. "Forgive her?" He shifted the collapsible cane he always carries in a pouch under his belt and laughed, a long, slow, dry laugh, the sort of laugh which needs no explanation.

Why is Fonda still an issue? After all, George Wallace, the former racist Governor of Alabama, who swore never to be "out-segged," and vowed to stand in the schoolhouse door to stop integration, was eventually able to command black respect and black support, because he expended prodigious effort in proving that his public change of tune was also a private conversion. Fonda, for all her suburban trappings, Hollywood stardom and entrepreneurial success, has only recently made the faintest attempt to make that connection with those she so outraged. Politics is a matter of honor and courage and accountability, and there can be no forgiveness until there has been an acknowledgment of wrong; unless, perhaps, the audience is tainted by the same wrong and has a vested interest in excusing the misdeed. Such behavior does not denote brave politics, such cowardice is not found in a hero. Rather, the hero must stand out front and lead, and not permit himself to be a straw figure propped up by followers for their often tawdry purposes. There we have Fonda: years ago, when the time was already fast slipping by, she ignored the demands that she repent, acting as though her critics would soon fade away and all would be forgotten. So it was with her defenders and supporters, many of whom had also sailed through the 1960s with a self-righteousness and selfishness that still rankles those subjected to its virulence and embarrasses those who recall their embrace of the decade's ugliest excesses with even a modicum of honesty.

Until Fonda herself apologizes authentically for her ignoble role in the Vietnam War, she will never come to terms with her critics—such as the Veterans of Foreign Wars, which in 1989 once again passed a resolution at its annual convention condemning both her past and present behavior.

Do not think this flaw is found exclusively in liberals. How many have accused Ronald Reagan of the same charges, that he let others fight for him using the facts he never learned and the history he never comprehended? How many have accused Reagan of hiding behind his office or his hearing aid or the roar of the helicopter? Never personally or professionally courageous, conscientious or principled, as has been made clear by his cooperation with HUAC, by his shady arrangement with the Music Corporation of America (MCA), by his startlingly poor relationship with his children, Reagan managed to adopt basic American values—family, honor, truth—on a grand scale, while not attempting to live up to these ideals. He embodied many a politician's inadequacy: the ability to love all of humanity better than those few people nearest and most in need of him.

Evidently, this is also the actor's trait, this separation between the private self and the public persona. In service to "art," the notion of reality takes second place to the "truth." In this fable, the truth is some vague, shining, worthier thing, deserving of veneration above all other considerations. However, the real truth is that this reverence often exists as a self-serving shield against ordinary responsibility, a craven means of evading less glamorous realities.

So how different are they, Fonda and Reagan? Both have serviceable though hardly stirring intellects, and in such minds these attitudes jelled and hardened. How else to explain their actions?

In 1972, in the midst of the Vietnam War, Fonda traveled to Hanoi to support the North Vietnamese cause, and met with communist officials, including vice premier. Incredibly, as the *piece de resistance*, she broadcast an appeal to American soldiers over Hanoi radio. Though she has denied urging U.S. troops to disobey orders, the CIA released transcripts of the broadcast:

Tonight, when you are alone, ask yourselves: What are you doing? Accept no ready answers fed to you by rote from basic training . . . I know that if you saw and you knew the Vietnamese under peaceful conditions, you would hate the men who are sending you on bombing missions.

Have you any idea what your bombs are doing when you pull the levers and push the buttons?

Should you allow these same people and same liars to define for you who your enemy is?

That was not enough for Fonda. She returned home, to America, and announced that the U.S. prisoners of war were not being mistreated by their Vietnamese captors, that the Pentagon was lying to the people. "I believe most (POWs) were treated amazingly humanely. Have you ever seen any other group of returning POWs who look like football players?"

Senator John McCain of Arizona, formerly Captain McCain of the U.S. Navy, held another perspective of the matter. McCain was a POW for almost six years and, as reported by columnist George F. Will, "One day his captors told him he would be taken to meet someone identified only as 'an American actress who is for peace.' "

McCain refused to see the actress. For his obstinacy, he "was confined for four summer months in an unventilated cubicle five feet long and two feet wide, and he was beaten and starved. Other prisoners suffering similar abuse also were made to suffer Jane Fonda's voice: the North Vietnamese piped into the cells recordings in which she urged prisoners to actively oppose U.S. policy, and told the world how well the prisoners were being treated."

Once again, the actor's credo at work: "Facts must never be allowed to interfere with the truth. Actors must rely on their feelings."

Now for Ronald Reagan and just one example of his capacity to willfully disregard what was true and real. One of the more shameful episodes of the Reagan era occurred in 1985 in the course of a Presidential trip to West Germany to commemorate the 40th anniversary of V-E Day. Always on the lookout for a photogenic site suitable for Reagan and the folks back home, the White House rejected Bonn's suggestion of a Nazi death camp and chose a German cemetery instead, later discovering that S.S. troops were buried there. To most people, it was an inexplicable mistake from the crack Reagan advance team, which only compounded the blunder with Reagan's active assent, by proceeding with the visit to Bitburg against the anguished pleas of Holocaust survivors and many others in America and around the world.

Though overlooked by the press at the time, the inexplicable becomes quite comprehensible when one remembered an incident that occurred a couple of years before Bitburg. As Garry Wills related in *Reagan's America: Innocents at Home*, Reagan consistently claimed a war record and war experiences that did not jibe with his posting in thoroughly safe Hollywood, making propaganda films and appearing at war bond drives. This inventive habit (which of course Reagan has always extended to everything he says) proved a bit awkward when the President told Israeli Prime Minister Yitzhak Shamir that he had been assigned by the Signal Corps to film the Nazi death camps. Reagan's tale did not stop there, nor his claims, according to Wills: "He kept one film, since he felt that the authenticity of the Holocaust would one day be questioned, and sure enough, one day he had to show the film to convince a skeptic. The story was so movingly told that Shamir repeated in detail to his Cabinet, from which the Jerusalem newspaper *Ma'ariv* printed it." Two-and-a-half months later, Reagan repeated the same story to Simon Wiesenthal and Rabbi Marvin Hier. Lou Cannon, *Washington Post* columnist and Reagan biographer, wrote an account of both meetings in the newspaper.

The White House damage control team shifted into high gear, and the incident was contained with apparently minimal fallout. Yet the President's death camp yarn—fiction brought to life by Reagan's desire that it had happened, by his insistence that what he believed, or what he did or witnessed in the movies—was on the record.

Thus, when the Bitburg controversy exploded, the President's aides were desperately determined not to change the setting, despite the criticism. As Wills wrote, ". . . those who did the initial planning had to remember their strenuous containment of the death camp stories Reagan had already told. They did not want that can of worms opened again. Acute awareness of that danger helped blind them to other, even greater ones, so wary were they of the power of Reagan's storytelling ability and the trouble it can cause a nervous staff. War movies are hell."

Reagan knew better than Holocaust survivors. Fonda knew better than American POWs. Everything Reagan and Fonda did was a foreshadowing of what we have witnessed in the highhanded attitude of celebrities that their supposedly special facility with emotions is a legitimate substitute for factual and intellectual knowledge. Both Reagan and Fonda had no difficulty insisting that their individual visions, however limited, managed to encompass the essence of the grander truth. Astonishingly, both Reagan and Fonda were held up by noted intellectuals and activists as perhaps the leading representatives of their particular ideological strains, with the former gaining the most powerful office in the world.

More than astonishing, it is frightening. Reagan and Fonda gladly hurried to center stage, but their handlers had to promote them and their audiences accept them.

Why? Is this the best we can do?

I drove out to Bacon Creek Park, two hundred and forty acres on the border between Sioux City and farm country. It was mid-September, and though the summer was fading, the sun was still strong and the temperature in the eighties.

The park is set around a lake, grassy hills framing the crystal blue water, trails leading off into a nature preserve of woods and animals.

Friends and families were scattered about, enjoying the lovely day. Four teenagers pushed a boat into the tranquil lake. A father baited a hook for his boy. A little girl attempted to show her younger brother how to hit a baseball. Several mothers talked while watching their children play on the swings and slides. A group of people of all ages finished a picnic, plates and food scattered about. An elderly couple, the gentleman in tie and Panama hat, sedately walked their small dog.

A sign near the start of the trail announced "The Woodland Community": "Many trees form the canopy and understory below. Trees and the shrub layer provide shelter and food for animals, birds, and insects. Fungi and decaying leaves create rich humus, ideal for new seedlings. Look among the dead leaves to see if you can spot some wildflowers. You are a visitor to the citizens who live and work here. Take time to meet them." The sign had been erected by the Sioux City Kiwanis Club.

I walked around the lake and suddenly realized I hadn't heard a police siren or car alarm or boom box since my arrival in Iowa. Instead, I was listening to the sound of my feet walking along the earth, cracking twigs and rustling dirt. That might not seem like a big deal, but where I live, one usually thinks about such things only when creeping around the apartment in the middle of the night, trying not to make too much noise and wake the kids or cat or neighbors. Outdoors, there is something immediate and tactile, alive and exciting, in the realization that the loudest sound you hear is the sound you are making by simply being there. I don't mean to make too much of this; no revelation accompanied the moment. It was simply different, and nice, and made celebrities and politicians, and the ploys and problems of D.C. and L.A. and N.Y., seem very far away on this perfect Sunday afternoon.

And yet, of course, it was precisely this place and these people that D.C. and L.A. and N.Y. expended so much energy to win over. And, in a sense, they had won here, because a celebrity, one of their own, had been accepted as a bona fide politician and elected to Congress. But did Grandy's victory really mean anything beyond a personal triumph? I had my doubts.

Grandy recognized the advantages and disadvantages of his unique position.

"Most candidates spend about seventy-five cents out of every dollar just to get people to remember their names," Grandy had told a reporter during the campaign. "That's already done for me, even if they just remember that I was one who played on 'Love Boat.' "

"People feel comfortable with me because they know the character Gopher," he said to another correspondent. "These are humorless times out here and they perceive Gopher to be of good spirit. But that's not enough to get elected. I'm serious about the problems out here and I've versed myself on the problems. People know me from television, but I don't want them to know the candidate from television. People need to distinguish the candidate from the character."

Grandy learned the district and the issues, and talked at length during the long campaign about farm credit, set-asides, price supports, groundwater contamination. Once in the House, he wasted no time in demonstrating to his constituents that they had chosen well. A member of the Agriculture Committee, ". . . Grandy worked hard on farm credit legislation," stated the 1990 *Almanac of American Politics*, "but probably got more publicity off a couple of casework items: he helped farmer Arlo Van Veldhuizen save his favorite cow, Old Mama, from slaughter under the whole herd buyout program, and he got an extension of a deadline for a widow to redeem expired PIK certificates she found in her husband's drawer. Grandy also serves on Education and Labor where, among other things, he sponsored an amendment to allow vouchers under the Democrats' ABC child care plan to be used for religious schools. He took a major political risk by becoming the only House member in dovish Iowa to vote for contra aid. And he conducted 93 town meetings across the district.''

In 1988, Grandy defeated an opponent offered up by the dislocated Democrats, ''a kid,'' Van Carter explained and dismissed. Grandy trounced the kid sixty-four percent to thirty-six, this in a district that Bush carried by just ninety-eight votes out of 198,330 cast.

So the congressman has his seat, and probably for a while if he likes. From the inception of his political career, Grandy has been smart. He has had no illusions about what has gotten him to a place where he can run for high office, and it is not his Harvard degree.

''If there were no Gopher,'' the candidate acknowledged to *People* long before his victory, ''there would be no Fred Grandy for Congress.''

However competent Grandy may turn out to be as a U.S. Representative, is this the path we wish more politicians would follow? Is this the preparation we hope more of our leaders would undertake to ready them for power and responsibility?

The sun was sliding back to earth now, and the afternoon's heat had cooled to a soft warmth. The adults were packing up the gear, fixing to leave, while the children were running and laughing and shouting with an extra intensity, aware that the day was ending and wanting to squeeze the last bit of fun from their time.

After my spring and summer in the world of celebrity politics, I knew what I had seen but wasn't exactly sure what it had proved. Lately, I had been trying to wrap up a few loose ends. I called Dallas from my hotel and explained to the public relations representative of Kimberly-Clark that several people had told me that they believed that the corporation had pulled its advertising from Ed Asner's television series because of his politics. The flack's voice was cold and her answer succinct: ''We have no comment.''

I phoned Laurie Battin from Medical Aid for El Salvador. She said a delegation from the board of Young Artists United had been in touch with her and were interested in sending a group to El

Salvador. From the description, this wasn't going to be just any group, but a star-studded caravan. There was a problem, however; though the board members wanted to shift YAU to a more aggressive and politicized posture, they were concerned that others on the board and in the general membership would object.

I learned from a YAU source that the board was grappling with another, even more pressing dilemma. It seemed that the young but practical show biz executives were worried about the insurance consequences of dispatching their comrades to a war zone. Current thinking was kicking around one possible a solution: YAU would supply the people, but Medical Aid would act as the organization responsible for their welfare.

There was an amusing sidebar to this. I had been planning to include in this book a group that was politically oriented, though neither activist nor partisan, and settled on the Show Coalition, which describes itself as "An Entertainment Industry Network for Political Education."

The Show Coalition is powerful enough to be invited to Senator Christopher Dodd's yearly "Washington Seminar." Each spring, the Connecticut Democrat holds a series of meetings and briefings at which high-ranking politicians and officials mingle with some of Dodd's high ranking constituents—not only to inform the latter, but of course to impress them.

It was unclear to me why Dodd had invited the Show Coalition to his two-day program. After all, as members of the group do not reside anywhere near Connecticut, it could reasonably be assumed that they did not know or care a great deal about the issues confronting the Nutmeg State.

A Dodd press aide informed me that the Senator had invited the group as a "favor to the organization . . . at the request of someone." I suggested that the invitation might have had something to do with Dodd's hopes of raising some big Hollywood money for his re-election campaign fund. The aide responded with what is sometimes referred to in government circles as a non-denial denial. "There was no *quid pro quo*."

It sounded like the group could soon become tired of just educating and was gearing for action. Not too surprising some months later, an article in the *Los Angeles Times* reported that the Show

Coalition was shifting its emphasis "from talk to action." Consequently, I passed up the Show Coalition for YAU, which would soon have its own changes to consider.

YAU was heading in a predictable direction, and another crop of Hollywood types was entering the political arena. Whatever else, I was not apprehensive that we were in jeopardy of contending with any imminent shortage of outspoken celebrities.

Generally, in politics, conclusions are not conclusive, only a head start on the next problem. So it is with the American citizenry today, confronting a world consumed by change. In our effort to grab hold and steady ourselves, we shall continue to muddle along, seeking solace and hope from wherever and whomever we can find it. Now we look to celebrities with increasing frequency. It is symptomatic of a failing, of promise unfulfilled. A person or a nation seeks refuge in fantasy only when reality offers scant comfort.

Though our fashion in heroes can slide this way and that, those values that proclaim society's priorities must remain constant. When times appear to be less dangerous, then it seems all right to make do and get by, to become wrapped up in frivolous matters and frivolous people. Consider the 1920s, with its apparently endless prosperity and flamboyant styles, and leaders who seemed solid and smart and turned out to be weak and wrong. When the Depression and war shattered the illusion, the flamboyance collapsed but the foundation held firm, and we elected a great champion, who found other champions, and who all together led us through the night. That is how great nations respond, how great peoples react, whether in 1932 or today or two hundred years ago, when the colonies turned to the Founding Fathers to seize their freedom.

It has become a truism that the 1980s resembled the 1920s, with the contemporary accent on greed and self-absorption, and with the bill coming due. Perhaps this pessimism is unwarranted. Perhaps nothing will go awfully wrong ever again, or perhaps desperation and conflict will swallow us once more. Then we shall see if our society still remembers what is fundamental and important, and if we are still able to summon forth men and women to uphold those beliefs. That is the way of a vigorous society, which constantly refreshes its national character through the dreams of a handful of its offspring. It is not a question of strength or size or wealth or technology, it is a matter of faith. That is why Rome, the capital of the civilized world and home and protector of millions of citizens and slaves, finally died with barely a sigh, easily devoured by the barbarians, because no one was left who believed in the Empire, because, in H.G. Wells's phrase, "that more subtle thing, the soul of the nation," had been neglected and lost, because a long roll call of extraordinary leaders had been replaced by fools and pretenders and jesters.

So there we end, and begin. No number of celebrities running for office or attending political conventions or marching or speechmaking or fundraising will change anything. The power is not with them, nor will it ever be. They are merely symbolic of where we stand, they only serve as a barometer of what we believe and want and deserve. In this light, finally, we can discern a real role for celebrities in our political life, a role only they can play, a role in which we do not wait for them to lead but watch as they reflect our hopes and fears.

A storm might come to our shores, or explode from within, but for now it was peaceful and quiet, particularly on a hill at dusk at Bacon Creek Park, Sioux City, Iowa. I was going home the next day, back to New York City, to the turmoil and noise. For a few more moments, while there was still time, I leaned back on the grass and enjoyed the serenity and the scene, celebrities forgotten.

In the airport terminal, I saw some familiar faces on the magazine rack in the gift shop. Melanie Mayron of "thirtysomething" smiled from the front page of *USA Today*, having won an Emmy. A happy Jane Fonda adorned the cover of *Ladies Home Journal*, the tag underneath announcing, "She talks about the pain of her divorce and reshaping her life." *US*, which bills itself as "The Entertainment Magazine," featured an article about Sam Donaldson, who, it promised, "sounds off on politics, balancing work and family and his newest venture 'Prime Time Live'."

"You gonna buy one?" the woman behind the counter asked, watching me flip through the periodicals.

I put *US* back on the rack. "I don't think so."

I sat on the plane and started to review my notes. It was going to be a long ride; the route home rambled from Sioux City, Iowa, up to Sioux Falls, South Dakota, down to St. Louis, Missouri, and over to New York, New York. I settled in and relaxed.

But the story wasn't quite done.

It was a short but bumpy commuter hop to Sioux Falls and most of us got off for a few minutes to stretch our legs. When we were called to board, I walked over to get on line and saw, garment bag slung over his shoulder, new passenger and honorable member of Congress from the great state of Iowa, Fred Grandy.

This was too good to be true. Grandy's election had been one of the pinpricks which had whetted my interest in writing the book, and his office had been one of the first I had phoned. There was a neat symmetry to his showing up on my journey home from my last stop.

I bided my time to approach until he was buckled into his aisle seat—a captive audience, you might say.

I told him I was just returning from his district, where I had talked to his constituents about their representative. I also mentioned that he had declined my request for an interview.

Grandy expressed polite interest in my work and blamed his chief aide, his gatekeeper, for my failure to obtain an audience. I accepted his explanation without comment; after all, he did not owe me an interview and it was standard operating procedure for politicians to dodge responsibility for such mildly unpleasant, insignificant decisions.

Our conversation rambled as conversations between strangers do. This was neither press conference nor ambush, so I didn't ask the congressman about the political implications of the show biz connection, or about campaign contributions from his Hollywood colleagues, or about the juicy rumor that when Grandy first moved back to Iowa he rented all the furniture for his new house, declining to buy until he was sure he had won and was, therefore, staying.

Rather, as our discussion drifted from my work to his and back, we started to chat the way they do on those network TV personality shows, posing those questions which seem intimate but are really big fat comfortable targets for any pro.

I asked him what it was like going from one very public profession to another.

Grandy shrugged, replying that it didn't bother him. "Let's face it," he said. "Nobody goes into either business to be anonymous."

That included journalists, Grandy continued. More and more, he said, politics revolved around the media, as politicians increasingly grasped that their individual and ideological successes depended on how effectively they could use those cameras. More and more, media stars relished and stretched the limits of their influence on the political process. More and more, the techniques and manner of politicians and press resembled one another, and both owed a lot to show biz.

"Have you seen Sam Donaldson's new show?" Grandy asked. "That's not the old Sam, this is the new, nice Sam. He's coming closer to being what I was when I was an actor."

I said I was willing to bet that Sam would not appreciate that description.

I told Grandy that the buzz in Sioux City claimed that the House was just a pit stop for him, and he already had his eye on a Senate race. He laughed at the idea without actually denying it, simply stating that he was busy and content with his current job.

After a while, I walked back and sat down, quickly jotting notes. Finished, I relaxed and watched as we approached St. Louis, the lights of the city twinkling out of the night.

Something was pulling at me, some last, unanswered question. I tried but couldn't put my finger on it, and then the wheels touched down. Everybody who wasn't going on to Toledo had to get out and change planes, and that meant practically everyone. Standing in the aisle, the last question suddenly hit me.

Unfortunately, I was trapped, waiting my turn to move forward. Grandy was a dozen yards nearer to the exit, and I labored to keep him in view.

I finally freed myself from the plane and hurried down the corridor, pausing to check the gate for my New York connection. Grandy was strolling right ahead, garment bag in tow. I ran over.

"There's one thing you've got to tell me," I said.

"Sure," Grandy responded affably, still walking.

"Bottom line," I said: "Which is more fun, politics or show biz?"

The congressman smiled. "Oh," he replied, before turning down a different corridor for the Washington gate. "Politics is a *lot* more fun."

It was probably a small point, and his answer was certainly predictable. Still, I thought as I headed for my flight home, I was glad he had said it.

The way I figured it, if all this settled only one question, that was one worth settling.

Index

237